The Land of the ETHEROW

Stories of Industry
and People in Longdendale

by

Neville T. Sharpe

CHURNET VALLEY BOOKS
1 King Street, Leek, Staffordshire. 01538 399033
email: picture.book@virgin.net web: freespace.virgin.net/c.hinton/

© Neville T. Sharpe and Churnet Valley Books 2000

ISBN 1 897949 68 5

Printed in Malta by Interprint Limited

Acknowledgements

I must thank the Tameside, Stockport and Derbyshire Local Studies Libraries for their unfailing assistance in unearthing information. I must also commend Joan Bone and Jean Gent for their extremely interesting histories of Broadbottom and Compstall respectively.

Also by Neville T. Sharpe

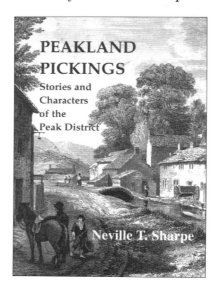

CONTENTS

Bibliography

The Railway Navvies by Terry Coleman.
Notes on Glossop History by Robert Hamnett
The History of the Manchester Waterworks by J.F. Bateman.
Roman Roads in The Peak District by Peter Wroe.
Reminiscences of Mottram by William Chadwick.
Traditions of North East Cheshire by Thomas Middleton.
The Victoria History of Cheshire.
A History of Peak Forest by Rev. Chas. Kerry.
Salt Ways From The Cheshire Wiches by W.B.Crump.
Stone Upon Stone by Rev G. Purcell.
Memorials of Charlesworth by Rev Hosken.
Ludworth Moor Colliery, The Mine and the Men
                by Geoffrey du Feu and Roderick Thackray.
New Mills History Notes by a number of authors.
The Andrews and Compstall Their Village by R E Thelwall
Survey of the County of Derby by John Farey.

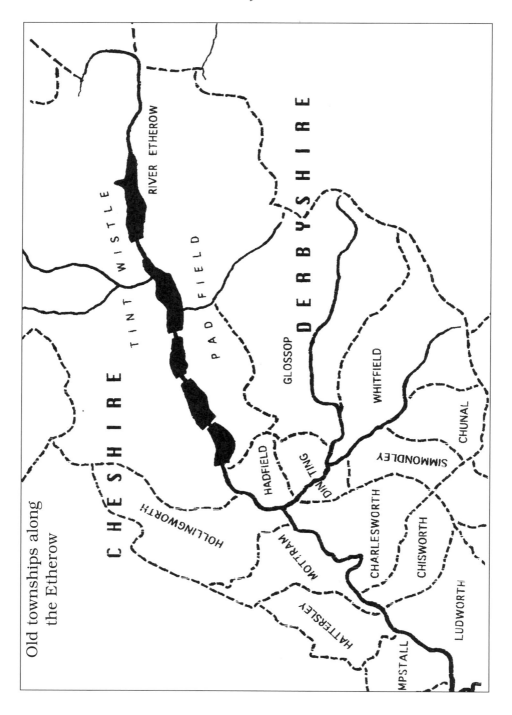

Old townships along
the Etherow

RIVER ETHEROW

WISTLE

TINT

PAD FIELD

C H E S H I R E

D E R B Y S H I R E

GLOSSOP

WHITFIELD

CHUNAL

HADFIELD

DINTING

SIMMONDLEY

HOLLINGWORTH

MOTTRAM

CHARLESWORTH

CHISWORTH

LUDWORTH

HATTERSLEY

MPSTALL

PREFACE

The book begins with a brief history of the valley before exploring the old trackways and roads and describing the great engineering works of Victorian times which altered the whole appearance of the district. If I seem to have spent an inordinate amount of time on the 19th century it should be remembered that this was when Longdendale was such a centre of great activity. Although the general plan is to follow the Etherow downstream from its source, I have not hesitated to turn off in pursuit of an interesting story. You will discover details of dark deeds of the past; disasters which have devastated the area; once thriving villages now virtually disappeared; solidly built farmhouses which provided a living for dozens of families reduced to ruins; and decayed industries, once the main source of wealth.

To help give a clearer picture of what Longdendale was like 150 and more years ago, maps showing the principal features of those days have been included. Wherever possible, I have given the names of the people involved, from all stations in life. No matter how humble, their efforts have made a contribution to the region. You will find characters both respectable and disreputable; and perhaps I should also admit that some are included because their antics are too amusing to be omitted.

It is a matter of lasting regret that I did not spend more time listening to old work people before they passed away and that I cannot remember more of what those I was privileged to know told me. But information turns up in the most surprising places - while encyclopaedias and works of reference seem to contain every scrap of information except the tiny snippet I am trying to unearth, I have been incredibly fortunate as I walk around the district in striking up conversations with the right people. It may be a chap quietly fishing by the canal, or a retired road sweeper, or a man who spent a good part of his life in some industry which closed down long ago. Often I never get to know their names but again and again they turn up some detail that I have been seeking for months. It is sometimes a surprise that the workman on the shop floor seems to have had a better idea of what was going on than the management.

Memories stretch back much further than we think; I can still remember my grandfather describing the scene in the Yorkshire village where he spent his boyhood when the stagecoach thundered through with the post horn going full blast, dogs barking and chickens squawking as they dashed out of the way, and minutes later the place as quiet again as if nothing had ever happened to disturb its peace.

Why bother to write a book like this? Because as Longdendale changes from an industrial to a residential area a whole way of life is lost. Soon most people will have no notion of everyday existence even fifty years ago. "Somebody should write it all down before it is too late!" A lot of the information here comes from old newspaper reports. But the Victorians were not the ones to write a sentence if they could write a few pages; therefore I make no apology for cutting whilst hopefully retaining the gist.

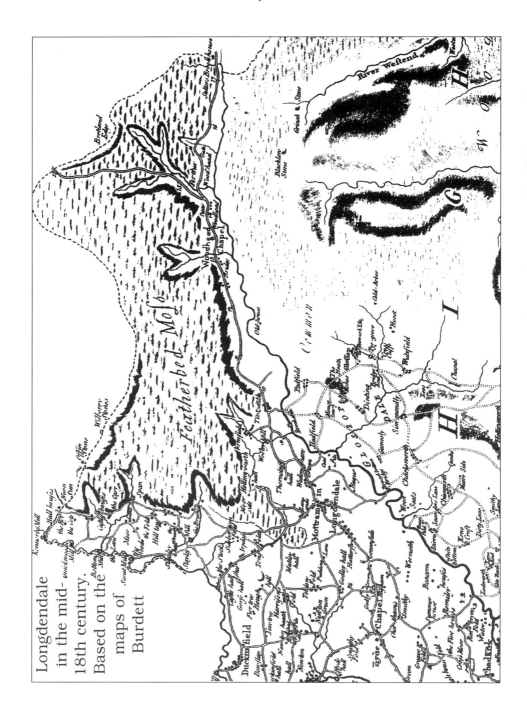

Longdendale
in the mid-
18th century.
Based on the
maps of
Burdett

CHAPTER ONE
A BRIEF EARLY HISTORY OF LONGDENDALE

One of the advantages of living in Britain is that you are surrounded with thousands of years of history. No matter where you walk from the tops of the high moors to some narrow alley in the inner city you are virtually certain to stumble across something of interest, from ancient earthworks, to street signs reminding us of trades and places long forgotten. The best way to discover details of local history is put on a pair of stout boots and get out and about to meet interesting people, of whom there is no shortage. This is the way to fill in those gaps with fascinating stories which are not to be found in even the best local studies libraries.

Travelling by main road through the Longdendale Valley today has become a testing experience as you follow a string of juggernauts stretching as far ahead as you can see, with little hope of overtaking due to the narrowness of a trunk road whose origins date back long before the days of the stagecoach. As you crawl along, not daring to take your eyes off the traffic for an instant, you could fail completely to even gain a glimpse of what was once a considerable stream, or of the efforts of generations of men.

Over the centuries the Etherow Valley has seen Stone Age peoples; fierce Celtic tribesmen; Romans trying to impose their particular brand of civilisation; Anglian and Norse invaders; squabbling medieval barons; pack horse trains; turnpike roads with coachmen, innkeepers and ostlers; the rise and fall of a great textile industry; railway and reservoir navvies, whose civil engineering works transformed the appearance of much of the valley. All have left their imprint for those who are prepared to look for the evidence.

Most of Britain's rivers have names of Celtic origin; the further you move north and west the more the Celtic names preponderate. It is easy to understand why this should be so in Wales and Scotland, but when names such as Avon and Derwent are to be found in the heart of England it calls into question the way history has been taught in the past. Many of the place names of England suggest that the various invaders lived alongside the existing population once they had claimed land for themselves. How else did the old names survive? Are we expected to believe that the Saxons asked the Britons the names of the rivers and hills before driving them out?

The Etherow is reputed to have had a Celtic name as did those other tributaries of the Mersey, the Tame and Goyt. I stress the word reputed because this is the opinion of learned men who have studied the subject in depth, although it might be more accurate to describe the information as being an educated guess. The difficulty is that most European languages have a common origin and words for everyday objects such as water, hill, or ford might once have been more easily recognisable between different peoples. Just to add to the confusion, Mersey is an English name.

What has the river been called in the past? In the Rolls of the Forest of Peak dated 1286 outlining the forest boundaries, Etherow is spelt Ederou; and in an MS written by Anthony Bradshaw about 1600, the Etherow is the Water of Tedder. These two records would certainly suggest that Etherow rather than Mersey was the original name of the river.

On some maps, the river we know as the Etherow is clearly labelled the River Mersey. Saxton's map of 1577 gives its name as "Marsee". On Burdett's map of 1763-7 the river is called the Etherow, but a few years later on Aikin's map of 1795 it is labelled Mersey yet again. It would be interesting to know exactly how such changes occur. I suspect the mapmakers asked the local citizenry for this information which could explain a great deal. Folks living in the upper reaches of the valley would know it as the Etherow and have no inclination to change the name as they travelled downstream, while those moving in the opposite direction would start out beside the Mersey and be equally sure of what the correct name was!

When does the Etherow become the Mersey? Is it when it joins with the Goyt at Watermeetings? Or a little further downstream where the Tame adds it waters? I will leave you make your own decision; it is my intention to start at the source and finish at the junction with the River Goyt, a fall of 1,285 feet or 392 metres in a distance of around twelve miles, or rather more, if you follow every bend and twist of its course.

It might be pertinent first to mention the matter of the river once being blocked at the gorge spanned by Broadbottom Arches so that much of Longdendale and Glossop dale was one large lake. But this is a matter of greater interest to geologists than historians as the Etherow cut its way through this barrier at a very remote date.

The whole area was once forested and the stumps of trees can still be found even on the highest land, usually protruding from under the peat. In the years before the moors were opened once more to the public, these remnants of trunks and roots were much more common and I can only think that such oddities attracted the attention of walkers who felt impelled to pull them up. Moorland fires have also contributed to their disappearance. Examination of the peat under a microscope reveals the presence of pollen from hazel and other trees. Petrified hazel nuts can also be found in considerable numbers in certain localities. The climate must have been more equable in the days when there was tree cover, one has only to enter a piece of woodland on a windy day to realise how much warmer it is there.

The peat was only formed a few thousand years ago and built up a blanket over the original soil protecting items left lying on the surface. With the denudation of the peat in recent years, flint chippings and tools from the Stone Age have been exposed. Since flint does not occur naturally in the area it follows that it must have been carried from a distance and worked into shape on the spot. A minority of these stone tools are made from black chert which occurs much closer in the Wye Valley, but chert does not keep such a sharp edge as flint. These flint tools can be found in large numbers if you happen to find a site where Stone Age men toiled away. So common are they that one might gain the impression that there was a whole gang of men chipping away, but the Stone Ages lasted for thousands of years so there was ample time for fragments of flint to accumulate. The feature that I find most striking about my own small collection is that the pieces have retained a sharp edge after thousands of years; no doubt due to being protected from erosion by the peat. Many of the pieces of flint are just the waste produced when trying to fabricate some axe or arrowhead, but many are useful small blades which could have been used to scrape skins or cut meat. Others take the form of thin slivers perhaps 20mm or so long which if secured at the end of an arrow shaft with resin would have made a weapon deadly to small game.

Finding them is something of an art. You could walk over the area for years and never see a one, but once you find the first and get your eye in, as it were, then you will start to spot them frequently. Usually they appear at the edges of the peat where it has been washed away or eroded by sheep or human feet, but I know of one site which was exposed by boys on a "Tarzan" swing cutting a groove in the earth with their feet.

Mesolithic flints in the form of blades, flakes, cores, microliths and scrapers have been found on Boar Flat, above Ogden Clough, on Arnfield Moor, Tintwistle Knarr and Butterley Moss on the northern side of the river. Most of the sites where flint knappers were at work seem to be between the 320 and 440 metre contours, but sites at a lower altitude may well have been obliterated by building work and cultivation. A later Neolithic barbed and tanged flint arrowhead was also discovered near Tintwistle. There are few records of finds on the Derbyshire side of the river, probably because no one has bothered to make a thorough search.

Whilst on the subject of antiquities, I must mention Torside Castle. This mound which lies just off the Pennine Way at SK077966 is a matter of some controversy. There are those who contend that it a purely natural mound and that similar ones occur in the area, while others believe that it is the handiwork of man. Having done my share of walking over the high moors around I cannot claim to have seen a similar phenomenon, and Torside Castle certainly stands out from the surrounding heather moor if only because its grass covering is of a different colour and texture. The manner in which the moorland streams flow almost round it to form a moat is also suggestive of a man-made earthwork. Another point which might just have some bearing on the matter is that the Anglo-Saxons used the word "portway" for their trade routes and leading from the Ashop Valley we have the River Alport heading in the direction of Torside Castle, and continuing on the same tack we eventually arrive at Buckton Castle. Could it be that this was an ancient route whose reason for existence is long forgotten?

Torside Castle

At a later date, Britain was invaded by Bronze Age Celtic tribes who doubtless intermixed with the original inhabitants after establishing themselves as a ruling elite. There are folks in the community who like to think they are descendants of these ancient Celts, yet others will tell you of their Norman ancestry. It would be most enlightening if we really knew whose genes we were perpetuating; almost certainly a very complex mixture indeed. In addition to the Stone Age peoples, and the Celts, we have had Romans, Saxons and Danes. The position is made even more complicated by the fact that the Romans employed auxiliaries from various parts of the Roman Empire to garrison their forts, and from what we know of the pursuits of soldiers of any era, they can only have added to the diversity!

We have the Romans to thank for giving us our first written history, but I intend to wait until dealing with the Roman fort near Gamesley before describing their impact in any detail. After the Romans departed in A.D. 407, until the Domesday Survey of 1086, we have no written record of what happened in the area, apart from details of the struggles between the Anglo-Saxon and British kingdoms which appear in the Anglo-Saxon Chronicles, .

We can only surmise how people lived in that interval with battles between the Romanised Britons, the Picts raiding over the border, the Irish raiding across the sea and finally with the invading Angles who eventually gained the upper hand. Presumably the inhabitants would exist by rearing sheep and cattle which could be moved rapidly into a safer spot when marauding bands were in the vicinity.

The boundary of the ancient Forest of Peak as set forth in the forest pleas held in 1286 followed the course of the River Etherow from its meeting with the Goyt at the aptly named Watermeeting, to the point where Far Small Clough joins it just to the west of Saltersbrook. The boundary then followed Far Small Clough and continued due south, until, after about a mile, it reached the head waters of the River Derwent which also marks the Derbyshire-Yorkshire boundary for its first few miles. Thus it follows that at least half of the area under consideration was once part of the Forest of Peak.

The Forest of Peak had been a hunting ground of the Saxon Kings before the Norman conquest, but it is William the Conqueror's Domesday Survey which gives us some early information about Longdendale. The English did not submit willingly after the Battle of Hastings and for years William was occupied in suppressing revolts which culminated in the "Harrying of the North" in the years 1069-70 when his armies laid waste to the whole area between the Humber and the Tees with a terrible slaughter of men and cattle. Crops, houses and farming implements were burned to stamp out the possibility of further resistance. After laying waste to the Vale of York he marched from Leeds over the Pennines into Cheshire, his army destroying anything in its path.

The Norman Conquest has left a legacy which at first seems strange. The landed English certainly objected to losing their estates and resistance continued for many years, but without a capable leader this resistance must eventually have been recognised as futile . The only possible way forward was to make the best of the situation and adapt to the new conditions and imposed leadership. The odd development is that William became the most popular Christian name for boys for many years and remains common to this day. Perhaps the explanation lies in the respect for the King or strong leader which had always been part of the Celtic and Germanic ways of life. The early tribal kings had been men who could attract a band of warlike young men to follow them in raids on neighbours and the sharing in the plunder. A leader who failed in battle would soon be deposed if only because his followers would soon find a replacement, perhaps joining with those who a short time previously had been their enemies.

The devastation caused by the "Harrying of the North" lasted for years and when the Domesday Survey was carried out we find that there were only three entries for that part of Longdendale which was formerly in Cheshire and four for the opposite bank of the Etherow.

Richard of Vernon, besides other land, held one hide in Hollingworth and one virgate in Tintwistle which were taxable. In Hollingworth there was woodland two leagues long and two leagues wide, whilst in Tintwistle there was woodland four leagues long and two wide.

Werneth was recorded in the Domesday Survey as being a manor held by Hugh Lupus, Earl of Chester. In Werneth is woodland 3 leagues long and 2 wide.

In Padfield Levinc had one carucate of land; in Hadfield Eilmer had four bovates; in Charlesworth and Chisworth Suin had one carucate of land; and in Ludworth Brun had four bovates of land.

All Longdendale is waste. There is woodland, unpastured, fit for hunting. The whole 8 leagues long and four leagues wide. Before 1066 worth 40 shillings.

This sparsity of entries is hardly surprising since with a much smaller population at that time there was plenty of land which was more productive and easier to farm in nearby lowland Cheshire.

A league is usually reckoned at 1.5 miles which would mean that the area considered to be within Longdendale was approximately 12 miles long. As the crow flies this is the distance from the Lady Cross to Compstall. The size given for Tintwistle seems correct, but that for Hollingworth seems too big until we note that Mottram-in-Longdendale does not appear in the survey which suggests that it had been utterly destroyed.

Lady Cross at the summit of the Woodhead Pass

In his *History of Peak Forest*, the Rev. Charles Kerry tells us that in medieval times Longdendale included twelve manors: Ludworth, Chevensworth, Chisworth, Hadfield, Padfield, Coelhal, Thornset, Hayfield, Dinting, Glossop, Whitfield, and Kinder. Longdendale then comprised no less than 32 square miles. One feature that should be noted is that almost without exception the oldest parts of these townships were located where they were safe from flash floods. Living in close contact with nature our ancestors were not lacking in common sense in such matters. It was the building of mills alongside the river and streams that led to the erection of workers cottages close by such as at Waterside, and Brookfield.

The expression "fit for hunting" gives some idea of what the area was like 900 years ago. The area of the three Black Cloughs just above the former Woodhead Station probably gives an even better one because it is still well wooded and seems to form an ecosystem of its own, very different from the countryside immediately surrounding it. For some reason this portion of woodland has been preserved; it stands as reminder of the days when the valley was a hunting ground and 'a squirrel could travel from Mottram to Woodhead without ever needing to descend to the ground'. Today we think of a forest as a large tree covered area which is just an example of how the meaning of a word can change. From the Conquest onwards, English law defined forest as those parts of the country which the king reserved for his own hunting.

Longdendale means "The long hollow of the dale," a very good description of the country. Woodhead is of course, the head of the wood, Broadbottom requires no explanation, but the origins of the names of other villages are not so obvious. Tintwistle was Tengestvisie in the Survey but the inhabitants insist in calling it Tinsel, and they ought to know. The name Tintwistle is something of a puzzle, in Old English "twisla" meant a fork in a river, or the junction of two streams. The only such meeting thereabouts is a mile and a half away at SK009952 where the Etherow meets the Glossop Brook, which is surely too far for Tintwistle to be named after it. A "worth" was Anglo-Saxon for a place enclosed within a hedge for purposes of defence. Places with this ending are common around the boundaries of the old Kingdom of Mercia particularly near the boundary with Northumbria. Presumably these names date from the days when there were raids across the borders to steal cattle and slaves.

William was fond of hunting and there is a distinct possibility that he hunted in Longdendale on occasion. It is more likely that his illegitimate son, William de Peveril, also enjoyed the sport frequently since William gave his son the grant of the Manor and Forest of the Peak. In effect William Peveril was the King's head gamekeeper as Head Steward.

The peasant farmers living on the Derbyshire side of the Etherow and thus within the bounds of the Forest would have to suffer their crops being eaten by foraging deer which they were forbidden to kill or even drive off their crops. The proscribed penalty for breaking the Forest laws was mutilation but all the evidence suggests that this was always commuted into a heavy fine, because the Lords of the Manor saw greater benefit to themselves in this income than in chopping off some unfortunate peasants ears or nose. The humanitarian aspects of the matter would have not caused them a seconds thought one suspects. These fines became such an important source of income that eventually the preservation of game was of secondary importance.

The foresters and peasants had to eat so at certain times of the year in specified areas they were allowed to graze cattle, sheep, and pigs on payment of a rent. With the passage of time the foresters built themselves cottages within the Forest and with them small gardens. These were illegal but once again, instead of some dire punishment, a fine and subsequent rent would be imposed which once more added to the Lord of the Manor's income. Thus over the centuries the original purpose of the Forest was whittled away.

The Forest laws may seem harsh, but in medieval times the King depended heavily on the game he killed in the hunting season to feed himself and his retinue. This is why it was regarded as such a serious offence to encroach on the Royal Forest or destroy the game within it. Furthermore hunting was the sport of kings and kept his warriors occupied and accustomed to swift action in the field when they were not engaged in war.

In England the king was the greatest landowner, and he fed his court either by wandering from estate to estate eating its produce, or by arranging for wagon loads of produce to be brought to his halls. From the laws of King Ine of Wessex in the late seventh century we have the following list: "As a food rent from 10 hides: 10 vats of honey, 300 loaves, 12 ambers of Welsh ale, 30 of clear ale, 2 full grown cows, or 10 wethers, 10 geese, 20 hens, 10 cheeses, an amber full of butter, 5 salmon, 20 pounds of fodder and 100 eels."

From the end of the 12th century, it is clear that the crown looked upon the forests not so much as a hunting ground as a necessary source of revenue. Rents, fees, and fines had become more important than game; however indifferent he might be about hunting, no king could relax the forest law because he could not afford to lose the income it gave him.

From old records we learn that in 1318 the Foresters of Langdenedale were Thomas son of Thomas le Ragged; Roger de Melner; Richard le Ragged, of Chisseworth; and Richard Broun. Notice that by this date folks were acquiring surnames. But for the constant vigilance of the King's foresters, people of all ranks would gradually encroach on the forest until it eventually disappeared. Houses, barns, and other buildings were constructed on the cruck pattern and usually oak was the timber selected for this purpose because of its strength and durability. Hence we find:

Bailiwick of Longdendale. (1285) The wood of Coumbes has been damaged by the people of Charlesworth (fined 2s) and Chisteworth. They must respond for 18 oaks.

The wood of Langeden has lost 20 oaks. The underwood here is worse than elsewhere. The King's wood of Holynewood is wasted and destroyed by the sale made by Thomas de Normanvyle by the King's order.

Basingwerke; it is presented by the regarders, that the King's wood of Langdene has been injured since the last pleas to the extent of 50s by the Abbots of Basingwerke, who are dead, and by the Abbot that now is, and that he must answer for the injury done there in his time. That the same Abbot held there a certain carpentered house 100 feet in length and 15 feet in width which his predecessors had raised out of the same wood.

The Abbot was present in court, and declared that he ought not to be 'amerced' nor blamed for this; that the pastureage of the wood in leaves and herbage was his; and moreover that this wood was outside the Regard.

Cruck built houses were built to a standard pattern, thus a peasant would only require two pairs of crucks spaced about 16 feet apart. This gave room for his team of four plough oxen along one side and his family along the other. Based on these dimensions the Bishop's house would have had seven pairs of crucks. This seems to have been of considerable importance because the length of a house appears so often in old documents. One explanation is that the tax levied depended on the number of crucks. Hence the peasant had no incentive to build his house any larger than was absolutely necessary, and indeed, here we have the basis of our present unsatisfactory system of rates which it seems impossible to alter and for which apparently we have to thank the Saxons!

In the Civil War between King Stephen and Queen Matilda (1135-54), Peveril's son or grandson found himself in an awkward position. His feudal superiors were the King, Henry de Ferrars, Earl of Derby, and Ranulf, Earl of Chester; as he held lands from all three. Ranulf, first supported the King and then turned to Matilda; by playing one side off against the other he achieved a position of semi-regal independence. When Ranulf turned to Matilda, the Earl of Derby promptly joined Stephens side. Peveril chose to support the Earl of Derby and the King. He was taken prisoner at Lincoln, fighting on Stephen's side and Matilda took his castle at Nottingham, but in 1142 Peveril's men surprised it at night and expelled all the adherents of Matilda from the town.

Ranulf of Chester died in 1153 reputedly poisoned by Peveril who then fled to a French monastery when he was attainted by the new King Henry II. The action of attainder held that a man's blood was stained or corrupted and therefore his estates were forfeit and he could neither inherit nor transmit by descent. These could be the consequences of a sentence of death or outlawry in respect of treason or felony.

In 1165 when Henry II advanced northwards, Peveril fled from Yorkshire to a monastery near Nottingham where he received the tonsure and assumed the monastic habit. But on Henry's approach he again fled - and was not heard of again.

In the Anglo Saxon Chronicle describing these times we read:

"Every powerful man built his castles and held them against him and they filled the country full of castles. They oppressed the wretched people of the country severely with castle building. When the castles were built they filled them with devils and wicked men.

Then, both by night and day they took those people that they thought had any goods. men and women, and put them in prison and tortured them with indescribable torture to extort gold and silver, for no martyrs were ever so tortured as they were...........

I have neither the ability nor the power to tell all the horrors nor all the torments they inflicted upon wretched people in this country and that lasted the 19 winters while Stephen was King, and it was always going from bad to worse. They levied taxes on the villages every so often. and called it protection money. When the wretched people had no more to give, they robbed and burned the villages, so that you could easily go a whole day's journey and never find anyone occupying a village, nor land tilled....they said openly that Christ and his saints were asleep."

Most of the action in this civil war would bypass such a quiet backwater as Longdendale unless a body of armed men wanted to use the pass across the Pennines. There is a tradition of a battle during this period between the forces of Stephen and Matilda on the aptly named War Hill. Mouselow is ideally situated to control the passage through Longdendale and Glossop-dale and may well have been fortified by local tribes before the Roman occupation. The generally accepted view at the moment is that it may have been brought into use as an unlicensed castle by Ranulf - King Stephen lacked the dogged persistence needed to subdue the baronial castles or the ruthlessness to make himself feared by the barons.

Why is there so little trace of a castle at Mouselow today? Stephen was replaced by one of the strongest, most ruthless and imaginative of medieval kings. Henry II rode about his kingdoms with a team of judges and a gallows mounted on a cart ready to dispense immediate justice. At the Northampton council of January 1176 Henry II divided England into six circuits and appointed three judges for each circuit. If he decided a castle was unlicensed and was to be demolished then down it came forthwith, or the owner might find himself dangling from the end of a rope. One can easily imagine that the local peasant farmers with Ranulf dead and Peveril safely out of the way, would be only too willing to help by removing the stone for their own use.

In the Assize of Northampton 1176, we find:

8. The justices shall see to it that where castles have been demolished, that they have been wholly demolished, and that those which have still to be demolished, are well and truly razed. If they fail in this, the king will wish to have the judgement of his court upon them, as scorners of his command.

By 1157 Glossop existed as a Manor within the Forest of Peak and the Abbot of Basingwerke had become Lord of the Manor. Henry II's charter states

"In free and perpetual alms ten pounds value of land in Longdendale namely Glossop with the church that is there and with all lands and things relating to it just as William Peveril had it in the time of Henry my grandfather."

There appears to be no information as to the ownership of the Cheshire portion of Longdendale from 1086 until 1311, when Thomas de Burgh sold it to the Earl of Lancaster. The Earl of Lancaster was not to remain in possession of Longdendale for long. The Earl, together with the Earls of Hereford, Warwick, and Arundel was one of those who in 1312 put to death King Edward II's favourite, Piers Gaveston. Gaveston was dragged from Warwick Castle to Blacklow-hill, about two miles away and beheaded. The King did not forget this dark deed and when the opportunity came he had the Earl of Lancaster beheaded at Pontefract.

Longdendale then reverted to the Crown. The lands were afterwards granted to the Holland family, and on Maud marrying Sir John Lovell, the latter became the owner. Another Sir John Lovell was a knight who fought at Bosworth Field in 1485, where Richard III, the last Yorkist King, was slain. Unfortunately for Sir John Lovell and his heirs, he was on the losing side. The estates again became the Crown's again and were given by Henry VI to Sir William Stanley for the part he took in the battle which contributed greatly to the victory. Not many years later, Sir William Stanley was a participator in Perkin Warbeck's rebellion of 1499, and suffered attainder for his pains. Longdendale was then given by Queen Mary to the Wilbrahams from whom it passed to the Tollemaches.

Many of these former owners of land in Longdendale have been men prepared to take very prominent parts in the history of the country, even at the risk of losing those lands or worse still, ending up the shorter by a head. As ever we know little or nothing about their tenants, but they would certainly take up their bows and bills and follow the local landlords to fight under their banners. We are fortunate in that P.P. Burdett and Dr Aikin produced maps of the area as it was around the 1760's and 1790's respectively. These maps were drawn to scale fairly accurately and there is little difficulty in recognising the places named today.

Mr Burdett made maps for both Derbyshire and Cheshire which in each case finished at the county boundaries. Thanks to the computer it has been a relatively simple matter to combine these two maps to produce one covering both sides of the valley. Once away from populated areas and roads, Mr Burdett seems to have let his imagination have free rein. For example he has shown a river running north from the Ashop which almost reaches into the Etherow Valley!

Presumably the spelling of place names was a good try after listening to the pronunciation of local folks. Wedneshough appears as Wedneshaw which is exactly as older locals pronounce it today. The Offin Stone must be Alphin and Wilberry Stones is almost certainly the Wimberry Moss stones, not far away. I doubt if Mr Burdett tramped over these wild moors, it is more likely that he preferred to take the descriptions from gamekeepers and others familiar with the area.

Another striking feature is the number of water mills along the River Tame and Goyt and their tributary streams at this early date. There are ten mills shown as compared with only two on the Etherow. There could be a number of reasons for this disparity; a smaller population, a greater distance from markets, and the problems in raising capital in the days before banks.

On the Derbyshire side of the Etherow the routes appear to be nothing better than packhorse tracks joining the hamlets. With the building of better roads many of these tracks have disappeared or become footpaths. There is for instance a track shown leading from Monk's Road to Simmondley; this was probably what remained of the Roman road from Edrotalia to Buxton. Anyone who has witnessed the effects of a cloudburst sweeping down the Dingle will know why no trace remains today.

Approximately thirty years later Dr Aikin's map was published in a book entitled "Thirty to Forty Miles round Manchester". The most obvious change is the appearance of Turner's, Sidebottom's, and Kelsey and Marslands just to name a few of the cotton factories that were springing up along the banks of the Etherow. It is also interesting to note the size of Mottram as compared with Dukinfield and Hyde. When studying these maps allowances must be made for changes occurring during the time the maps were being drawn which means that they really give a picture of the area a few years before the date of issue.

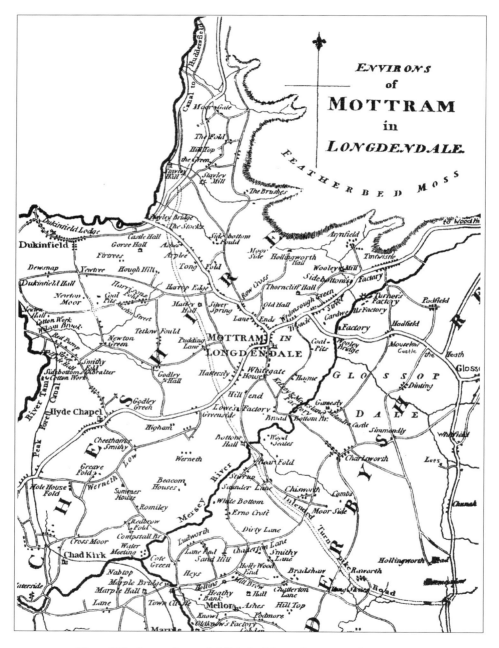

Simplified version of Aikin's Map showing the region
at the end of the 18th Century

CHAPTER TWO
FROM SOURCE TO WOODHEAD

Like many rivers which have their origins on the high peat moors, the source of the Etherow is difficult to pinpoint exactly. Redhole Spring (SE125012) just above the 460 metre contour line is the most promising candidate, but the stream which rises at (SE131015) near Wike Head at around 480 metres and flows down Wike Gutter to join it in Upper Head Dike is another worthy contender. Before the alterations to the county boundaries in 1974, Redhole Spring was in Cheshire while the source of the stream flowing from Wike Head is in Yorkshire. There is another tiny stream which also rises on Wike Head close by the first, but this stream flows east down Dearden Clough and into the River Don. Thus a drop of rain falling on Wike Head, right on the watershed of England, eventually, months later, ends up in the Irish or North Seas.

Whatever the location of the true source, these tiny streams combine to form the Salter's Brook at a point some 120 metres above the now disused Woodhead Tunnel. The source can best be examined by walking from the road bridge at Saltersbrook, but there is no route worthy of the name of path, and stout boots and limbs are essential to make one's way through the soft black peat. The high moorland is usually saturated except after prolonged dry periods making it easy to understand why there were such problems with excess water when the Woodhead Tunnel was being driven through.

At this altitude you are in the realm of the Golden Plover and the Red Grouse. The Golden Plover is usually to be seen and heard as it stands on some tussock at a safe distance making its plaintive piping cry. If you try to approach its lookout, it flies swiftly to another, always keeping you in view. The Red Grouse on the other hand, often lets you approach until you could almost touch it, relying on its natural camouflage, and at the last moment when you are about to step on its hiding place, will sudden rocket out from under your feet with whirring wings and crying "go-bak, go-bak." I get the distinct impression that red grouse are nowhere near as common as forty or fifty years ago when the moors were shot over on a regular basis, and the gamekeepers patrolled with shotgun under arm on the lookout for birds of prey, foxes, stoats and weasels.

The red grouse may have diminished in numbers, but the birds of prey have made a real come back. The area has plenty of old disused quarries and rugged cliffs which make ideal nesting places for peregrines and kestrels and it is not unusual when walking on the higher ground to find the remains of pigeons with the identity rings still attached to their leg bones. Occasionally a buzzard can be seen circling high above on constant lookout for an unwary rabbit or mountain hare. With their mastery of the air currents, these predators can be over the summit of the Woodhead Pass at one moment, and shortly afterwards be quartering the Upper Derwent Valley a couple of miles away.

Airshaft above the Woodhead Tunnel

Standing on the moorland just above where the Redhole Spring wells out from under the peat it is possible to make out signs of man's past efforts. To the south east, one of the air shafts (SE129008) of the Woodhead Tunnel stands out like some ancient stronghold, with water vapour almost always issuing from the top; a constant reminder of the great days of steam. To the east across the stream is an embankment whose regular outline signifies that it is surely man made. A closer examination shows that the rocks making up this flat topped bank are all jagged because they were produced by blasting. Every piece of rock being laboriously hauled to the surface by steam engine and bucket when the tunnel was being bored through deep in the bowels of the earth below.

At one time a tower stood on the moor above this embankment (SE136012). It is still marked on the map and was also on the line of the tunnel, presumably some sort of ventilator. It was very different from the other air shafts, much taller, looking more like a chimney. Perhaps the topography caused down draughts with a shorter air shaft. All the air shafts are slightly offset from the line of the tunnel to minimise the danger of debris falling down the shaft, endangering rail traffic below. In stark contrast to these reminders of Victorian enterprise, the television mast at Holme Moss can be made out in clear weather some two and a half miles away to the north west.

The reason for the name Redhole Spring is far from obvious. The water is not reddish, at least not on the occasions when I have paid a visit, but is certainly discoloured. There are other streams in the district which are distinctly red due to the presence of iron. Usually these moorland streams clear rapidly as they bubble along but the nascent Etherow remains cloudy for over a mile before it clears on mixing with cleaner waters.

In his report to Manchester Corporation on the feasibility of building the reservoirs in Longdendale, John Frederick Bateman stated that:

"Within ten or twelve miles of Manchester..... there is a tract of mountain land abounding with springs of the purest quality. Its physical and geographical features offer such peculiar facilities for the collection, storage and supply of water for the use of the towns and plains below, that I am surprised they should so long have been overlooked. There is no other district within reasonable limits, nor any other source from whence water may be obtained which will bear comparison with it..."   Later in his report he stated that:

"the streams in dry weather were very small and particularly clear and pellucid; walking over the hills whenever I had found, by following the stream as it flowed, that it invariably lost all taste and colour within half a mile or so of the place at which it escaped from a stagnant swamp; whether this was by admixture with spring water in its course or by exposure to the atmosphere in a running stream, I did not pretend to say, but it was a fact which I had repeatedly observed, and which anyone might go to the hills and observe for himself."

Although in general this statement is correct, the quality varies considerably as it emerges from boggy peat, or suddenly wells up out of the ground. In some places it has a distinctly oily appearance and in others is crystal clear. While it is true that the water clears as it runs along, it still has a peaty colour and taste when it reaches the reservoirs. In those places where the water appears to come straight out of the earth, sometimes gushing out in a considerable flow it seems to be of excellent quality and such springs are worth remembering by the serious walker, as they flow even after a prolonged period of drought, and best of all, make a decent cup of tea into the bargain.

For the first half mile or so the infant Etherow flows East-South East before turning south and passing under the high arch of the Salter's Brook Bridge. Built in 1830 for the new turnpike road, this bridge is worth a closer study; for a start it has without a doubt, the finest collection of mason's marks in the area. Hardly a stone is without an initial or some other distinguishing mark. A cross, a key, a square with diagonals, a star, a circle with inscribed cross or a pair of compasses. Every mark a reminder of some long dead craftsman who took a pride in his work. The subject of mason's marks is one where everybody seems to know all about it until you ask a few searching questions when they suddenly fall silent. There is nothing arcane about mason's marks;

Saltersbrook Bridge. Note outlets for water from the road surface.

Packhorse Bridge, Saltersbrook, on the old turnpike road.

the accepted explanation is that a man made his mark as he finished each block and the marks served to indicate how many stones he had dressed as a basis for payment. One snag with this explanation is that there are several stones in the Saltersbrook bridge with two different marks.

Mason's marks have certainly been in use for centuries because the same, or very similar marks are to be found on mediaeval cathedrals as on bridges built in the early 19th century. In the case of sandstones, masons try to lay the stone on its natural bed as this enables it to withstand the elements for longer without flaking off. Could the marks be a guide to the stone setters? Further, marks which consist of a letter and a number of vertical strokes might be an indication of where the stone was intended to go. I suspect that this is a subject which needs a lot more investigation. Why for example have

Masons' marks Saltersbrook Bridge

Broadbottom and Dinting Viaducts a fair selection of mason's marks, whereas on the bridges along the branch line to Glossop or at Saint James' Church in Whitfield, built at the same time, I cannot find a trace of one. The practice certainly had not died out in 1883 when the Torrs Bridge at New Mills was built.

Another notion is that a son would use his father's mark when he took over from him but before this he would use a similar mark., often his father's mark with an extra line. A further reason for mason's marks was to indicate which faces of individual stones were to align with others to simplify construction, but these marks may not be visible on the exterior. Every one of the old bridges in Longdendale over or under the railway track are worth an examination in search of mason's marks. Do not expect to see a mark on the exposed face of every stone, they could just as easily be on a face hidden from view.

I do not know where the stone for Saltersbrook Bridge came from, but it is clearly different from the millstone grit to be found in the immediate area. Designed to carry horse drawn traffic, it is a credit to its builders that it somehow manages to cope with a procession of heavy lorries. But this unintended use has wrought its toll and from time to time stones on the parapet have fallen into the watercourse below, where some of them still lie. They have been replaced with different stone - some of the present parapet have horizontal lines chiselled into it, typical of bridges nearby over the Rivers Porter and Don. Another feature of this bridge, which shows that the builders knew their business, is that the arch is high enough to accommodate a sudden flash flood.

On the north side of the parapet, in mid span, was a boundary stone marking the division between the ancient Townships of Tintwistle and Thurlstone, and formerly between Yorkshire and Cheshire. Because of the vibration from heavy traffic, this stone cracked around 1994 and was poorly repaired by the crack being pointed up. Crossing the bridge on 3rd August 1999 I noted that the boundary stone was cracked wide open once more and within a fortnight the larger piece had fallen off and been conveniently dumped over the parapet into the stream bed.

Saltersbrook Bridge. Boundary stone between Tintwistle and Thurlstone.

The 1897 Ordnance Survey map shows a bench mark at 1284 feet on the bank of the brook just above the bridge which indicates that the stream has descended around 300 feet already. This mark took the form of a brass peg fastened to a rock. The bench mark is not shown on modern maps and the brass peg disappeared some years ago, almost certainly carried away in some sudden spate. The ruins of the Miller's Arms can still just be made out to the north of the A628 at the Yorkshire end of the Bridge. This rather gaunt building was demolished around 1930 and was the meeting place for the Shepherd's Society whose members met to return stray sheep to their rightful owners; many a traveller must have been glad to rest there after tramping up the valley.

Saltersbrook got its name because it was on one of the old saltways from Cheshire leading into South Yorkshire. There is little to be seen of the hamlet of Saltersbrook today, apart from the foundations of buildings, but the Victorian

Miller's Arms, Saltersbrook.

Ordnance Survey maps clearly show two Saltersbrooks a short distance apart. The hamlet which once stood on the Yorkshire side of the road bridge is marked as Saltersbrook while Old Saltersbrook is indicated a short distance away besides the older turnpike and packhorse trail, just beyond the packhorse bridge as the track climbs up on the Yorkshire side heading for the Lady Cross.

The reason for the existence of a tiny hamlet in such an inhospitable spot was to cater for the needs of the packhorse men and later the carters, coachmen and travellers on the turnpike road. There was a need for stables so that horses could be changed, and for ostlers to care for the horses. The tumble-down remains of the dry stone field walls once used to pasture the coachmen's and jagger's horses can still be made out around Saltersbrook.

There were once at least eight inns along the road between Tintwistle and the Plough and Harrow at the summit of the Woodhead Pass. In addition to those already mentioned were the Crown, Angel, George and Dragon, Commercial, Quiet Shepherd and the Bull's Head. Inns named the Shepherd and Crook and the Royal Oak also appear in some records. I cannot place them, but of course it is not unknown for inns to change their names.

The Plough and Harrow, built around 1812 and closed in 1851 after a short life for an inn, was at a spot still marked on the map as Fiddler's Green. This name was acquired because of the blind fiddler who use to play there for the entertainment of customers. One night this fiddler, having drunk rather to well, got lost on the moor and ended up at Ronksley in the Derwent valley where he was found by the locals. He was most upset having lost his fiddle during this terrible ordeal, but it was found by shepherds a month later and returned to him.

On the older track a little to the east of the packhorse bridge stood Saltersbrook House which was an inn from 1795. It was used by railway labourers, but once the twin tunnels were completed in 1852, it closed. Parts of the walls are still standing and in a corner of one of the old rooms is a hole through which it is possible to gain access to the cellar where the meat hooks are still to be found in the ceiling. Until recently there was the stone base of a cheese press close by the Saltersbrook Inn. Its disappearance is something of a mystery - it is not the sort of souvenir someone would put in their rucksack.

Ruins of Saltersbrook Inn.

At one time these inns would brew their own ale on the premises and one wonders where they drew their water from, as the Saltersbrook and the stream down Lady Shaw Dike are not crystal clear. There are no wells indicated within the hamlet even on the 6 inch Ordnance Survey maps but that is no guarantee that wells did not exist. If the pack horse trail is followed towards the Lady Cross you will pass the site of Lady Cross Farm and in the cellar you will discover a clear spring of water.

Approximately a quarter of a mile downstream from this packhorse bridge the Etherow grows still further by the addition of the water from the three Small Cloughs. The most westerly of these, Far Small Clough, which flows due north, forms the boundary between Derbyshire and Yorkshire and before 1974 three counties met at this point. At one time the area was notorious for the staging of prize fights since the contestants could easily move over the county boundary and continue to trade blows. Only a combined effort by all three police forces could put a stop to their activities. Manchester Guardian 4th May 1839:

PRIZE FIGHT: One of those disgusting and revolting exhibitions, which we had hoped were at length in disfavour with what is called "the sporting world", was fought on Tuesday, at Woodhead in Cheshire. The Pugilists were "Jemmy Russell" of this town, and "Bob Heald," of Stockport; the fight was for £50 a side, and it is stated that the roads leading from Manchester and Stockport to the scene of action were thronged with equestrians, pedestrians, and vehicles of every description. Betting was in favour of Heald at starting; and after pommelling each other through 52 rounds, occupying an hour and five minutes, Heald hit Russell down, on which his seconds gave in, and Heald was declared the winner. Where were the magistrates and constables of the neighbourhood?

The next copy of the Guardian carried the following apology:

THE LATE FIGHT NEAR WOODHEAD: In giving an account of a disgraceful pugilistic encounter which took place near Woodhead, in Cheshire, last week, we made a remark upon the remissness of the magistrates and constables of the neighbourhood in not taking proper measures for preventing so disgraceful an exhibition. As this would appear to censure the Cheshire magistracy, we have been requested to state, that though Woodhead is certainly in Cheshire, and though the fight took place near it, yet the spot on which the offence was committed is in Yorkshire, where the Cheshire magistrates have no authority. The fact was, that Capt. Clarke, of Hyde, hearing of the intended fight, rode over to Woodhead, and actually prevented it from taking place there, as was originally intended; on which the parties moved a few miles further into the adjoining county of York.

On the 27th of September, 1867, George Fletcher, of Sheffield and James Rawlins, of Hull fought for a purse of £100. Again on 12th of November Henry Kimberley, of Birmingham and Arthur Chambers of Manchester battled for a stake of £50. On this occasion, Superintendent Moran and a posse of police surrounded them and arrested the principals - a feather in the cap of the constabulary as the construction of the Manchester Corporation reservoirs was still in full swing and crowds of hard drinking and hard fighting navvies would swell the spectators and cheerfully mix it with the police given any excuse.

Leaving Saltersbrook hamlet and the former junction of the three counties behind, the Etherow now flows roughly due west gathering water from various side cloughs on the way. Travelling downstream the left bank is in the Township of Padfield for seven miles and the right is in the township of Tintwistle for eight. For most of the way there is no path and the going is extremely rugged until the point where the three Black Cloughs add their clear waters. On the west side of the clough is a path leading to a line of shooting butts which after the first steep ascent gives an excellent access onto Bleaklow. Even if you do not wish to walk so far, on a summer's day it is worth climbing the first portion to reach a position level with the tops of the oaks and birches and listen to the warblers singing among the tree tops. If you follow the path higher onto the moor, there is a good chance of seeing flocks of twites fluttering ahead along the edge of the path, and on more than one occasion I have seen a merlin flying swiftly over the heather. Moments of pure magic.

A little further downstream we pass the now sealed entrances to the Woodhead railway tunnels and the platform which is all that remains of the former railway station. Water flows constantly from the tunnels to add once more to the Etherow which can now seriously claim to be considered a river. When one thinks how much more water is added from Howden and Crowden Brooks and the stream flowing down Torside Clough plus the other minor streams one realises that the Etherow must have been a far more impressive river by the time it reached the confluence with the Glossop Brook in the days before its waters were impounded and piped away to Manchester.

Woodhead Tunnel entrances

CHAPTER THREE
TRAVEL IN THE PAST

This is an ideal point to examine some of the old routes which passed through the area because it is easier to trace their path in the upper reaches of the valley than further down where they have been hidden by reservoirs, railways, and buildings. The Longdendale Valley provides a natural, if exposed route across the Pennines and must have been used since the earliest times. The really old tracks kept to the higher ground which afforded much easier going than the marshy overgrown valley bottoms. This would apply to Stone Age man carrying his flints and skins, and later during the Bronze and Iron Ages, when Brigantian tribesman were moving their cattle through the valley.

No mention of ancient tracks would be complete without broaching the subject of Ley Lines. I try to keep an open mind about the matter, whilst at the same time keeping my eyes open for anything unusual. Not having Alfred Watkins vision, I cannot say that I have ever come across much evidence for tumuli, standing stones, ancient crosses and churches falling into any sort of exact alignment, but on the other hand I have come across standing stones with a chisel edge at the top which aligns very well with some distant landmark, and I found them wholly by accident when ley lines were the last thing on my mind. Standing stones are to be found everywhere and the mapmakers consider them to be of sufficient importance to mark their positions. Some are explained as former gateposts in walls that have long disappeared, but others seem to be without purpose and I am sure that no one would go to the trouble of setting up a heavy stone in a vertical position with all the hard work involved, just for the fun of it. When we consider that many ancient standing stones and crosses have been smashed or carted away to be used in walls and buildings, it is remarkable that so many remain. The notion of using a standing stone or other landmark as an aiming point when walking across open country makes sense and it is a useful device when crossing difficult stretches of moorland where it is almost impossible to walk in a straight line because of deep groughs in the peat.

Real roads arrived with the Roman invasion. Throughout the Roman Empire, roads were laid out in a carefully planned system to link both civil and military centres of occupation, to ensure rapid communication. A careful survey of the ground was first made by skilled engineers to decide the best practicable route. Generally, permanent roads were not constructed until an area had been completely pacified as they were intended for the use of state officials and merchants, but naturally, use by the military sometimes had to take precedence.

There is a popular notion that any old track is of Roman origin. The Romans would not have gone to the trouble of building a road without having some definite purpose. Their roads were needed to march reinforcements between forts quickly, or supply their forward bases with grain. The Romans possessed formidable artillery in the form of ballistas and catapults which needed roads to move them quickly over distance when some strongpoint had to be reduced. Bearing all this in mind we have to ask why should they need to make a road through the upper part of Longdendale? The most likely reason is to reinforce Penistone and other forts in present day Yorkshire from the their camp at Gamesley. Once the Brigantes had been pacified and it was no longer needed the road would be allowed to fall into decay. The distance from Edrotalia to Penistone is 16 miles, a days march for a foot soldier.

The popular notion that all Roman roads were arrow straight is a misconception. In rugged country such as the Pennines or the Lake District, they had to take the most direct route available, changing direction in order to gain some advantage such as avoiding waterlogged valley bottoms. Straight alignments were certainly a characteristic of Roman roads in easier country, but if a road had to follow a ridge or a river, the road took the most convenient course. The real purpose of the straight road was for convenience in setting out. Sighting marks could be quickly aligned from one high point to the next. Roman roads nearly always make a change in direction upon high ground at points from which such sighting could be done. Where the road is straight for a long distance there are slight turns on intermediate hill tops.

Wherever possible paving was constructed from local materials, although suitable stones and gravel might be transported for a few miles. It is not therefore possible to select one type of construction as typical. Once the route had been surveyed and marked out, the surface was cleared of vegetation and loose material, then levelled. Drainage ditches were dug at either side, and the material from these could be used in the foundations if it was suitable. On the subsoil the various courses were laid; these might consist of sand covered with mortar on which slabs were laid, or cobbles set in lime mortar; The whole surface was kept in place by kerbstones. It was usual to add a top surface of fine gravel where this was available locally.

The only evidence we have for a Roman presence higher up the valley is the fortlet at Highstones which may have been a marching camp; and a note by Robert Hamnett, the Glossop historian as follows:

"In 1838, in removing the soil near to a stone quarry in Hooley Wood, Padfield, a large number of Roman coins in base silver were found. Only five were taken particular notice of, and these were three of Alexander Severus and two of the Empress Julia Maesa. In 1881 they were in the possession of William and James Sidebottom. They were lent to Mr Beaumont, the Mayor of Warrington, but were never returned. Copies of them are in the Warrington Museum. The late John Hyde Roberts had some; his father was one of the finders. Thomas Thornley, of White Mill had others, but he went to Australia and took them with him. A Silver Denarius, Emperor Alexander Severus, A.D. 231-235, was found in Bank Street Hadfield. The dates of the coins are evidence of a lengthy Roman occupation of this district."

I have failed to discover a living soul who has the vaguest idea were Hooley Wood is, or was; neither does the name appear on any map. I suspect it must lie somewhere under the waters of Rhodeswood or Torside Reservoirs.

In Roman Roads in the Peak District, Peter Wroe writes:

"The discovery of a probable fortlet at Highstones in the Longdendale Valley is indicative of a road from Edrotalia towards the east. The most likely line for such a road would be northeastwards from SK012951, just below the fort, to SK021960 on the crest of the hill shoulder and part way along Stanyforth Street, Hadfield. From there a turn is made more easterly following existing roads as far as SK024961, where a northeasterly course is resumed. The turn is made to avoid low ground ahead. Unfortunately this new alignment coincides with the railway, which itself is taking the only level and straight way through. At the end of this mile, SK035972, the course is problematic. A line from there to a point south of the fortlet(?) is possible with minor modifications to cope with bad ground and would cross the Etherow at about SK056983. The site of the fortlet(?) lies at SK064990. It may be that the railway, which follows the same course towards the Etherow, has destroyed much of the Roman road."

Clearly Mr Wroe doubts the authenticity of a Roman fortlet at Highstones.

One other place name which could have a Roman connection is Windy Harbour. There are those who hold that names such as Cold Harbour and Windy Harbour referred to places where it was possible to gain some shelter in inclement weather. In many instances these names occur along known Roman routes, but some would argue that this is mere coincidence. There are few things academics love better than to rubbish each others pet theories, when they might be better employed in the field with a trowel, but we need not get drawn into such scholarly battles, far better that we proceed cheerfully on our way leaving them to pound each other about the head with ancient texts and documents.

In the Middle Ages goods would still have to be carried on the backs of men or horses, and just like the Stone Age men, these would take the easiest route. Any hill walker knows that it it usually easier to gain altitude steadily by following the sides of a valley than by trying to march straight up hill and down dale. It is also possible to make much faster progress by following the simplest track, even a sheep trod, than to force a way through ling and bracken. The packhorse men would find the easiest track and the later turnpike roads followed a similar line. Thus the packhorse route in the higher portion of the valley would cross the Heyden Brook to the north of the Nine Holes Bridge and then climb up the side of Pikenaze Hill and proceed up the north side of the valley gradually climbing and then follow the contour of Longside Edge until it crossed the line of the modern road just before Saltersbrook and dipped into the valley to cross the brook at the packhorse bridge.

From here it climbed up past Lady Shaw Farm and on to the Lady Cross at the summit. One can imagine the relief of the jaggers on reaching a point from where it would be mainly downhill for the rest of the trip. About half way between the Saltersbrook Inn and Lady Shaw Farm the track divided with those heading for Dunford Bridge turning north.

From the earliest times, one commodity worth carrying for considerable distances was salt, required in large quantities for preserving meat and other food through winter. In these times there were no facilities to shelter and feed stock through the winter months, so animals were slaughtered and salted down. The salt industry was firmly established in the days of Edward the Confessor, the Cheshire wiches being owned jointly by the King and Earl Edwin who shared the tolls in the proportion of two to one. The industry continued after the Conquest, details of the wiches being included in the Domesday Survey. Later still, the Abbey of Basingwerke in Flintshire was a monastic owner of salt wiches. The packhorse trade in salt continued until the 18th century when canals and turnpikes gradually put them out of business. Some indication of the former importance of the salt trade can be gathered from the number of salt place names along the routes; Salter's Gate; Salter Edge; and of course Salter's Brook. The surname Salter is yet another reminder of this ancient trade.

Salt would be collected from the Cheshire Wiches by the cart or horse load and carried through Stockport, Mottram, and on through Longdendale en route for South Yorkshire. Before the recent alterations to the county boundaries, the whole of this route as far as Saltersbrook would be in Cheshire much of it along the spur of the county that penetrated into the hills between Yorkshire and Derbyshire. This odd shape to the old county was intended to protect the interests of the Earls of Chester who gained considerable wealth from sales of salt and who had no wish to pay tolls to pass through other counties.

In addition to salt, such items as tools, nails and chains not manufactured locally were worth carrying. Lead ore was also carried from the rakes to bole hills for smelting and casting into pigs, and when woollen cloth was woven locally to supplement the farmers income, it also could be moved by packhorse. The pack horses carried not only merchandise, but passengers on occasion.

In such difficult country as the Pennines, the transport of heavy goods presented a very real problem which could only be overcome by using packhorses. Each horse would have a pair of panniers strapped to its flanks which loaded would weigh around 240 lbs. and as many as fifty horses might make up a train under the control of the jaggers, as the men in charge were known. As well as large packhorse trains, travelling salesmen such as chapmen, swallers and badgers would carry their wares with the aid of one or two horses In the 17th century country people would visit the nearest market town from time to time for essentials but luxury items usually had to be brought from a distance by pack horse. Newspapers and books were also sent in this way.

One advantage of the packhorse train was that it made its own track across moorland and where very muddy conditions had to be contended with only narrow roads and bridges were needed. Moorland streams presented no real problem as men and horses just waded across. The problems arose when two trains met, so the horses would have bells fitted to their harness to give warning of their approach. In many parts the path was so narrow there was not room for two loaded horses to pass each other, and quarrels between the drivers of packhorse trains were frequent as to which of the meeting convoys was to pass into the dirt and allow the other to pass on the bridleway. The pack horse men were hardy fellows who had to contend with the elements as well as thieves, and it was not unknown for whole trains of pack horses and jaggers to be lost in blizzards in exceptional winters.

In addition to the salt names mentioned earlier, Badger-gate, Jagger lane and Limer's Gate are indications of old tracks used by packhorses, the names being derived from the occupations of these folks. Another small entrepreneur who would use a packhorse was the higgler who made the round of farms buying fruit, eggs, cheese or other goods which he could carry to the nearest town and sell on the market or from door to door. The higgler acquired his name because he was prepared to haggle over the price. A hebble is an old dialect word for a plank bridge, and a holloway is the result of the passage of countless feet and hooves cutting a deep gash in the earth, especially on hillsides where the disturbed earth would be constantly washed away.

Even when the turnpike roads were built, they would only give access to major towns or villages along their route so packhorses would have to be used

The first turnpike along Longside Edge.

to collect cloth from outlying handloom weavers, or move farm produce to market. John Farey in 1817 said that *"Pack horses are still used in North Derbyshire and were muzzled to prevent them from grazing alongside the packhorse routes."*

Another transport activity contemporary with the later days of the packhorse was that of droving. The days of the packhorse were numbered with the building of turnpike roads, but droving continued until the railways were built and took over the long distance movement of cattle and sheep. Before that time huge herds of beasts on the move were a common sight with as many as 200 cattle or 2000 sheep driven as a single herd. Such large herds could only move slowly, from six to twelve miles a day being typical. Despite the relatively short distance covered on a daily basis the total distances from farm to market could be hundreds of miles; from Galloway in Scotland to London for example. The drovers were interested in keeping the animals in good condition so as to command the best price at market. It was possible for a drover to earn considerable sums of money as some of their wills testify. They usually took payment in the form of some of the animals in the herd so as not to be a tempting target for highway robbers by carrying cash.

On their way to supply the rapidly growing towns of Lancashire and Yorkshire with beef and mutton, the drovers used tracks with which they were familiar keeping to higher land to avoid enclosed farmland in the valleys. With the gradually enclosure of common land and the building of turnpikes they were forced to alter their routes in an effort to avoid payment of tolls, but they had to follow a route which gave them access to inns, markets and overnight grazing. In some parts of the Pennines particularly on the limestone, drove roads have survived as unsurfaced tracks known as green roads. A large number of inns along country roads were closed years ago but we still have reminders of these long lost occupations in such names as The Bulls Head, Drovers, Highland Laddie, Packhorse, and The Woolpack.

Farmers still have the right to drive their animals along public roads even if we only see them using this facility to move beasts from one field to another. This is why when the motor ways were built, legislation was thought necessary to ban certain types of road use and why special bridges or tunnels had to be constructed for the use of farmers whose land was split by the new roads.

In feudal times the cost and duty of keeping roads in repair was thrown upon the districts through which they passed, and every householder was liable to work on the roads as often as required. If he had horses he was obliged to furnish a team. The liability to work was upon all and was compulsory. Naturally such unpaid work was unpopular and the roads were in a terrible state. Let it suffice to say that those working upon them were popularly known as the "King's Loiterers." Parliament passed an Act in 1691 to the effect that roads should be of a minimum standard; those leading to market towns should be even, level and at least eight feet wide, whereas horse causeys for packhorses should not be less than 3 feet wide. This legislation failed to achieve its objectives and eventually the roads were improved by turnpiking.

In 1732 an Act of Parliament under George II was passed for the turnpiking of the old track from Manchester to Saltersbrook and in 1741 there was a complementary Act providing for the road to be continued from Saltersbrook to Doncaster through Penistone and Barnsley with a branch to Rotherham. Burdett's map of 1763-7 shows it passing through Mottram, Tintwistle and Woodhead en route. From Mottram the road went to Stockport via Greenside and Gee Cross, or to Manchester by way of Stalybridge. This first turnpike road followed the line of the ancient packhorse route passing over the packhorse bridge and on past the Saltersbrook House Inn in Old Saltersbrook.

Early bridges were built of wood and packhorse bridges were not generally built of stone until the 17th and 18th centuries. The bridge is wide enough to allow for the passage of small carts, but much of the traffic would be on foot and larger carts would have to ford the stream beside the bridge. The earliest reference to the Lady Shaw Bridge is in 1695.

This packhorse bridge has recently been restored, dry stone walls rebuilt and a good surface put on the track. These improvements have made matters easier for the walker or cyclist but in so doing have hidden the original surface. These early roads were made by laying broken stones on top of the existing track which were pressed into place by the passage of wheels, hooves and feet.

Gradually the stone would sink into the softer ground and the surface remade by spreading more stone which in turn would sink in again. Now you know the reason for all those poor folks busily breaking stone in the workhouse. It is often possible to detect the course of one of these old turnpikes by the feel of the stone chips under your boots or by striking them with the tip of your walking stick. The first turnpike had milestones marked with Roman numerals. If there were any of these milestones in Longdendale, none remain today, but there is a well preserved example at SK152999 beyond the Lady Cross marked XX for the twenty miles still to go to Rotherham.

We may know the date when the road was turnpiked, but the route is far older as revealed by the fact that for some six miles east of Saltersbrook the ancient road forms the boundary between the townships of Thurlstone and Langsett. In an ancient document the bounds of Thurlstone were given as "from Hertclyffe Crosse by the Heyghweye to the Ladye Cross and from Ladye Cross by the well unto the Salterbroke."

In 1768 an Act was obtained for the turnpiking of a road from Huddersfield to Enterclough Bridge and in 1792 a further Act was passed for the Chapel-en-le-Frith to Enterclough Bridge road. The name Enterclough hardly merits a mention on a modern map but Enterclough quarry is about half a mile west of the nine holes bridge and Enterclough Bridge, or what is left of it, now lies under the cold waters of Woodhead Reservoir.

The Chapel-en-le-Frith to Enterclough Turnpike is still with us. Burdett's map of 1763-7 gives no indication of any route leading from Glossop along the south side of the Etherow, but Aikin's map of 1795 showing the environs of Mottram shows just such a road starting from the Heath. The preamble to the Act indicates however that there was already a road of sorts in existence.

As far as Longdendale is concerned the Turnpike followed the same route as the modern road from Glossop for most of the way and at map reference SK088995 it swung north to meet the existing Manchester to Saltersbrook road at the former site of the George and Dragon Inn. The railway passed over it at SK058981 where there was a level crossing and again at SK078989. When the Woodhead Reservoir was finished the last section of the road was submerged and the route then lay over the top of the dam, more or less as at present.

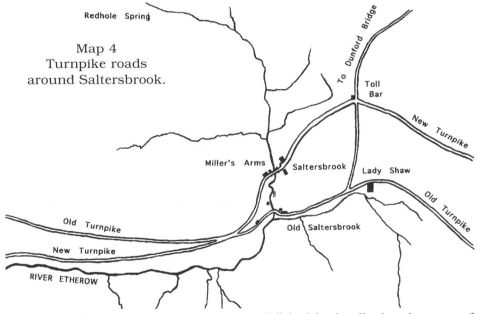

When the factory system became established in the district, the want of good highways was soon recognised, and a number of manufacturers, owners, and occupiers of land obtained an Act of Parliament entitled:

"An Act for repairing and improving the road from the town of Chapel-en-le-Frith to or near to Enterclough Bridge, in the County of Derby; and also the road from the village of Hayfield to Marple Bridge, in the said County, and also the road from the village of Glossop to a certain gate, called Claylands Gate, in the Township of Longdendale, on or near to the side of the turnpike road leading from Mottram to Woodhead, in the County Palatine of Chester."

Preamble: Whereas the road leading from Chapel-en-le-Frith to or near to Enterclough Bridge, in the County of Derby, to communicate with the road already made from the township of Huddersfield, in the West Riding of the County of York, to Woodhead, in the County Palatine of Chester, and from thence to a bridge over the River Mersey, called Enterclough Bridge, on the confines of the said County of Derby; and also the road leading from the village of Hayfield, in the County of Derby to Marple Bridge, in the said County Palatine of Chester; and also the road leading from the village of Glossop, in the said County of Derby to a certain gate called Claylands Gate in the Township of Longdendale, on or near to the side of the turnpike road, leading from Mottram to Woodhead, in the said County Palatine of Chester, are in a ruinous condition, and in many places narrow and incommodious for passengers and carriages and cannot be effectively amended, widened, altered, diverted, improved, and kept in repair, by the ordinary course of law; may it, therefore, please your Majesty that it may be enacted, and be it enacted by the King's most Excellent Majesty by and with the advice and consent of the Lords spiritual and temporal, and Commons, in this present Parliament assembled, and by the authority of the same. That John Armitage, here follows the name of 147 others, shall be, and they and their successors to be elected in manner herein after mentioned, are hereby appointed trustees for amending and widening, altering, turning, improving, and keeping in repair the said several roads, and for otherwise putting this Act in executancy. And be it further enacted that the said trustees, or any five or more of them, shall meet together at the house of Joseph Brocklehurst, in Hayfield, on the first day of June, 1792, and proceed to the execution of this Act, and shall adjourn themselves from time to time, and place to place, as they, or any five or more of them shall think most convenient.

The Tolls on the Chapel-en-le-Frith to Enterclough Turnpike.:

For every horse, or other beast of draught, drawing any coach, landau, chaise, Berlin, hearse, chariot, curricule, chair, or chaise marine, wain, cart, or other carriage, travelling the said whole road from Chapel-en-le-Frith to Enterclough Bridge, the sum of fourpence, from Hayfield to Marple Bridge the sum of fourpence, and from Glossop to Clayland's Gate the sum of fourpence, and for every horse, mare, gelding, mule, or ass, laden or unladen, and not drawing, travelling the whole road from Chapel-en-le-Frith to Enterclough Bridge, the sum of one penny, and from Glossop to Clayland's Gate the sum of one penny.

For every drove of oxen meat cattle, travelling the said whole road from Chapel-en-le-Frith to Enterclough Bridge, the sum of one shilling and threepence per score, and so in proportion for any less number; from Hayfield to Marple Bridge the sum of one shilling and threepence per score, and so in proportion for any less number, and from Glossop to Clayland's Gate the sum of one shilling and threepence per score; and so in proportion for any less number, and for every drove of calves, sheep, swine or lambs fivepence per score.

And be it further enacted that no toll shall be demanded or taken at any gate or turnpike to be enacted by virtue of this Act for any wagon, wain, cart, or other carriage, or any horse or or other beasts, laden only with coal, and carrying such coal from Ludworth, Chisworth, and Simmondley Pits, in the Lordship of Glossop for the use of owners and occupiers of land in the said town of Glossop only, or within the precincts thereof.

And be it further enacted that no victualler or retailer of ale or beer, cider, or spirituous liquors shall be capable of holding any place of profit under this Act."

The first meeting was held, according to the Act, on the 7th day of May, 1792, at the house of Joseph Brocklehurst, Hayfield. Among the trustees present were Edward Bennett, Henry Cardwell, Robert Cardwell, Thomas Hadfield of Croyden Brook, Rev. Ralph Kinder, Samuel Oldknow, Robert Thornley, Robert Thornley junior. At this meeting, James Mander Esq., of Bakewell was appointed clerk at a salary of £20 a year; Charles Calvert of Glossop, the treasurer, at a salary of 25 guineas per year. At a meeting on the 24th of the same month, Mr. Joseph Hill, of Hope, was appointed the surveyor of the road from Hollingworth Head to Enterclough Bridge, and the branch from Glossop to Clayland's Gate, at a salary of £50 per year. It was ordered that:

....the road from Hollingworth Head to Enterclough Bridge, be made and carried on from the North side of the old road near the plantation, continuing that road by certain stakes now on the common and so through the village of Chunal, as the old road now runs to John Bramwell's Banks, and so through Joseph Bramwell's field and John Bennett's Rye Croft, by Mr. Charles Hadfield's mill, and so in a direct line to Hollin Cross Lane and on that lane through Robert Fielding's field on the Little Moor to Bridge End, and continuing the old road to the East side the Pitstead in the Royle Meadow, and thence in a direct line to William Bennet's field, and so cross the road in a direct line through certain fields to James Garside's house, and so over Winterbottom's Reddish Intacks to the old road that leads to the Low Quarry into Roger Goodison's field, and so to Runnot Intack near Thornley's sough, and so to Ogden Clough, and as the stakes are fixed at Torset above David Sykes' house and under William Sykes following the old road, and so through the Pasture Wood and Kid Field Woods to Enterclough Bridge.

...that the road from Glossop to Clayland's Gate be made and carried on continuing the old road over to the intended turnpike above the Smithy, and so as it is proposed to run as far as Winberry Hill, leaving the main line on the West side of Winberry Hill in a direct line to Allman's Heath old road, and continuing that road to Redgate Head, and thence through certain closes on the North side of the hill of Marley Brow, as the stakes are fixed on the old road at the bottom of Marley Brow, and thence following the old road through Hadfield to Woolley Bridge, and thence entering the Earl of Stamford's land as the stakes are fixed on the old road leading towards Clayland's Gate and deviating from that road near the gate to a point opposite the Gun public house, where it is proposed to fix the gate in the turnpike road leading from Mottram to Woodhead.

At a meeting held at Edward Pickford's Bull's Head, Glossop, on the 14th June, 1792, it was ordered:

....that the inhabitants of the following places liable to do Statute labour do and perform for 1792, the following days' labour:- Chunal and Whitfield, three; Simmondley, one; Glossop, three; Padfield, three; Hadfield, four days.

27th February, 1793.

Ordered that a chain be drawn across the road at or near Abraham Broadbent's on Allman's Heath, within Hadfield. 22nd April, 1793; Ordered that a chain be drawn across the road at or near the Fulling Mill in the Township of Glossop. 29th May, 1793; Ordered that Joseph Hill, one of our surveyors, do immediately apply to a magistrate to obtain a summons to bring James Rhodes, the surveyor of highways of Hadfield, to a proper account for the performance of Statute duty within the Hamlet of Hadfield, aforesaid.

17th February, 1794.

The tolls were sold to the highest bidder for twelve months, the collectors entering into the possession of the Toll Bars on the 1st March. Israel Warrington, for Glossop Toll Bar, paid £91; G. Goodison, for Hadfield Bar, £61; John Collier, for Torside Bar, £30. Mr. Goodison failed to keep his agreement, and the tolls for Hadfield Bar were let to Abraham Clark for £54. Proceedings were ordered to be taken against Mr. Goodison.

Ordered that a side gate be placed across a certain highway in Hadfield, called Moor Lane, from this day, and the tolls allowed by the Act be received there. Ordered that the river below Moodsbottom Bridge be piled to prevent carriages travelling to the coal pits. 6th July, 1795.

The trustees met with difficulties in making the road, and the cost was more than any of them anticipated, and for many years they were constantly obtaining loans. The office of treasurer and clerk were combined and the salary reduced. The traffic however, increased, and we find from a report of the Commissioners for enquiring into the state of the roads in 1840, that £558 8s. 7d. was paid yearly to the bond holders, being 5% interest on loans.

The tolls were sold annually, and in the advertisements the sum the tolls were sold for at the last sale was always stated, so that we get a very good idea of the state of trade by the sums the tolls fetched.

Not everyone was delighted with the improved roads, there could be local opposition from farmers, carriers and local small businessmen such as colliery owners who objected to paying the tolls, preferring to put up with the roads as they were. We have only to travel to New Mills to find a good example of how far certain local interests were prepared to go. Time and again the toll bars were uprooted and thrown into the river by mobs inflamed by drink handed out by those who wanted the tolls abolished.

These early turnpikes knew their share of desperate deeds:

"The Hue and Cry, and Police Gazette" 6.5.1815. Woodhead Toll Bar Murder:
"On the 10th April, the toll bar house at Woodhead, Cheshire, was broken into, by some villains, who cruelly murdered Hannah Hampton, who kept the bar, and robbed the house of a considerable sum of money, a silver watch numbered 94, with the name David upon it, and a cheque of Messrs. Jones, Fox and Co. for £82. A reward of £50 has been offered for apprehending the perpetrators of this horrid crime."

In 1830 the new turnpike road through Longdendale was constructed which the modern road follows, although some alterations were necessary when the reservoirs were built. As many as a 1000 carts a day went over the new

Devil's Elbow on Chapel to Enterclough turnpike.

bridge which is not all that surprising when you consider that until the construction of the Woodhead Tunnel in 1845 all passenger and goods traffic had to pass this way. The inns along the route must have enjoyed a brief heyday. One of the old milestones can still be seen at 046984 besides the concessionary path alongside Rhodeswood Reservoir. The stone on the face of this milestone is flaking off and all that can be made out is "miles to ...." The missing words could be Manchester or Woodhead or Barnsley (most likely Manchester 15, Woodhead 3). There could well be more stones cast down in the past - it might be worth searching the sides of the old route at mile intervals from this stone.

With the great increase in the textile and other trades the number of stagecoaches plying for trade increased rapidly in the 1820's. The Manchester Guardian carried advertisements for new coaches travelling to Derby, Sheffield, and Liverpool. At the same time new coaching inns were built to cater for the growing trade. This was the golden age of the stagecoach as it swept through previously quiet villages with the guards resplendent in their red coats and with a bugle hanging by their side. These colourful proceedings were gradually to come to an end as the railways spread across the country a few years later.

But travel along the Turnpikes was not always an unalloyed delight:

A late pious dignitary being at his diocesan seat, in a part of the country where the roads were uncommonly bad, went to pay a visit to a person of quality in the neighbourhood, when his coach was overturned in a slough and although his grace received no damage, it was beyond the power of the servants to extricate the carriage. As it was far from either house or village, and the weather bad, the coachman freely told his master, that he believed they must stay there all night. "For," he said, "while your Grace is present, I cannot make the horses move." Astonished at this strange reason, his lordship desired him to explain himself.

"It is," said he, "because I dare not swear in your presence; and if I don't, we shall never get clear." The good Bishop, finding nothing could be done if the servant was not humoured, replied, "Well then, swear a little, but not much." The coachman made use of his permission, but without limitation; and the horses being used to such dialect, soon set the coach at liberty."

The Times 31.10.1822:

"The blowing of the horn by the coachmen and guards of our mail coaches, on the Turnpike Roads, which has usually been considered a sort of nuisance, is now, by the persevering labours of these ingenious gentlemen, converted into an instrument of public gratification. Most of the guards of the stagecoaches now make their entrance and exit to the melody of some old national ballad, which though it may not be played at present in such exact time and tune as would satisfy the leader of the opera band, is yet pleasant in comparison to the unmeaning and discordant strains which formerly issued from the same quarter."

The coming of the railways may have put an end to the stagecoach but when the goods and passengers had reached the station they still had to be carried to outlying towns and villages so that coaches and carriers were still needed. The following is a list of a few of the local carriers who plied their trade between Stockport and villages in Longdendale. The Ardern Arms was a favourite starting point because it was, and still is, close to Stockport Market.

Pigot' Directory; 1838

To Ludworth, Ralph & John Hudson, from the Red Bull, every Friday.

To Mottram, William Hill, from the Ardern Arms, Mersey Street, every Friday.

William's Directory; 1845

To Mottram, from Ardern Arms, John Chatterton, Friday.

White's Directory; 1860

To Broadbottom, Jas Oldham, From Ardern Arms, Friday

To Hollingworth, William Hill from Ardern Arms, Friday.

Worral's Directory; 1872.

To Chisworth, Joseph Booth from Ardern Arms, Friday.

To Ludworth, John Hudson from Ardern Arms Monday, Wednesday, Friday.

The horse and cart was still in regular use for local deliveries of milk, coal and groceries till the 1940's. You could drive through today, unaware of the history underfoot and to either side. Just to leave the main road for a spell and walk along one of these old trackways is to enter another world. If you keep your eyes open you will find remnants of old dwellings besides the track and there is something very evocative in sitting in such a spot and trying to imagine what life was like 200 years ago for the hardy folks who once lived there.

CHAPTER FOUR
WOODHEAD

"The few inhabitants of Woodhead cultivate small farms with extensive sheep walks. The public houses depend upon travellers, few of whom pass without calling, and indeed it would be imprudent for them to neglect feeding their horses here, as they have no other opportunity of doing it for a considerable distance, especially on ascending to Bretland-edge."

This was how Aikin described matters in 1794 and he probably wrote all that could be written at the time. Bretland-edge now appears on the map as Britland Edge Hill which is the high point to your right as you climb the steep ascent from Woodhead on the way to Holmfirth.

Adventures At Woodhead

Before proceeding any further downstream it might be as well to pause and take a look at the tiny hamlet of Woodhead, since even the quietest spots have known their moments of excitement. When the tunnel was finished a fine station was built at Woodhead which resembled a small castle and the tunnel entrance was ornamented with matching battlements. The whole structure was far too grand for such a remote spot and the number of passengers likely to use it. Today only the platform remains not far from the blocked tunnel entrances.

A Bully Gets His Deserts

The troubles began when a burly ruffian walked into the waiting room at Woodhead Station, threw a shovelful of coal onto the fire and announced that he was staying for the night. Without more ado, the stationmaster told him to clear off, at which the scoundrel snatched up the shovel and stuck the station master on the arm inflicting a nasty wound. Not to be easily outdone, the station master locked him in the waiting room and caught the next train down the line in order to inform the Glossop police of the outrage. Before changing trains at Dinting he informed the stationmaster there of his little difficulty.

By this date, Woodhead had become part of Charlesworth Rural District and was thus outside the jurisdiction of the Glossop Borough Police. With the police unable to be of any assistance, the stationmaster, a persistent man, set out once more, this time heading in the direction of Charlesworth.

Meanwhile, back at the Woodhead Station events had moved on apace. The waiting room door was stoutly made but the surly fellow had eventually managed to escape by smashing it down. He then sought to get out of the district by jumping on the next available train which proved to be a bad move because

Woodhead station in its heyday.

the station staff at Dinting were on the lookout for the ruffian and overpowered him after a struggle before carting him off to Glossop Police Station.

The Glossop Police could still do very little, but at this crucial moment the troublemaker took it into his head to strike the Chief Constable, Mr Hodgson, a heavy blow behind the ear. This was a most unfortunate turn of events since the Chief was a huge man well used to handling such fellows and promptly responded by giving him such a blow in return that he was unconscious for an hour and a half. When the miscreant appeared in court next morning, the magistrate fined him one shilling, his considered opinion being that the bully had been punished sufficiently already. Shortly afterwards, the Chief Constable was awarded a medal for his excellent service.

The Perils Of Hunting

Here is a story which illustrates a lifestyle which we have almost forgotten.

One morning in January, 1893, a band of intrepid hunters from the head of the valley set out in pursuit of a fox which had been raiding the district. The ground was frozen hard with a thin coating of snow when Reynard was spotted on the hillside above Crowden Station and men and dogs set off in hot pursuit up the hillside. The steep sided valley was no place for hunting on horseback; the only way the job could be done was on Shanks's pony.

The dogs were close on Reynard's heels when he disappeared into thick mist on the higher ground, so close that the men swore they could hear his pads as he ran across the crisp ground. But foxes did not get their reputation for cunning without cause and before long men and dogs were hopelessly lost on the tops. None of them possessed such a sophisticated item as a compass. The party roamed for hours until at last they heard what was thought to be the trickle of a stream - unless it was Reynard sitting nearby, chuckling at their predicament.

Eventually they reached what they took to be the head of Torside Clough and followed it downstream hoping to reach some farm or track. Good progress was made along a sheep trod until darkness overtook them and they counted themselves lucky to spot the lights of a farm ahead. It was six that evening when they arrived tired and hungry at Alport Castles Farm.

From that remote outpost they made their way through the darkness for another three miles until they reached the Snake Inn where they feasted on bread, cheese and beer. The landlord entertained dark suspicions about the dishevelled looking gang who were all strangers to him. There had been a spate of robberies in the Hope Woodlands and he decided to keep a wary eye on them.

There was little point in setting off for home since it would be long after midnight before they could reach Glossop and they had no wish to walk all the way to Woodhead after the tramping they had already accomplished. The hunters asked the landlord if they could stay until the early hours of the morning and then set out for Glossop with the intention of catching a train to Woodhead. The landlord still had doubts about them and did not relish the thought of a band of armed robbers staying overnight, but eventually relented and allowed them to sleep in his shippon where there was pile of old sacks. The hunters thought his treatment of them somewhat shabby as they had spent a considerable amount on food and drink, and would have preferred to stay in the warmth of the inn, but they could only make the best of the situation and spent the next few hours huddled together under the sacks in the shippon.

At least they managed to get a little sleep which was more than could be said for the landlord who stayed up until they left at around two o'clock in the morning, dreading that at any moment he was to be the victim of vicious robbers. As they set off once more they had the satisfaction of seeing the lights of the inn still shining indicating that the landlord had missed his night's sleep. On reaching Glossop about six in the morning after another seven mile tramp they came across a policeman who took them along to the Police Station in order to have a closer look at them. When they entered the Police Station they were able to see themselves for the first time since they slept in the shippon.

They were white from head to foot, the landlord having thoughtfully let them sleep on a pile of flour sacks.

It was a long time before they were allowed to forget their hunting adventure; first they had to endure the strictures of their wives and then run the gauntlet of the jibes of their fellow workers next day.

The George and Dragon, Woodhead

The George and Dragon Inn was well placed for business at the meeting of the new turnpike roads from Chapel and Huddersfield with the earlier Manchester to Saltersbrook road. Situated close to the toll-gate its importance was further emphasised by a milestone bearing the inscription Barnsley 18 miles, Huddersfield 13½ miles and there is still a well for the horses built into the wall by the road junction.

The building was claimed to date back to 1647 and anyone complaining about problems along the road today might pause and consider what it must have been like a hundred years before the construction of the turnpike. The pub was closed on 8th January 1961 by Manchester Corporation and then demolished, probably because of the expense entailed in dealing with water purity problems. A petition with 3,500 signatures was presented to Manchester Corporation in an effort to save the place, but failed to sway the city fathers. The inn may have gone almost forty years ago but many folks still remember it together with Mrs Annie Bagshaw and her husband Eddie.

Eddie Bagshaw was a well known local character; I remember him as the ever cheerful foreman of the unloading gang at Maconochies over fifty years ago. He always had a lump of chalk in his pocket and after each wagon was unloaded he would draw a cartoon figure on it.

He also enjoyed a game of cricket, being a useful spin bowler for Crowden. There was a time when nearly every church and chapel had its own cricket team playing in the Sunday School League, and after World War II when religious attendances fell off, several local companies fielded sides in the Industrial League. The standard of play may not have been of the highest, but there was certainly plenty of entertainment. I can still remember some of the comments of the spectators to this day. Of one thing you could be sure, the games would never last long enough for the umpire to miss the last bus. If there seemed any possibility of this happening, his finger would go up at the slightest hint of an l.b.w. or run out. Alas many of the chapels and companies are no longer with us and the fields are now lost under housing estates.

Eddie's father was Harry Bagshaw who played for Derbyshire for many years and is buried together with bat, ball, wickets and bails, in the celebrated cricketer's grave at Eyam. According to his epitaph he was still playing at the age of 64. His wife, Jeannie, and Eddie Wingfield Bagshaw are interred in the same grave. Harry Bagshaw's parents kept the Royal Oak in Tintwistle when Harry was a lad so the Bagshaws had a long connection with the district and the licensed trade.

During the exceptionally hard winter of 1946-47 a number of motorists stranded by a blizzard were making the best of the situation sitting round a roaring fire in the George and Dragon with the Bagshaws serving refreshments and Mrs Fazackerley playing the piano.

Cricketer's grave, Eyam

Suddenly the door was flung open and an officer and six soldiers covered in snow staggered in.

"Where on earth have you lot come from?" enquired Eddie Bagshaw. "We have been on an exercise on Bleaklow and made for your light across the valley." "Aye, but how did you manage to get across the valley?" "We walked straight across the flat snow covered meadow." The "meadow" of course was the frozen surface of Woodhead Reservoir!

An unusual hostelry about three quarters of a mile north of the George and Dragon along Holme Moss Road was the Tollemache Arms which was a teetotal inn. The building is long demolished but the site is still easy to pick out on the right hand side of the road shortly before you reach Heyden Bridge. It was once regarded as a treat for the more well to do to set off in a wagonette for a day trip to such an establishment.

Tollemache Temperance Hotel.

An Unwelcome Visitor

High Peak News; Woodhead, 27.6.1874:

On Saturday last a man made his appearance at Woodhead, who manifested very strange conduct. He threw off his hat, and part of his clothing, talked very incoherently and gave other signs of mental derangement. The men were all shearing at Picknas and the women and children were so alarmed that most of them locked their doors by way of protection. He got onto the Waterworks where he remained for some time shouting and praying.

When anyone approached him, he cried out, "Stand back, I am doing a great work, you will soon see signs and wonders in the heavens."

Towards night he got onto the railway line, when the Station Master had him secured. Sergeant Cooper and two constables went to Woodhead in a conveyance on Sunday and removed the poor fellow. It is said he came from Wigan.

Saint James' Woodhead

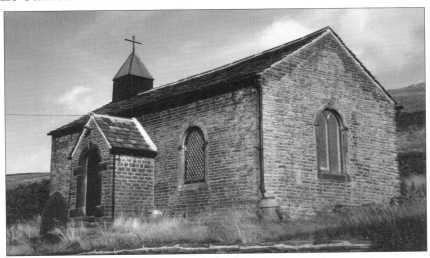

Saint James' Chapel, Woodhead celebrated its 500th anniversary on June 7th 1987. The stonework may not be in pristine condition today, but it does not look old enough to have been there for 500 years, despite having been repaired several times during its long existence.

A Chapel at Woodhead is certainly very ancient. Sir Edmund Shaa, Lord Mayor of London, left money in his will of 1487:"I will have two honest priests one of them to sing his mass and say his other divine service in a chapel that I have made in Longdendale, in the County of Chester; and to pray especially for my soule, and for the soules of my father and mother, and all Christian people; and I will that he have for his salary yearly for evermore, the sum of £4 6s 8d; and I will that the other honest priest be a discrete man, and coming in grammar."

In later medieval times it was thought that the best way to shorten one's time in purgatory was to endow a chantry chapel, where a chaplain would sing daily masses for his benefactor's soul for a number of years, or even in perpetuity.

Sir Edmund also endowed Mottram Church and Stockport Grammar School. He is thought to have been a local man born in Stockport or Dukinfield; as such he would be familiar with the difficulties faced by travellers in such a remote spot. There is some disagreement as to whether the original Chapel was built in the same place as the present one. It could be that the first, probably wooden, Chapel was built at place once known as Robin-i-Meers about three-quarters of a mile higher up the valley by the river.

An unheated building, exposed to the elements would soon decay without regular attention. Through the centuries it has relied on the support of the local farmers who could never have been very numerous. In 1730 these local benefactors added money to a few legacies and Queen Anne's Bounty. According to Robert Hamnett their names were commemorated on a plaque in Mottram Church but I can find no trace of it today.

When the Chapel was rebuilt it appears that the old timbers were used and as a result, on Sunday, May, 22nd 1825, the roof fell in with a dreadful crash, breaking down the pulpit and a great number of the seats. When the chapel was opened for afternoon service the woodwork of the roof was observed to have given way and it was considered unsafe to proceed. Mr Thomas Thornley, of Vale House, was consulted as to the best means of securing it, and he had only left the chapel a short time when the whole lot fell in.

The porch is a comparatively recent addition being added as a memorial to local men who died in the First World War. In addition to these building problems, the bell was stolen on the 1st March, 1854 by some of the railway navvies, presumably for the value of the metal. It was robbed of its bell more than once and in 1994 some depraved scoundrels even went so far as to steal the stone slates from off the roof.

It is interesting to stand in the graveyard and examine the inscriptions. The spelling of local spots varies considerably: Croddin (Crowden) and Picknas (Peaknaze) are just a couple of place names which give a clue as to how they were pronounced in the past. To this day some local folks still use the pronunciation Picknas. The names on the gravestones are all still common in the district: Dearnaley; Moorhouse; Robinson; Bower; Hall; Newton; Garlick; Garside; Doxon. One inscription which is a little different is that of John Bower who died in Hamburg in 1836. What is the story behind this inscription? Perhaps John was a seaman who died while his ship was in Hamburg. Several of the railway navvies are also buried here and their address is given as Woodhead Tunnel.

On his 1763-7 map, Burdett shows the Chapel beside the first turnpike road with a couple of buildings to the east of it. Certainly in the past there were more farms and other habitations in the higher reaches of the valley.

Before travelling further downstream and examining the great civil engineering works and factories which transformed its whole appearance it might be as well to take a brief look at a way of life which has long disappeared. In the popular imagination, farmers live on their losses, all the time pleading poverty when actually doing very nicely. The reality can be very different; hill farming has always been a hazardous occupation, with a reasonable living being made in the good years and many being forced off the land in the bad. Two hundred and fifty and more years ago, most of our ancestors worked on the land as farmers or farm labourers. Their lives were of unremitting toil on the land from dawn to dusk. If they were not working for some farmer, then they were tending their own cottage garden. At night, there was only the light of the fire or a rush light. One benefit of not being able to read was that they did not damage their eyesight and therefore rarely needed spectacles.

The only cereal crops that would grow were oats and barley - wheat could not be grown successfully in such a cold damp climate. Such staples as potatoes and turnips had still to be introduced. The barley would be used to brew small beer and the oatmeal for oatcakes and porage. One of the great advantages of these foodstuffs is that they are easily dried and can be stored for long periods.

As schoolchildren we used to play a game at school which had a chorus, "Nor you nor I nor anyone knows, where oats and beans and barley grows."

The significance of the song was lost on me at the time, but of course it is a reminder of just what local people relied on to keep them alive. I must admit to a partiality to Derbyshire oatcakes, but have reservations at the thought of eating them for every meal. The roast beef of Old England did not appear too often on the tables of the poor whose meal was more likely to consist of oaten bread and cheese.

For confirmation we need only look at an inventory of the goods left by these hard working folks. Besides very simple items of furniture such as boards and trestles, we will usually find an ark used to store oatmeal, and foodstuffs such as butter, cheese, oatmeal and malt. The fork did not reach the eating tables of Britain until around 1620 and the spoon followed in mid century. Beds were a luxury of the wealthy, ordinary folks slept on the floor on a pile of straw. Their houses which have long been torn down would be built on the cruck pattern, glass was so valuable that folks fortunate enough to have any moved the panes

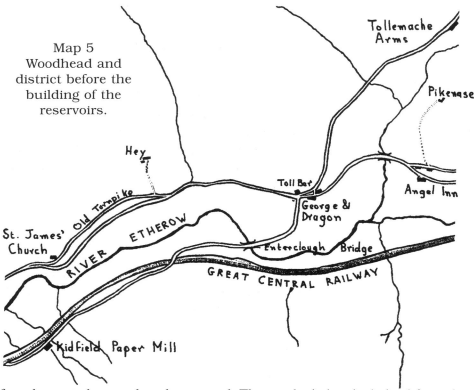

Map 5
Woodhead and district before the building of the reservoirs.

from house to house when they moved. The word window is derived from the Old Norse "vindauga", or wind's eye; which is a good description of what it must have been before the introduction of glass.

There must have been a wide disparity in the types of farming between those in the valley bottom and those in an exposed spot like Lady Shaw Farm, close to the summit of the pass. The best soils would be lower down, and there was some shelter from the winds that come whistling down Longdendale in winter as if straight from Siberia. I have sat among the ruins of Lady Shaw Farm on many occasions waiting for the billy to boil and pondering on what sort of hardy people once eked out a living in this inhospitable spot. Presumably they depended mainly upon sheep farming with perhaps a cow for milk and a few chickens scratching around the farmyard supplying eggs and the occasional table bird. The odd hare would help to fill the pot. When the first turnpike road passed by, they may have added to their income by supplying travellers. Schooling and church attendance must have been a very hit and miss affair and totally out of the question in really inclement weather.

CHAPTER FIVE
THE COMING OF THE RAILWAY

Local manufacturers were handicapped in their business dealings when compared to their rivals in Manchester who were already benefiting from the opening of the Liverpool to Manchester Railway on the 15th of September, 1830. These competitors, owing to the reduced cost of the carriage of raw materials and finished goods, were able to undercut them in the markets. Manufacturers in Ashton, Hyde, Broadbottom and Hadfield still had to transport the raw cotton and the finished cloth from Manchester to their factories and back by horse drawn wagon. Naturally local mill owners were the keenest to see a railway opened between Manchester and Sheffield and were later to form an influential group among the directors. Further advantages likely to be obtained were supplies of good cheap coal from Yorkshire, and access to the port of Hull and Europe. In an effort to offset their disadvantage they banded themselves together to construct such a railway and the following item appeared in the Sheffield Iris a fortnight before the Liverpool to Manchester Line opened:

The Railway - The construction of a railroad between Sheffield and Manchester, appears now to be considered as certain. We understand that on Thursday a deputation of five gentlemen from this town, met a deputation from Liverpool, at the Royal Hotel Manchester, when the requisite surveys were ordered to be taken, and other measures adopted, for bringing before parliament this undertaking at the earliest convenient period of the ensuing session. We are informed that there have already been numerous applications from persons anxious to become shareholders.

At first they were unable to raise sufficient capital. A meeting was held at the York Hotel, Manchester 5th June 1833 at which 302 proprietors holding 2,576 shares notified their wish to decline all further interests in the concern, and as no applications had been received for new shares to fill up the vacancies, the committee considered it altogether impracticable to carry the Act into operation. Subscriptions were £85,000 short of the capital required by Parliament. It was unanimously resolved to dissolve the company and abandon the undertaking, and to return the Treasurer's balance to the subscribers.

This failure did not deter all of the subscribers; some time later another committee was formed, and Mr Charles Blacker Vignoles, a military engineer, was authorised to draw up a scheme for a railway. On 5th January 1836 a public meeting was held at the York Hotel, King Street, Manchester, to consider Mr Vignoles report on constructing a railway without the use of inclined planes from Sheffield to Manchester, with Mr David Harrison, of Stalybridge, in the chair. The previous day at a Sheffield meeting it had been agreed to form a company with a capital of £800,000. The Manchester meeting agreed with the proposal, and many shares were taken up. On 6th June 1836 a general meeting was held at Woodhead, the capital subscribed being nearer £2,000,000 than £800,000. Shares allotted were 3,500 by the Sheffield Committee, 5,500 by the Manchester Committee, with 1,000 reserved. The Provisional Committee included the following well known local businessmen: Michael Ellison, George, Joe and William Sidebottom, John Cheetham, John Ashton, John Wood, Francis Sumner, John Dalton and James Rhodes. Among the reasons for building the line, the committee gave the following:

"It is needless to expatiate upon the advantages to be derived from railway communication, through districts so populous, so rich, and so important in a manufacturing point of view, as those on the projected line; and from uniting Sheffield with the port of Liverpool, where a very large proportion of the manufactures of the former place are shipped, promoting and expediting as it will be the intercourse between Manchester and Sheffield, and thereby increasing the general trade and business of those places, and of the several towns and villages thus connected with them.

The present mode of conveyance for goods to and from Sheffield and Manchester is by wagon, and the time occupied in the transit is about forty hours; there is not the most remote possibility of any competition by water, and consequently the exclusive carriage of merchandise and minerals between the two termini, which can be taken by the railway at two thirds of the present cost and in one-tenth of the time, may be calculated upon as a prolific and unfailing source of revenue."

It was hoped that only two miles of tunnelling would be required.

On the same date as the report of this meeting the Manchester Guardian carried an announcement of the establishment of the Locomotive Engine, Steam Engine and Carriage Company intended to meet *"..the great, extensive, and continued demand that will shortly be made, not only in England, but upon the continent of Europe, in America, and in India, for locomotives, steam engines and carriages..."* Mr Vignoles had an interest in this company as well.

Despite the arguments put forward, there were those who had their doubts, particularly as to the cost of crossing the moors and tunnelling in areas where there was little or no chance of collecting revenue. "Why should the inhabitants on this side of the Yorkshire hill be burdened with their proportion of such an expensive extended line, when the whole of the line, for their own individual welfare, is over a country unusually unfavourable in every particular?"

A well attended meeting of the committee was held at the Norfolk Arms, Glossop, on Friday, 1st July, 1836, with George Sidebottom, in the chair, when a deputation consisting of the Master Cutler of Sheffield, and several other gentlemen, visited for the purpose of informing them that they had formed another railway company with the intention of connecting Sheffield with the port of Hull, and to be called the Sheffield and Humber Railway, and to state their readiness to open a direct communication between Manchester and Hull. Naturally this scheme made the Manchester to Sheffield railway even more attractive as a business proposition.

At this meeting the allotment of shares was finally agreed upon, and referred to a committee to issue circulars to the subscribers. It was agreed to advertise for an efficient secretary at a liberal salary, and instructions were given to the engineers to complete their surveys without delay. Railway construction still being very much in its infancy it was also determined that the country should be resurveyed separately by Mr. Vignoles and Mr Joseph Locke, each to furnish estimates. The Parliamentary contract was to be prepared forthwith, and every necessary step taken for the purpose of applying to Parliament for an Act the next session to carry out this project.

The Sheffield, Ashton-under-Lyne and Manchester Railway Company was thus formed. Later after various amalgamations the line was to be the Manchester, Sheffield and Lincolnshire Railway; the Great Central; the London and North Eastern; and finally British Railways.

The directors and shareholders might be in a state of euphoria over the new 'railway' but some members of the public were not so well satisfied as the following letter of complaint shows;-

Manchester Guardian; 23.10.1830:
"Sir, Can you or any of your correspondents inform me, whether I can obtain compensation from the directors of the Liverpool railroad for a serious injury to my clothes, by the hot ashes thrown out of the chimney of one of their engines, whilst on a journey up here? My case is not a solitary one, for I find there are hundreds complaining of valuable shawls and dresses being burned. Would not the annoyance be removed by the engine pushing the carriages before it?"

Not such a daft idea, and the letter goes on to make the point that the railway company are charging twelve times as much to convey a ton of passengers than for an equivalent weight of cotton despite the fact that the cotton has to be stored in warehouses and handled by porters whilst the passengers conveniently load themselves onto the train. Finally, the writer makes the interesting suggestion that a company be formed for packing poor folks in cases and forwarding them on the railway as freight at 6d per head.

On Friday, 24th September, 1836, a meeting of the committee of the railway was held at Glossop and Lord Wharncliffe took the chair. Mr Vignoles made a highly favourable report. Mr. Locke was not yet prepared with the report of his survey, and another meeting was therefore appointed for the 14th October, when it was expected both engineers would be fully prepared. Instructions were given that in the meanwhile the Parliamentary notices should be given.

At a meeting of the directors on 24.12.1836, Lord Wharncliffe was in the chair once more and the following local businessmen were among those on the board. George, William, Joe, and James Sidebottom; Michael and Thomas Ellison, James Rhodes and John Wood. Several of the directors have been portrayed as philanthropists and performers of good works - but we shall see another side to these gentlemen in due course.

At the meeting the shareholders were informed that the separate surveys by Vignoles and Locke had been under consideration and that from these reports a map of the proposed route had been prepared and would shortly be delivered for their information. It was also stated that *"As proof of that importance (the railway) to the manufacturing country between Manchester and Woodhead, in the article of coal only, it is sufficient to state, that the same coal which is selling at 8s. 6d. in the neighbourhood of Ashton-u-Lyne and Stalybridge, is now the value of one shilling only in the neighbourhood of Penistone."*

On 16th March 1837 the Railway Bill passed the committee of the House of Commons, was reported next night, and was expected to be read a third time after the holidays. There being no opposition, the Bill was only in committee for three days. On 3rd May 1837, the Sheffield and Manchester Railway passed its principal stages in Parliament, establishing itself as an eligible mode of transit over and through the backbone of the island.

The first general meeting was held at the Cutler's Hall, Sheffield, on the 23rd November, 1837, with Lord Wharncliffe in the chair. The directors determined upon having only one line of rails through the tunnel, until the traffic should so increase as to render a second necessary; in which case it will either be laid in the same tunnel, or another single line tunnel will be made.

On the 27th February, 1839, the half yearly meeting of shareholders was held at the Albion Hotel, Manchester. The directors were able to announce that the engineers were at work staking out the line; that meetings had been arranged with landowners along the line and negotiations entered into for its purchase; and that much of the land required had been purchased on reasonable terms. All the land from Broadbottom to Saltersbrook for example had been purchased from the Duke of Norfolk. There was also a need for negotiations with canal and turnpike interests which the new line would cross.

It was proposed that stations be built at Guide Bridge; near the Peak Forest Canal for Ashton; Newton Green or Godley; Broadbottom; Dinting; Hadfield and Woodhead. The meeting ended with Engineer Vignoles' report in which he stressed his confidence that the project could be completed within budget, that the tunnel would be opened within three years and the whole line completed in the Spring of 1842.

In November 1839 a special general meeting of the shareholders was held in the Cutler's Hall, Sheffield for the purpose of determining upon the expediency of enforcing payment of arrears upon the calls already made by the directors, and also for the purpose of considering whether any and what remuneration the engineer may be entitled to receive in consideration of professional services in surveying and setting out the line.

In the report of the directors in February 1840, Lord Wharncliffe said:

"In presenting this report to the shareholders, the directors cannot avoid the expression of their regret, that, although nearly three years have elapsed since the Act of Parliament for making the railway was obtained, the progress towards its completion had not been such as they had hoped or expected. The directors therefore think it is their duty, as well to their constituents as to themselves, to enter into a short review of the difficulties which they have had to overcome. The causes of the delay may be stated as follows:

1. The estimated capital not having been wholly subscribed when the act was obtained.
2. The endeavours of a number of discontented shareholders to prevent the progress of the undertaking.
3. The large arrear upon the calls made by the directors.
4. The misunderstanding between the directors and their late engineer, Mr Vignoles.

With regard to the last difficulty the directors did not deem it either prudent nor desirable to enter into any detailed explanation regarding the misunderstanding with Mr Vignoles. It is sufficient to state, that it led to the resignation by that gentleman of his office of engineer in chief to the company. On this being tendered and accepted, the directors lost not a moment in opening a negotiation with Mr Joseph Locke, engineer of the Grand Junction, South Western and other railways, whose character for integrity and sound judgement, and whose reputation for practical skill in the construction of railway works, stand so high among members of his profession he may safely be regarded as second to none. The directors cannot omit to offer to the shareholders their congratulations on having secured the services of Mr Locke."

(At all the early meetings the directors insisted that all the proceedings should be as open and above board as possible. This seems to have been conveniently overlooked in the case of Mr Vignoles resignation.)

Mr Locke in his report to the shareholders said he had read the reports of Mr Vignoles and did not foresee any insuperable difficulties ahead. Steam engines were being installed at the shafts along the tunnel to speed the work.

The main obstacles to building the line were boring a major tunnel under the Pennines from Woodhead to Dunford Bridge, plus lesser tunnels at Hattersley; and viaducts at Broadbottom and Dinting. It was important to get the first section of the line into operation as quickly as possible to bring in revenue while these major works were in progress. As a result of their exertions it was possible to place an advertisement in the Stockport Advertiser of 26th November, 1841:

Sheffield, Ashton-under-Lyne and Manchester Railway. The public are now informed that a portion of this line, extending from Godley Toll Bar, near Mottram is now open.

Departure of Trains:-

Week days: Seven each way, 1st from Godley at 8.0am, last 7.17pm. First from Manchester at 8.45am, last, 8.0pm.

Sundays: Four each way, 1st from Godley at 8.0am, last 6.45pm. 1st from Manchester at 9.0am, last, 7.50pm.

Fares.

From Manchester to Fairfield: 1st, 8d., 2nd, 6d., 3rd, 4d. From Manchester to Ashton: 1st, 1s., 2nd, 9d., 3rd, 6d. Dogs with passengers 3d each.

Omnibuses will leave the Norfolk Arms three quarters of an hour before the departure of the second fourth and sixth trains for the Godley Station. On Wednesdays they will leave three quarters of an hour before the departure of the first train, and will meet the second fourth and sixth trains from Manchester.

On Wednesday, the 17th November, 1841 the line was opened from Manchester to Godley Toll Bar. 1,734 passengers, not including 400 of the shareholders in the undertaking, to whom free tickets were given, travelled along the line without the slightest accident or delay. The receipts amounted to £48 11s. 8d. On the Thursday 1,019 passengers were conveyed the same distance, the fares amounting to £31 7s. 6d.

The Hattersley tunnels proved more difficult to construct than the engineer anticipated because the route passed through a seam of sand, and as a result the opening of the line to Broadbottom was delayed until the 10th December, 1842, a fortnight later the viaduct being finished. The line was then opened to Gamesley, which at the time was known as Old Dinting. The Hattersley tunnels continued to be a problem and in the 1920's the tunnels were removed and replaced with the broad cutting that we pass through today.

On Thursday, the 17th March, 1842, the foundation stone of the viaduct over the River Etherow was laid by John Chapman, Esq., of Broadbottom, one of the directors of the railway, in the presence of many of the resident gentry, and others interested in this great undertaking, and a numerous body of workmen. The latter and the different agents were afterwards regaled with a substantial supper in the good old English style.

Original Broadbottom viaduct with wooden arches.

Dinting Arches around 1914 (T.W.Sharpe).

In Bradshaw's Journal vol iv., 1843, this account of the viaduct is given:

"The view before the reader delineates one of the most beautiful and stupendous works connected with railways to which engineering science has yet given birth. The line of the Sheffield, Ashton and Manchester Railway is carried over the River Etherow by a splendid viaduct in three arches, formed of stone and timber. The arches are composed of three timber ribs each, formed of three inch planks. put together on the laminating principle, with tar and brown paper between each layer. The centre arch is 150 feet span, and 40 feet versed sine. The western arch is 135 feet span and the eastern 120 feet; the radius of each being the same as the centre arch, so that the thrust upon the stone piers is rendered as equal as possible. The whole of the ribs are five feet in depth; those in the centre of each arch are two feet four inches wide, and those at the outside one foot ten inches. The spandrels are composed of timber framing, upon which are placed the main longitudinal beams, which carry the cross joisting and the half baulks upon which the rails and chairs are fastened. The cross joists are five feet apart from centre to centre. The three ribs in each arch are firmly braced together by diagonal and cross stays and wrought iron rods. The extreme length of the viaduct is 506 feet. Its length, however is inconsiderable compared with similar undertakings, and is not so remarkable a feature as the extraordinary height at which the trains and heavy engines used on this line are safely and rapidly carried across the valley below. The extreme height from the foundations to the top of the viaduct, is 136 feet -- more than ten feet higher than the viaduct under the Manchester and Birmingham Railway at Stockport, and about fourteen feet higher than the celebrated chain bridge over the Menai Straits. The quantity of stone used, is about one hundred and eighty six thousand cubic feet, and of timber about 41,000 cubic feet. The foundations of the piers and abutments are laid upon the solid rock. The piers at the base above the footings are fifty three and a half feet by twenty two and a half feet, and at the springing they are thirty five feet by fifteen feet. The stone which was brought from near Tintwistle is of excellent quality, and much superior to that from quarries in the immediate neighbourhood, and the whole of the work is solid ashlar. The timber is from the Baltic, all dressed with plane, and has been immersed in a solution of copper to render it impervious to the dry rot, or attacks of insects. The entire structure was designed by Joseph Locke, C.E., and executed under the management of Alfred S. Jee, Esq., the resident engineer of the company."

The whole, notwithstanding the turnouts of the workmen and changes of the weather, was completed and opened on the 24th December, 1842. The cost of the erection was about £25,000.

The viaduct at Dinting was of a similar construction but necessarily longer, the stone in this case coming from Shelf Quarry. The original bridges with their curved wooden arches were the reason why to this day we speak of Broadbottom and Dinting Arches. During the building of Dinting Viaduct several lives were lost. On May 31st 1843, William Stubbs, aged 22 was blown off the viaduct. On January 26th, and July 22nd, 1844, respectively, William Lowe, aged 24, and Robert Wilson, aged 26 were also killed when they fell from the Viaduct.

As soon as the Dinting Viaduct was finished the line was opened to Woodhead on the 8th August, 1844. The first train to pass over the Dinting Viaduct was driven by a man known as "Hell Fire Jack" owing to his daring mode of driving. On weekdays there were five trains; on Sundays seven trains from Woodhead to Manchester, and a corresponding number in the opposite direction, where conveyances met them at Woodhead to take passengers to the Yorkshire towns. The third class carriages were called "Stand Ups", there being no seats, and no roof, in fact they were little better than cattle trucks.

Third class passengers were first conveyed on British trains as early as 1838. In 1844, Gladstone's Railway Act was passed which attempted to do three things: to increase the direct control of the government over the management of the railways; to give it power to purchase them outright at a future date; and to compel them to provide reasonable minimum conditions of comfort for third class passengers. The companies and their shareholders howled and called it the "Railways Plunder Bill". The Bill ruled that the railways must carry third class passengers on at least one train a day in closed carriages with seats, at a charge of one penny a mile at a minimum speed of 12 mph. The railway companies often responded to this legislation by running these Parliamentary trains at the slowest speeds and at the most inconvenient times. It showed remarkable foresight on the part of the Government to see that at some future date they might need to purchase the railway companies.

The Timetable dated 29.4.1846. gives the following information:

Weekdays Hadfield to Manchester, 10 trains per day including 2 government trains; Sundays Hadfield to Manchester 6 trains per day including two government trains. !st class fare for this journey 2s. 6d; 2nd class fare 2s. 0d; 3rd class fare 1s. 1d; Government or 4th class fare 1s. 1d.

The Government trains were usually the first in the morning and the last at night and were the forerunners of the so called workmen's fares. A typical time for the journey was 50 minutes for trains stopping at all stations and 40 minutes for an express. For the 41$\frac{1}{4}$mile journey between Manchester and Sheffield the time was around 2$\frac{1}{4}$ hours for a stopping train, and 1 hour and 40 minutes for an express. Considering the types of locomotive available these were excellent times. At that date there were no stations at Ashburys and Godley, but there was a station half a mile from Guidebridge at Dog Lane, close to where the line crosses the High Peak Canal.

Manchester Guardian 10.6.1846;

The total number of passengers on line in Whitsun Week including the extraordinary number of 21,358 Sunday scholars was 101,600 as compared with 69,680 the previous year. The total monies received was £3,081.

The only stations of any size were Store Street at Manchester, (later known as London Road and today as Piccadilly), and Bridgehouses in Sheffield. Many of the intermediate stations started out as temporary structures and were replaced as business improved and cash became available. Bridgehouses Station later became a goods depot with the opening of Sheffield Victoria Station.

When planning a railway line it was desirable to pass through as many sizeable towns as possible to benefit from the passengers and freight. One glaring local omission was the then thriving cotton town of Glossop. This difficulty was surmounted rather neatly by the Duke of Norfolk. To save the expenses of an Act of Parliament, the Duke arranged for the construction of the branch railway from Dinting to Glossop as a private line, and on its completion sold it to the Railway Company. This saved a great deal of legislative time, but the Duke's understeward, George Tomlinson and a Manchester surveyor named Thomas Greenwood still had to visit London on several occasions between January 1844 and May 1846 in connection with the building of the branch line.

The making of the branch line began on 8th November 1842 with Charles Storey, John Pye, William Pye, and Septimus Storey, woodsmen employed by the Duke of Norfolk, clearing the land of shrubs and trees. On 25th June 1845 John Higginbottom was making the road to the railway station, and Daniel Higginbottom was getting stone. The branch railway was opened on 18th July 1845. Even when the line had been transferred to the Sheffield, Ashton and Manchester railway Company, the Duke still retained an important privilege at Glossop Station; his own private waiting room. It is still there just to the left of the old Victorian post box, but was walled up years ago.

The idea of someone building their own private line to connect with the main railway system may strike us as odd today, but when railways were first being constructed it was envisaged that short extensions would be built leading to private dwellings and that the owners would run their own locomotives and carriages on the line. While such schemes did not come to fruition, private coaches were loaded onto railway wagons. William Sidebottom who was a director of the Railway Company, and an M.P. had the London Express stopped at Broadbottom where he boarded together with carriage and horses and travelled in style to London. While the idea of private individuals running their own locomotives along a company line may have come to nothing, private companies did have their own rolling stock; the big collieries for example.

With the rapid increase in the weight of locomotives and trains it became necessary to strengthen the viaducts and in 1860 William Fairbairn's company rebuilt the timber viaducts without interrupting the passage of 70 trains daily.

In 1918, the Great Central Railway decided to tackle the weakness in the two old viaducts. Three extra piers were built under the Broadbottom Viaduct and seven piers at Dinting. John Moffat of Manchester was awarded the contract in January 1918 for the work at Broadbottom which cost £16,266, and John Price and Sons were given the contract for work at Dinting which cost £41,600 and commenced in October 1918. The work on both was completed in 1919.

The Woodhead Tunnel

The Woodhead Tunnel was one of the great landmarks of early Victorian civil engineering and the largest obstacle to building the line. It was not the first major tunnel to pass under the Pennine hills, that distinction belongs to the Summit Tunnel connecting Littleborough and Todmorden which opened 1st March 1841. The tunnel under the moors between Woodhead and Dunford Bridge was started in 1839 and completed in 1845. At the time it was the longest tunnel in Britain at three miles and thirteen yards. Eventually there were to be three Woodhead tunnels. The second tunnel was bored besides the first between 1847 and 1852, while the 20th century tunnel was opened on 3rd June 1954 after $5^{1}/_{2}$ years work. The intention of driving a tunnel under the Pennines was greeted with some scepticism, George Stephenson doubting whether it was possible - he said he would eat the first locomotive to pass through the tunnel.

The first chairman of the company, Lord Wharncliffe, cut and threw the first sod in a workmanlike manner with a ceremonial spade at Saltersbrook on 1st October 1838. Mr Vignoles cut the next, and was followed by each of the directors in turn. A cold collation was served in a large marquee erected adjacent to the spot. Vignoles first estimate of the cost of the work was £60,000 which he later raised to £100,000. The company were determined to spend as little money as possible and the welfare of the men came way down at the bottom of their list. They did eventually provide tents for 400 men working on the shafts on top of the moors at the Woodhead end of the tunnel who had been sleeping in the open. Most of the labour force had to exist in rough huts which they built themselves from mud and stones thatched with heather. Many of these were just squalid dens containing perhaps a dozen or more navvies.

If the company was not prepared to look after the navvies, then these were not the folks to sit there and do nothing. The Woodhead moors formerly abounded with game and poaching forays were frequent. A gamekeeper's duty was one not to be envied and on numerous occasions they were overpowered by sheer numbers. On the 13th August, 1838, there was even a desperate attempt to murder one of them. Poachers were prepared to travel for considerable distances in search of game or a farmyard fowl. One dark night, the landlord of the Plough and Harrow having lost a number of birds to these desperados decided to lie in wait for the fowl rustlers. When he spotted one of these fellows making off with a goose tucked under his arm, he let fly with a loaded musket, hitting the raider in the legs. The thief was later traced by the trail of blood to the navvie encampment at Woodhead.

Until parts of the line had been completed and trains were in operation the Company would have no income. Adverse weather and the heavy rains characteristic of the district added to their problems. In 1839 Company ran into financial difficulties which ended with the resignation of Lord Wharncliffe and Vignoles also leaving the company. The directors sued Vignoles and were not satisfied until they had bankrupted him in 1841. Besides supervising the work at Woodhead, Vignoles was working on several other lines, some as distant as Spain and Germany. In addition to the problems Vignoles was having in connection with the tunnel, the directors may have felt he was not giving his full attention to their particular project. Joseph Locke was appointed in his place and the work continued, often in fits and starts, as funds became available.

A little more must be said about Charles Blacker Vignoles lest it be thought that his services were disposed of through lack of ability on his part. He was one of the leading civil engineers of the age. Vignoles was born in County Wexford in 1793, a descendant of a Huguenot family. As a young man he spent some years in the Army, being wounded at the storming of Pointe a Pitre in the West Indies. He was for some time a prisoner of the French, but later released. He was with the rearguard at the Battle of Vittoria and was also present the same year at Bergen op Zoom. On being put on half pay in 1816 he went to South Carolina where he was engaged on a survey of that and neighbouring states.

Returning to Europe in 1823 he was employed by Messrs Rennie in 1825 on the projected railway to Brighton and also on the Liverpool to Manchester Railway. After working on the Oxford Canal and a branch railway from Wigan to Preston, he became, in 1832, the engineer in chief of the Dublin and Kingston Railway. In 1837 he designed a flat bottomed rail which rested directly on sleepers which became virtually standard on the continent. In 1841 he was elected to fill the new professorship of civil engineering at University College.

His problems with the Sheffield to Manchester Railway were largely to do with over reaching himself financially. He undertook to take up too many shares in the company and when the calls came in 1840 he was unable to come up with the cash. He was also at fault in underestimating the cost and time it would take to bore the Woodhead Tunnel. This was not the end of Charles Vignoles, he continued as a railway engineer until he retired in 1865, after being involved in the building of railways in Switzerland, Spain and Russia.

During 1842 the new contractors that Locke had started needed more men. The workforce had grown from 400 to 1000 and at one stage was as many as 1500, which made conditions even worse since there no proper sanitary arrangements and the men they were living little better than savages. Critics of the scheme suggested that the tunnel would never be completed and the estimated cost moved up to £200,000. Accidents were more frequent, partly due to the drunken behaviour of the men and partly due to the lack of simple safety precautions by the company. Twelve different faces were being worked simultaneously, two from each end of the tunnel at Woodhead and Dunford Bridge and the others from the foot of the five shafts bored from above and being driven in both directions. The deepest shaft measured 177 metres, and the work involved blasting through different types of rock, millstone grit, shale, red sandstone, and clay. Almost the full length of the tunnel had to be lined with masonry because of the treacherous nature of the rock. When money ran out the work stopped; when cash was available, the work went on day and night at the fastest possible speed with scant regard for safety. With the site being remote there were also problems with bringing up supplies, especially to the navvie encampments clustered round the vertical shafts on top of the moors.

Henry Pomfret, a surgeon who lived at Hollingworth was retained by the workmen who paid a small amount out of their wages as a voluntary contribution. He visited the site three times a week and was called out to deal with sickness or accidents. Accidents were all too frequent, often caused by reckless drunken behaviour; many men went to work drunk as a regular practice, partly no doubt because the working conditions were so miserable, with water running down the sides of the walls and the men often working knee deep in mud. To add to the discomfort, one day all work had to be suspended owing to a cloud of gnats entering the works and driving the workmen away!

Labour was difficult to recruit in such an out of the way spot with its lack of facilities, but wages were good when compared with those on construction work under more salubrious conditions. Joiners earned five shillings and masons six shillings for a ten hour day, while miners earned four to five shillings for an eight hour day. Matters were made worse by the custom of only paying every nine weeks, and paying in public houses. This would often result in a drunken riot which could last for days until they had no money left. At the Woodhead end of the tunnel there were two inns close by. As you face the tunnel entrance the Crown stood above on the left hand side close to the road. There is little trace of it today. The Angel was just over a quarter of a mile further down the turnpike road and the spot where it stood can still be made out just to the east of the Nine Holes bridge on the reservoir side of the road. The Miller's Arms and Saltersbrook House were also close at hand for those men working on the shafts. The men worked for tickets which could be exchanged for food and drink as a form of credit. The contractors made an extra profit on top of the already high prices they charged, since they ran the only shop available to the workmen. Thus the wages were offset by the high cost of food which had to be carted to the site. Matters were made even worse because the contractors made it easier for a man to get a beer ticket than one for food.

Pomfret, the surgeon, drew up a list of injuries which listed 32 men killed, many others maimed, and dozens of cases of serious fractures, burns, and dislocations. Many were caused during blasting plus the hundreds of minor accidents involving rock falls, trucks overturning and the like. It was the custom when a man was killed for each man to contribute a shilling to cover funeral expenses and leave a bit over for his widow. Neither the contractors nor the company paid any compensation to the families of men killed.

One virtually unnecessary cause of serious accidents was the use of iron stemmers. To blast a way through the rock, holes would be drilled at intervals and a charge of gunpowder rammed into place with the stemmer. If the iron struck the stone side during ramming and caused a spark the powder could explode and the stemmer be blown out like a bullet causing severe injury. The contractors and company directors might not be unduly concerned about the deaths and injuries, but stories of the shocking conditions were spreading abroad and eventually a Commons Select Committee was set up to investigate. When the assistant engineer Wellington Purdon was questioned about the use of iron stemmers he answered that the copper kind were too dear; it seemed that the company thought that the loss of a few men's lives was a risk they were prepared to take rather than go to the expense of costly copper stemmers. A similar state of affairs was revealed with regard to the use of patent fuses, and this time the excuse was that they took longer to use and would slow down the rate of progress. It seemed that the company worked to its own set of rules and so the men were left to toil on in desperate conditions. Inquests were a formality, Henry Pomfret was never called upon to give medical evidence as to the cause of death during the six years he attended to the workmen.

The clergy did little for the men's welfare. The root of the problem was that the tunnel crossed the boundaries of the parishes of Tintwistle and Penistone and the tunnel and airshafts were several miles from both churches. It would take a couple of hours for the Vicar from either to walk to the tunnel entrance. If a man was injured inside the tunnel the Vicar would have to walk over the moor to the airshaft entrance and be lowered into the tunnel in a an iron bucket by a steam engine at the top. This must have been a terrifying experience and there was always the prospect of the bucket striking the side and tipping out its human cargo. Not surprisingly, neither Vicar was anxious to claim the navvies as part of his congregation.

The line from Sheffield to Dunford Bridge opened to passenger traffic on Monday 14.7.1845, and on 15th November 1845 notification was issued of the intention in the next session of parliament to take powers to purchase the branch line to Glossop from the Duke of Norfolk, and also to take on the lease or purchase of the Peak Forest Canal. Despite all the problems encountered, work on the tunnel eventually came to its conclusion and on 20th December 1845 the Board of Trade Inspector rode through the tunnel and declared it fit to be opened to the public. Most of the navvies had left as the work came to an end and sought construction sites elsewhere, but the 300 left at the Woodhead end of the tunnel were treated by the Railway Company to a bullock roasted on a spit made from a length of rail and as much food and drink as they could possibly consume set out on tables in a large tent.

The directors as might be expected from their previous conduct, looked after themselves decidedly better. At ten o'clock next morning a train of twenty carriages left Sheffield hauled by two fine new engines. The passengers comprised the directors, engineers, shareholders, local gentry, and mayors from towns directly affected by the new line. After a halt at Dunford Bridge, the train passed through the tunnel to loud cheering and on over Dinting Viaduct which was another wonder of the age carrying the track high above Glossop-dale and on to Manchester arriving at a quarter past twelve where it was greeted by a band playing, "See, the Conquering Hero Comes."

Back in Sheffield that same evening the directors dined at the Cutler's Hall and toasted Engineer Locke and his assistant Wellington Purdon; Charles Blacker Vignoles, the man they had bankrupted, and all those who had been killed or injured were not considered worthy of a mention. The line opened to the public on December 23rd 1845. The Sheffield Iris gives this description:

"In the vicinity of Sheffield terminus large crowds had gathered to witness the first starting of some of the most splendid carriages that ever adorned a railway. To say nothing of the first and second class carriages, those of the third class are unparalleled for comfort and protection, being covered at the top and sides, and richly painted on the exterior. The guard box behind is sheltered on three sides and the top, so that even in the coldest season, this important functionary will be protected from the inclemency of the weather."

In July 1846 there was a scare when the Manchester to Saltersbrook turnpike road was washed down on to the line below by heavy rain pouring down Audernshaw Clough and carrying with it several huts occupied by workmen. The collapse of the road occurred in the early hours of the morning and the men were lucky to escape, running from the primitive huts with hardly a stitch of clothing on their backs. This incident caused a wild rumour to circulate in Manchester that the tunnel had caved in.

In 1847, work on the second tunnel was commenced. This cost less because the airshafts were already in position and during the construction of the first tunnel arches had been driven alongside it to give access to a second tunnel when it should be built, thus material excavated could be brought out along the existing line with comparative ease. Conditions were better and fewer men were killed as a result of accidents, but in 1849 there was an outbreak of cholera in which twenty eight died. At first the disease was thought to be dysentery but when men started to die and the doctor diagnosed cholera a panic began which was intensified when the men saw extra coffins arriving in expectation of more deaths. Within a few days there were only 100 left working of the 750 men before the outbreak. Some of the bodies were buried at the little Chapel of Saint James' at Woodhead and others at Christ Church, Tintwistle, further down the valley, The outbreak is still talked about to this day and local folks refer to it as the plague. In the north east corner of the graveyard at Christ Church is an area covered with heather which has no gravestones. This is reputed to be where the cholera victims were buried and why no one had been buried there since. Medical opinion of the time was that it was those of intemperate habits that were struck down - people with strength of character resisted the disease!

Even when completed the tunnels were unhealthy places being thick with smoke and anyone working on the track had to use lamps to see what they were about. Many suffered from lung disease because of exposure to the smoke and damp. Among railwaymen, the tunnels had the reputation of having *"the most fearsome atmosphere in the world"*. A signal box inside the tunnel had to be closed because no one was prepared to work in it, and train crews had to breathe through damp rags because of fumes.

Even when the line was completed, accidents occurred. On the 20th February, 1867 William Coffey, the station master at Crowden, was killed by a railway train. In addition to the deaths there had been 200 severe accidents, and 450 minor ones. 157 tons of gunpowder had been used to blast the way through.

The original tunnels were closed in 1956 after the line from Manchester to Sheffield, the first all-electric line in Britain, opened to traffic on 14th September 1954, after the new tunnel had been completed. The passenger service was withdrawn 5th January 1970. Freight traffic was withdrawn 18th July 1981 and the line abandoned. More recently Richard Branson has proposed to open a line from the Channel Tunnel through Sheffield and Manchester, and on to Liverpool reopening the Woodhead Tunnel on the way. The reaction of many is to hope he succeeds and wonder why a route between two major cities such as Manchester and Sheffield was ever closed in the first place.

The railway navvies have been popularly portrayed as a gang of ignorant, beer swilling roughs capable of any sort of mischief. It should not be forgotten that these were the very same fellows who rescued the British Army from the mess it had gotten itself into during the siege of Sevastapol. Consider also the skills required in ensuring that when working on a dozen different faces in the tunnel they all aligned exactly. When the tunnel was complete it was possible to stand at one end and see a tiny dot of light at the other. Not a bad achievement over a distance of more than three miles. Early railway cuttings, embankments and tunnels were cut with picks, shovels and crowbars, the only power being supplied by men and horses; monumental accomplishments by any standard.

At one time "sixpenny trips" were popular and gave people in Manchester an opportunity to get out in the countryside for a day. They also gave country folk the opportunity to make a few coppers selling them teas, etc. It was these trips that gave rise to the expression, "What do you think you are on - a tanner trip?" Less politely the visitors were known as "Manchester Gorbies, sixpence return." Long before the advent of the "tanner trip," there were outings to Woodhead. One memorable one was from Stockport, on 29th July 1865, when 2-3,000 Oddfellows came with two military bands. Another Yorkshire contingent were accompanied by the Thurlstone Old Prize Band.

Joseph Locke was born at Attercliffe near Sheffield on August 9th 1805. His father worked as a mining engineer and when Joseph was five the family moved to Barnsley when his father took a post at Gawber Colliery. Joseph went to Barnsley Grammar School and in 1919 took up an apprenticeship with William Stobart, a viewer at Pelaw Colliery, County Durham. While he was there that he met and became a lifelong friend of Robert Stephenson who was

serving an apprenticeship at Killingworth Colliery. Joseph had great faith in Stephenson's aims to establish a national railway network.

Joseph Locke

Locke's contributions to the advancement of railways were many. As a surveyor, he was a master of assessing the lie of the land, selecting the best route over difficult terrain. He never swayed from his maxim to take the most direct route while embracing as many towns as possible, and engineering the railway according to the traffic potential. Being aware of the power that locomotives would eventually develop led him to construct steeper inclines and thus often dispense with expensive tunnels and cuttings. He introduced his own heavy I section rail, mounted on wooden sleepers, the standard in Britain for a 100 years. This rail gave a much smoother ride than the rails mounted on stone blocks.

On the debit side of the ledger we must not forget that he was the man in charge of the Woodhead Tunnel project and as such must bear his share of responsibility for the lack of concern for the workforce.

Before leaving the railway there is one little story to tell which illustrates the life style of the wealthy during the closing years of the 19th century when the line was run by the Great Central Railway Company. Theodore Ellison and his friend Herbert Partington arrived at London Road Station. Herbert Partington boarded the 5.20pm train and waved cheerily to his friend Theodore as it drew out. Theodore Ellison, a grandson of Thomas Ellison, one of the original directors, promptly ordered a private train to Glossop which cost him the first class fare plus 5 shillings per mile. The 5.20 was shunted into a siding while his private train went racing past. Mr Ellison was thus able to greet his friend when he arrived at his destination.

CHAPTER SIX
CROWDEN

The promenade above Crowden station.

Enough of all this industry and hard work, it is time to take a look at the hamlet of Crowden and some of the events that have enlivened the place.

On what is now the Camping and Caravan Club's lightweight camping site once stood Crowden Hall which was demolished by Manchester Corporation in 1937. This ancient hall, built in 1692, was the home of the Hadfield or (Hatfield) family who were the local gentry for nearly 200 years.

Its existence would probably have been quickly forgotten but for a black sheep of the family born around the middle of the 17th century. John Hatfield appears to have spent his younger days walking and shooting amid the surrounding hills and in his late teens was sent to London in the hope that he might gain some education. His parents were to be disappointed. Young Hatfield was soon revelling in the pleasures of women and drink. Local legend has it that one New Year's Eve after returning from his London College, he walked over the hills to visit an old mystic who lived at the Brushes near Stalybridge and asked what the future had in store. Old Robinson is reputed to have said, "Powerful fates resistless hand, shall seal your fate in Cumberland."

We shall never know if there is any truth in the story, but it certainly did not interfere with his riotous way of life, marrying more than once, first to the daughter of the Duke of Rutland by whom he had three daughters. They lived in London where John had a wanton time living on his wife's income. After the death of his wife he soon found himself penniless and was speedily disowned by the Duke who regarded him as an utter scoundrel. Eventually his recklessness resulted in a spell in Newgate Prison for debt. His stay there is recorded in the prison records and his place of origin given as Mottram. He was bailed out by the Duke, but was soon back behind bars. A Devon lady discharged his debts, and he married her, leaving his children with relatives.

He soon tired of his new wife and set off under an assumed name with the intention of finding and winning the hand of Mary Robinson, the legendary lakeland beauty, whose father ran the Fish Inn on the shores of Lake Buttermere. The name he chose was the Hon. Alexander Augustus Hope. He claimed to be the Member of Parliament for Linlithgow and a Lieutenant Colonel in the 14th Regiment of Foot.

He soon found Mary and he must have been a charmer, because he courted her and married her at Lorton parish church in October 1802. After a short honeymoon at Longtown in Scotland, they returned to the Lakes. When the landlord of the Queen's Head where they stayed demanded payment, Hatfield made his first big mistake. He made out a bill of exchange which bounced. It led to an interview with a Mr George Hardinge who asked about his family and about his adventures in Egypt where he claimed he was wounded. Why did he sign his name A.A. Hope when Colonel Hope's name was only Alexander? Mr Hardinge sent for a magistrate and asked Mr Wood the inn-keeper to secure Hatfield's horses to prevent his decamping. The bill of exchange, coupled with the fact that he had been franking letters illegally - one of the privileges of Members of Parliament - led to a warrant being issued for Hatfield's arrest.

Hatfield was in desperate straits by this time but managed to effect his escape by boat across the lake to Borrowdale. It led to a a nationwide scandal and manhunt, before he was seized and thrown into a dark cell in Carlisle Gaol. On the morning of Monday, August 15th 1803, John Hatfield appeared at the bar before the judge, Sir Alexander Thompson. Hatfield's trial was fully reported in The Times of August 20th 1803:

Three indictments were preferred against the prisoner: The first charged him with assuming the name and title of the Hon. Alexander Augustus Hope and pretending to be an

Crowden Hall

Railway cottages at Crowden.

M.P. and with having, under the same name and character drawn a Bill of Exchange on John Crump Esq. for the sum of £20. The second charged him with uttering a false, forged and counterfeit Bill of Exchange. The third charged him with pretending to be an M.P. and brother to the Right Hon. the Earl of Hopetown and under that fictitious character, forged and counterfeited the handwriting of Alexander Hope in the superscription of several letters or packets, to avoid payment of the duty of postage.

One witness identified Hatfield and stated that he had entered the firm of Dennis, Hatfield and Co in 1801. Yet another witness said he had known the prisoner as John Hatfield when he was married to a lady by the name of Mrs Nation. The Rev. Nicholson told how he had met the prisoner when he attended the Chapel at Loweswater on Sunday September 12, 1802, and how he had accompanied Hadfield to Whitehaven to procure a marriage licence to marry Mary Robinson of Buttermere.

Hatfield was found guilty on the first and second indictments and ordered to be brought up on the next day Tuesday to receive judgement. The case had caused widespread interest and ladies and gentlemen within a radius of twenty miles of Carlisle crowded into the town to attend the trial. The judge did not mince his words.

"John Hatfield; after a long and serious investigation of the charges which have been preferred against you, you have been found guilty by a jury of your country. You have been distinguished for crimes of such magnitude as have seldom, if ever, received any mitigation of capital punishment, and in your case it is impossible it can be remitted. Assuming the person, name and character of a worthy and respectable officer, of a noble family in this country, you have perpetrated and committed the most enormous crimes. The long imprisonment which you have undergone, has afforded time for your serious reflection, and an opportunity of your being deeply impressed with a sense of the enormity of your guilt, and the justice of that sentence which must be inflicted upon you; I wish you to be seriously impressed with the awfulness of your situation, and to reflect with anxious care and deep concern your approaching end, concerning which much needs to be done: lay aside now your delusion and imposition and employ properly the short space of time you have to live. I beseech you to employ the remaining part of your time to prepare for eternity, that you may find mercy at the hour of death, and in the day of judgement. Hear now the sentence of the law."

His Lordship then put on the black cap and pronounced the death sentence.

John Hatfield must surely have had the words of the mystic ringing in his ears, because Carlisle was the county town of Cumberland, the county the old man had declared his fate would be sealed. After his return to prison he was visited by the poet Samuel Taylor Coleridge, who wrote later that he thought Hatfield "vain". William Wordsworth was with Coleridge, but did not enter the cell. He later wrote of Hatfield in the Prelude.

> "Unfaithful to virtuous wife,
> Deserted and deceived, the spoiler came...
> And wooed the artless daughter of the hills
> And wedded her in cruel mockery".

Although doomed, Hatfield had supporters, especially among the women of the area. Dorothy Wordsworth wrote in her journals while staying at Longtown: *"Here as everywhere else, the people seem utterly insensible of the enormity of Hatfield's offences. The ostler told William that Hatfield was quite a gentleman."* While awaiting execution, Hatfield kept himself busy writing letters for other prisoners, replying to the letters he received daily and making his peace with God. In a letter to the Rev. Ellerton he said: *"I am indeed sensible of the goodness of God, in granting me the abundant preparation I have had...."*

The Times whetted the public appetite for details of the case with reports from the condemned man's cell:-

2.9.1803: A letter from Carlisle mentions that Hatfield seems perfectly resigned to his fate. He does not seem to entertain the slightest hope of being pardoned. None of his relations have visited him since his condemnation. Neither before his trial now since has he ever alluded to his connection with Mary of Buttermere.

5.9.1803. Hatfield's appetite has failed him, he lives chiefly upon coffee. He applied this morning to one of the clergymen who attends him, Mr Pattinson, to recommend him a tradesman to make his coffin. Mr John Bushby of this town took measure of him and he did not appear to be at all agitated.

6.9.1803. Letter dated 2.9. 1803. I hope that by this time tomorrow all will be over for me; he was to be executed at 4 o'clock.

Finally in The Times September 7th:

Execution of Hatfield. Carlisle September 3rd. His irons were struck off this morning at 10 o'clock; soon after two clergymen attended and prayed with him for about two hours. At 3.30 he was taken to the prison lodge and his hands pinioned before he was taken to the place of execution. Hatfield was escorted to the gallows through a massive crowd where after speaking a few words, he adjusted the noose to his satisfaction and took the drop to eternity. He hung from the tree in the midst of a great number of spectators for one hour, when he was cut down and interred in St Mary's churchyard, the usual place for those who come to an untimely end, the parishioners of Burgh objecting to his being laid there.

Some indication of the nationwide interest in the Hatfield case is the fact that The Times was prepared to devote so much space to it at a time when the main story of the day was Napoleon's preparation to invade Britain.

The Hadfield family stayed on at Crowden Hall until the 1880's when the line became extinct. The Rev James Brooks, Pastor of Hyde Chapel from 1806 to 1854 describes visiting an old wizard, known as Robinson, who lived at the Brushes, near Stalybridge. He said:

I found him very penitent. He acknowledged that he knew no more than other persons, and repented of the deceptions he had practised. "But," said he, "the people would come to me, and I always took care not to say anything that would injure or cast suspicion on a neighbour."

I afterwards learned what his practice was. There was a large field sloping from the house. When a person was seen coming up this field, Robinson went into a back room, where he could hear what was said in the front room. His wife asked the person to sit down, saying her husband would be in soon, and she then questioned the person about his errand. When Robinson thought he had heard sufficient, he went out at the back door, took a circuit, and came up the field; and when he came in and seemed to know everything about the matter the person was astonished, and went away fully convinced that he was really a wizard.

The Camping and Caravan Club's lightweight camping ground at Crowden is ideally situated for serious walkers wishing to explore the region, or climbers heading for Laddow Rocks, or for a night's stop along the Pennine Way. In the days when I used to camp at the site, the warden was the most excellent Mrs White who had a wealth of stories to tell about the area. Her family had at one time farmed in Norfolk and had transported the complete farm, animals, equipment, fodder and family to the Ash Farm which formerly stood nearby at SK070992. The whole kit and caboodle was transported by train and arrived at the little station at Crowden from where it was but a cockstride to the farm. All that remains of Ash Farm today is a heap of stones.

The Manchester Corporation Waterworks was responsible for the destruction of many of the farms. Some are under the water and others which it was feared might pollute the water if left inhabited were ruined by the simple expedient of removing the roofs to let in the elements. These ruined farms furnish an opportunity to learn a little about the methods of building in the 17th and 18th centuries. An examination of the walls reveals that lime mortar was only used for the outer courses and that what can best be described as mud was used in the interior of the wall. Lime would be expensive in the days of packhorse transport and only be used where absolutely necessary. The method seems to have served well enough if the farms which are left are anything to go by. For outbuildings mud was used exclusively, and if a wall which at a first glance appear to be of a drystone construction, is examined more closely it will often reveal the presence of mud inside the walls. The wind and rain over the years having removed it from the outside.

With the wind in the right quarter in open country it is possible to hear people talking at a considerable distance, often long before they come into view. If you can hear folks in this way, just think how wildlife is alerted by a group of chattering ramblers. We are frequently advised not to walk alone on the high moors in case of accident, and very good advice it is too, but you will see and hear a lot more on your own than with a noisy party. A fox slipping into a patch of bracken, shortly afterwards a rabbit shooting out at the other side; a slim pencil of life as a bright eyed weasel disappears into a wall; the constant rustling in the grass on the bank beside you as the shrews go about their business. The countryside teems with life and most of it we miss completely.

There are plenty of stories of unusual sitings in Longdendale; of strange lights, of Roman soldiers marching in ghostly column, and best of all, of a strange creature living in the reservoirs. All that remains of Crowden Station which closed in 1957 is a little row of railway cottages. In one of them lives Mr John Davies who spent his working life on the railway, finally retiring as a signalman at Crowden signal box. One clear moonlit night, Mr Davies was returning from Glossop to his house at Crowden when just after rounding the difficult corner at Devil's Elbow he was alerted by an odd creaking sound as of something moving across gravel. He quickly came to a halt and looking back saw a huge whale-like creature come out of the reservoir and slither up the hillside. The strangest things of all about the monster were that it had two large white eyes and a curly tale. Such stories are naturally greeted with scepticism, but Mr Davies is not alone in his claim and living where he does he is placed better than anyone to see anything out of the ordinary. One thing is certain, if one dark night you are travelling that way and see a whale like creature slithering across the road, you would believe it as well.

WATER-SPOUT AT WOODHEAD

Manchester Guardian; August 10th 1900:

A great sensation was caused on Friday night by a serious block occurring on the Great Central main line by the bursting of a water-spout on the hills between Woodhead and Hadfield. The great volume of water swept down in an irresistible torrent bringing with it large rocks and trees, and piled up a huge mass of debris on the line, to a depth of as much as 15 feet. The unflagging labour of over 500 men was needed to clear the obstruction. The refreshment bars were kept open all night, but as everything eatable had been sold by midnight on Friday, it was only possible to obtain liquid refreshment. Mr Hunt, the station master, had a considerable number of the passengers in his own house to breakfast, but most passengers went breakfastless. About ten o'clock next morning special trains were made up and people taken to Manchester via Huddersfield.

A Mr Gore, sent the following letter to the Manchester Guardian:

"Sir, I notice in your account of the block on the Great Central Railway near Woodhead that it is stated that passengers travelling from Sheffield and stopped at the tunnel were sent back either to Penistone or Sheffield. This is not correct. The train from Hull, 3.25 pm due in Liverpool at 7.20 pm, spent from 6 pm. to 6am. on the line between Penistone and the tunnel. The train stood out on a bleak and exposed spot all night. It was bitterly cold and wet; no refreshment could be obtained, and the officials would not take the train back. I do not wish to complain of the block on the line, but I consider the action of the Company's officials in not sending the train back to Penistone or Sheffield inexcusable. My journey from Hull to Altrincham took 20 hours and 20 minutes, during the first 17 of which we were obliged to starve."

Another described his experiences more cheerfully:

"To be eighteen hours in accomplishing the 45 miles journey from Manchester to Sheffield by train is an unpleasant and probably unique experience. The Rocket would have blushed at such a performance, while all that our driver, could do was to curse the elements, and resign himself to fate and wait. Leaving Manchester at 3.30 with a light heart on holidays intent, we travelled well up to time, and not even the beating rain and howling wind could disturb our prospects. The line runs between the high hills on the one side and the Manchester Waterworks on the other, and it was here, between Hadfield and Crowden stations that misfortune overtook us.

We were travelling at a medium pace when suddenly a more vivid flash of lightning and a louder peal of thunder, together with an immediate application of the brake, caused us to jump up. Despite the driving deluge outside, heads quickly looked out of every window. Right across the line, to a height of ten feet, huge boulders were piled up and we thought what might have happened had the driver not kept a sharp lookout. Providence, in the form of a platelayer, had come to our aid. The sudden torrent had washed part of his home away; his furniture was among the debris on the line; and after saving his wife and family, he rushed to warn our train, which was overdue. (**This platelayers cottage once stood close to the Old Kidfield Paper Mill SK079991).**

As we could not go forward, our engine driver intended returning to Hadfield, but found that the cloud-burst had caused an even worse accident in our rear. We again thanked providence for our merciful deliverance, for had we been passing at the time, our train would have been hurled down the embankment.

So there we were for the night, hemmed in by the hills, the reservoirs, and the tearing torrents. What a situation! With no immediate prospect of reaching the small station at Crowden, some 200 yards ahead, and without food, our holiday happiness seemed to dwindle down to zero. Nothing they told us, could be done till the rain stopped. This was decidedly encouraging. After waiting two hours, the rain slightly abated and some ventured out to inspect the ruins. We came across two cases of soda syphons which had been stored at the platelayers house for some gentlemen coming for the shooting on the 12th. This find, together with a gentleman who was discovered to have a bottle of whisky with him, helped to comfort us slightly.

We examined the poor platelayers house. The whole lower storey with all it contained, was washed away. Only the side walls and upper storey remained. Behind us on the down line, beyond the block to our rear, we could see the smoke of at least four trains, but they, had a back door, and we had not.

After three more hours of waiting we managed to cross by the help of the boulders. The performance was risky but the ladies and children were carried across and we all reached Crowden station in safety. The accommodation was scanty in the extreme. There were only three houses close at hand belonging to the station master, the signalman and the porter. By the courtesy of the good wives of these men, whatever there was of bread, tea, and new laid eggs was procured for us, while the ladies and children were put up at their houses. For the men there was more weary waiting, as the rain was again coming down in bucketfuls, and no one would face the walk to the George and Dragon. Meanwhile we learned that the line was also blocked further ahead, just outside the Woodhead tunnel, which meant more delay, as that obstruction had to be cleared before the breakdown gang could reach us. These were already busy at the obstruction in our rear, but darkness and continuous rain necessitated their relinquishing work till daylight.

One by one the male passengers sought the comforts of the George and Dragon whilst I remained at the station trying to get some rest out of the six inch wooden seats which lined the waiting room walls. Then the station master told us it would be noon on Saturday before we could be sent on to Sheffield. That was the climax. Here were the precious moments of our holiday slipping away in the vain attempt to persuade ourselves that wooden seats were feather beds.

Then I and another made a resolve. We would at daybreak walk to Penistone, a distance of twelve miles over the peaks, to catch the 7.20 train to Sheffield. When day broke we took a last survey of the blocked line, over which the torrent, now only some six feet wide, was still running. We then started our walk, not a very cheering idea after a sleepless night, to be accomplished on a steep road and an empty stomach. The rain had now ceased, and the fresh wind and the exercise increased our appetite. Our one goal was the breakfast table at Penistone. But our spirits were not low; they rose with the road beneath us. The walk was delightful, and though we met no human beings, the grouse, which were very plentiful, and the grazing cattle, were good company. We saw the glorious sunrise, and after that saw occasional labourers going to work. Poor fellows! We at least had no work till Tuesday.

For the last two miles of the journey we used the railway track. Once an official stopped us, and told us we were trespassing, but on showing him our tickets he enjoyed the joke, and agreed with us that 1d per mile was a good price to pay for the privilege of walking. On reaching Penistone we found the station full of passengers bound for London who had been delayed all night. A good breakfast soon put us on a proper footing again, and we eventually completed our journey."

The Manchester Guardian report contained the following piece of invaluable technical information which you might with benefit contemplate for the next flood you meet, as you cling to the rooftop and watch your belongings sail down the street.

"It is a fact mathematically demonstrable, that if the velocity of running water be only doubled its power of moving and transporting rocks is increased 64 fold, while if the velocity is trebled the moving power is multiplied 729 times".

The work of clearing away the debris from the line near Woodhead was accomplished on Tuesday. The first train to reach Manchester after a thorough clearance had been effected was the 2.45 from Sheffield, which arrived shortly before five o'clock.

The heavy rains added greatly to the stock of water in the Longdendale Reservoirs. During a 24 hours, which included Friday night, the fall as shown by the rain gauges at Woodhead was 3 inches. This was the heaviest fall in the records of the waterworks department. The existing supply which had been sufficient for 72 days was so augmented that it became enough for 101 days.

Just over a mile to the west of Crowden village beside the A628 stands Quiet Shepherd Farm, once better known as a public house of the same name. In the days of the old turnpike road there were some desperate characters at large. If local legend is true then some of the landlords were not much better. The story is that John Wesley intended to stay at the Quiet Shepherd Inn as he travelled the country preaching, but he was so disturbed by the villainous appearance of the landlord and his spouse that he departed in the middle of the night fearing to have his throat cut while he slept. Your academic historian my protest that there is no record of such an event in Wesley's extensive journal. Not all that surprising really as John Wesley seemed to prefer giving accounts of people who came to howl down his words and throw missiles which invariably missed him and struck other troublemakers to his rear.

Above Highstones Farm are Highstones Rocks, probably best approached via the "Lad's Leap". I would like to see any lad leap across that gap! The rocks are a vantage point giving wonderful views along the valley. From here on a clear day you can see right to the Lady Cross; and looking in the opposite direction you can make out the site of the Roman fort at Edrotalia. Below are yachtsmen enjoying themselves on Torside Reservoir, and across the valley walkers making the steep descent beside Torside Clough as they travel along the Pennine Way. After crossing Torside dam the path passes Quiet Shepherd farm before turning north heading for the summit of Black Hill. At one time the Crowden hills resounded to the rifle shots of the Territorials practising on the ranges below the footpath. Across the valley is the imposing Loft End Quarry which is most easily reached by the cobbled track from Saint James' Chapel and a further up the valley are Laddow Rocks, a favourite destination of climbers.

Looking down on Crowden today with its few houses it is hard to imagine that it once had its own football and cricket teams, a school and a busy pub called the Commercial. Who knows what the future holds for us? If a motorway ever passes through it could end up as the site of a service station serving the needs of modern travellers in the same way as the pub served the coachmen and carters.

CHAPTER SEVEN
BUILDING THE RESERVOIRS

The Woodhead Tunnel had hardly opened to traffic before another huge civil engineering project disrupted the life of the Longdendale Valley. Manchester, was by this time the rapidly growing centre of the cotton industry, with a desperate need for a supply of pure drinking water, particularly urgent because of the high death rate among its poorer residents especially children.

In the time of Elizabeth I Manchester was supplied with water by an old conduit built by a Mrs Isabel Beck. By the end of the eighteenth century this conduit had been lost to the town *"by means of encroachments and improper diversions of the spring, added to the mismanagement and total neglect of the trustees and officers appointed to keep it in repair"*. Various meetings were held to rectify this situation, but without making any worthwhile progress.

Sir Oswald Mosley, the local Lord of the Manor, made efforts to alleviate the situation and set up a pumping engine by the Medlock to pump water into two small reservoirs at Beswick, but the population grew so rapidly that by 1823 it had reached around 200,000 souls. Sir Oswald's reservoirs soon proved inadequate and larger reservoirs were constructed at Gorton

Before 1838 Manchester was owned by the Mosley family and run by the Court Leat under a continuation of medieval laws. In that year the town was incorporated, and a council duly elected, an event spurred on by the national uproar which followed the disgraceful Peterloo Massacre. Until that date, its day to day government was in the hands of men whose only qualification was their establishment background. In 1807 Sir Oswald Mosley had offered to sell his manorial rights for £90,000, The town elite consisting of High Anglicans countered with an offer of £70,000 and the deal fell through. He made a further offer to sell in 1818 which was again unsuccessful. At the root of the problem was the fact that the money to buy the manorial rights would have to come from the shopkeepers and small business men who were supporters of the High Anglicans, while the chief beneficiaries were likely to be the textile workers who would be contributing little and were mainly of the Non-Conformist persuasion, and the cotton masters who were likely to take over the running of the city. These events were all part of the wider struggle for the reform of Parliament and universal suffrage.

The water problem was becoming worse because with more and more

Kidfield Paper Mill today.

Quiet Shepherd Farm.

houses and chimneys belching smoke the Irwell and Medlock were turning into stinking sewers and water collected in rain butts was as black as ink. The short term solution to the water shortage was to be found in nearby Longdendale and the River Etherow with its fast flowing feeder streams and high rainfall.

In 1846 the Manchester Corporation obtained an Act of Parliament to build the Longdendale Reservoirs; and in subsequent years they obtained several Amendment Acts, principally in 1862 when they decided on great extensions. By an Act passed 22nd July, 1846 they were obliged to discharge 75 cubic feet of water per second for 12 hours of every working day for the benefit of the Vale House, Tintwistle, Bottoms Lodge, Waterside, Best Hill, Broadbottom Mills, and Hodge Printworks. (approximately 20,000,000 gallons) By 1835, the steam engine had become the predominant form of power in nearly every cotton town; but in a few places, Glossop-dale and Longdendale being typical examples, the ample water supply meant that water power still continued to be economical. A reliable supply of water was vital to the cotton masters who needed it to not only to power their water wheels but for various cleaning processes in the dyeing and printing trades. If the bulk of the water flowing down Longdendale was to be impounded and piped away for the use of Mancunians then it would have serious implications for many of them. Naturally they opposed the plans for the reservoirs, but eventually had to settle for remuneration in the cases where their mills and property were to be inundated. Even when the Corporation had bought out and demolished these mills, those downstream were still entitled to compensation water and this was to lead to difficulties in years to come.

Some idea of the extent of the former use of water power is gained from the following figures for mills along the nearby Glossop Brook: Hurst Mill, 35 horse power, 57 feet 6 inches fall; Wren Nest Mill, 30 horse power, 19 feet 9 inches fall; Brookfield Mill, 25 horse power, 19 feet 3 inches fall. Along the Etherow reliant on water were Valehouse Mill, Bottoms Mill, Waterside Mill, Botany, Broadbottom Mill, Hodge Printworks, Hodge Cotton Mill, Compstall Mill, and of course other mills further downstream in Romiley and Stockport.

The building of Manchester Corporation Reservoirs meant the end for many of the farms which once provided a living for dozens of folks right along the valley. Some were submerged under the water while others were bought out and destroyed by the Corporation. The reason given at the time was to prevent pollution of the water by men and beasts. The public were excluded from the area of the reservoirs for the same reason. Relatively recently, on occasions

Bottoms Lodge Mill.

Paddling in the water supply.

when large numbers of railway workers were employed on work near the reservoirs, inspectors would check to make sure that there had been no contamination of the supply. Today, there are yachts on Torside Reservoir, footpaths giving access round most of the others so that folks can throw sticks in the water for their dogs to fetch, and on fine weekends, children happily paddle in the feeder streams.

On the 3rd August, 1848 work was commenced on Woodhead Reservoir, the contractors being Richard Thompson and Sons, Blackburn, who had 1,400 men employed. Disputes about the price to be paid for the land taken were settled mostly by arbitration. Mr George Hyde's of Tintwistle Hall being the first case settled. Mr Abel Buckley, of Ashton-under-Lyne, was the arbitrator. It was stated in evidence that "the Hollingworth estate, sold in 1831 for £11,250 consisted of 630 acres, some of it moorland, but with 200 acres of good land." The landlords naturally tried to get all they could for their lands, and the Corporation to pay the least.

Working conditions for the men employed on the project were better than had been the case only ten years earlier on the Woodhead Tunnel. Unlike the railway shareholders, personal profit was not the motive of the Manchester Corporation, although they certainly wanted the work carrying out as efficiently and cheaply as possible. Also they did not have the problems of having to keep raising extra capital to keep the work progressing. They knew they had the resources of the ratepayers of Manchester behind them whose numbers and wealth were growing apace. A real bonus would ensue when the pure water started to flow and Councillors would be able to bask in the publicity which is the very lifeblood of the politically minded. Those were the days when Mancunians could say with pride, "What Manchester does today, the rest of the world does tomorrow."

To accommodate the navvies and their families, wooden huts were erected on the northern side of Rhodeswood Reservoir in a shanty town known as New Yarmouth. Those living there were fortunate, for by no means the whole workforce was able to use such accommodation, many lived in huts built of turf and stone thatched with heather and with potato sacks for doors. Nevertheless living in the valley was a much more comfortable proposition than struggling to survive on the top of the moor round those airshaft entrances.

The building of the reservoirs is associated with the name of John Frederick Bateman the famous water engineer who fortunately has left us a complete record of the project complete with detailed drawings and

New Yarmouth.

specifications. John Frederick Bateman was the eldest son of John Bateman of Ockbrook near Derby. His mother was the daughter of the Rev. Benjamin La Trobe of the well known Moravian settlement at Fairfield, near Ashton-under-Lyne. He was born 30th May 1810 at Lower Wyke near Halifax. The La Trobes were descendants of a noble French refugee family.

Bateman served an apprenticeship with a Mr Dunn of Oldham who was a surveyor and mining and civil engineer, and in 1833 he commenced business on his own account as a civil engineer. In 1834 he investigated the causes of the floods in the River Medlock, which led him to study hydraulic questions closely. In 1841 he married Anne the daughter of Sir William Fairbairn, the famous ship builder. By 1859 he was sufficiently wealthy to purchase Moore Park estate at Farnham where he lived until his death in June 1889. In 1883 Bateman assumed the name of La Trobe by royal licence. In 1878 and 1879 he was President of the Institution of Civil Engineers.

John Frederick Bateman.

The Manchester Corporation Reservoirs in Longdendale were not the first Civil Engineering projects on which Bateman had worked. In 1836 the mill owners of the Upper Bann in north eastern Ireland asked Bateman and Fairbairn to regulate the River Bann's flow because they were having problems with the erratic flow at various times of the year. These two Engineers adapted a natural lake into a reservoir to impound flood waters by building an embankment.

In nearby Glossop dale a group know as the Glossop Commissioners which consisted mainly of mill owners, obtained an Act of Parliament in 1837 empowering them to construct the Glossop Reservoirs which were intended to provide power for the water wheels driving their mills. Public drinking water was not one of their priorities. It was their intention to build three reservoirs to be called Chunal Wood Reservoir, Shelf Reservoir, and Hurst Reservoir; but the rapid development of the steam engine was making water power redundant and only the Hurst Reservoir was actually constructed in 1838. The engineer was Thomas Ashworth and his surveyor was the 28 year old John Frederick Bateman. It is quite remarkable how young some of the Victorian engineers were to be entrusted with such major works. These men were tackling work of a size and complexity previously unknown and were forced to rely to a large degree on their intuition rather than any body of earlier experience. The very notion of a dam bursting and flooding the valley was sufficient to ensure that they erred on the side of excessive caution. This is why so much of the work is characterised by its obvious strength and why it stands to this day performing its original purpose.

The contract for the work on Hurst Reservoir was advertised for tender in the Manchester Guardian at the end of May 1838.

THE GLOSSOP RESERVOIRS - CONTRACT FOR WORKS - TO BE LET, on Monday the 25th day of June next, at eleven o'clock in the forenoon, at the house of Mrs Wagstaffe, the Norfolk Arms, in Howard Town, within Glossop Dale, in the County of Derby, the EMBANKING, PUDDLING, STONING, MASONRY, and other work, of the Hurst Reservoir, in Glossop Dale aforesaid. The earth consists of upwards of 90,000 cubic yards. The plans, specification, and working drawings, will be ready for inspection, on and after the 6th day of June next, at the office of Mr J F Bateman, civil engineer 48 Pall Mall, Manchester, from whom any further information may be obtained. The commissioners do not pledge themselves to accept the lowest tender, and the contractors must be prepared with satisfactory security at the time of letting.

THOS. ELLISON, Clerk to the Commissioners
Glossop, 25th May, 1838

The successful contractor for the building of Hurst Reservoir was Samuel Taylor who was later to obtain the contracts for building Arnfield and

Hollingworth Reservoirs. We read articles about cotton masters who made fortunes, or the splendid lives of great landowners, but too little attention is paid to men of the calibre of Samuel Taylor without whose skills, vast civil engineering projects would not have been possible. Samuel was born in Saddleworth and started his working life as a stonemason. From 1822 to 1825 he was an innkeeper in Hadfield at the Spinner's Arms but then returned to building work and progressed so well that by the census of 1851 he describes himself as a Contractor for Public Works. In 1865, he tried to set up his son as a cotton master at Bury me Wick Mill in Chunal, but the venture failed. There must be hundreds of similar men whose skills and foresight took advantage of the opportunities at the time, but whose names are now largely forgotten.

There is a letter in Manchester Central Library dated June 1845, which contains the following interesting detail: "*The Commissioners of Glossop Reservoirs have paid Taylor within £50 of his claim on them.*" A successful contractor could do very well indeed for himself. Samuel Taylor built Ryecroft House in Manor Park Road in 1851 and when he died in June 1866, his estate was worth around £4,800.

Constructing the reservoir dams in Longdendale was only part of the work; conduits had to be built to allow water to be transferred from one reservoir to another to allow maintenance work to be carried out, culverts and bridges, residuum lodges to allow the sand and peat washed down in times of flood to settle out, and last but by no means least, a tunnel under Mottram to deliver the water from Arnfield Reservoir to the reservoir at Godley.

Work on this tunnel was started in 1848 at the same time as the dam for Woodhead Reservoir. When completed the Mottram Tunnel was 2,772 yards long, 6 feet high, and 6 feet wide. The fall is five feet per mile. There are five airshafts along the tunnel and two of them can be seen from Edge Lane. On 19th October 1850 water was allowed to flow through, and Mr JE Bateman, CE, the engineer to the Corporation, Messrs J Manson, and J Molyneux, the resident engineer and superintendent of the tunnel, Messrs George Hill, resident engineer, and Samuel Taylor of Glossop, passed through the tunnel in a flat bottomed boat. The journey was accomplished in one hour and forty minutes.

The tunnel is drained and inspected on an annual basis, but during 1998 the events of the official opening were re-enacted and parties passed through in boats once more. On average, some 24,000,000 gallons a day pass through this tunnel, but when necessary it can cope with double that quantity. This figure gives us a very good idea of the size of the Etherow before the dams were built,

Pikenase from Woodhead Dam.

Waterchute, Woodhead Dam.

since it is larger than the amount of compensation water.

To ensure that the dams would hold water, in the centre of each was a core of puddled clay. A trench was first excavated across the valley and gradually filled with wet clay which was trodden into a plastic waterproof mass by men in clogs with sacking wrapped round them. The puddled clay core rose steadily with the rest of the embankment. The man supervising this essential work was called the puddle tinter. Perhaps the word puddled, meaning stupid, comes from this occupation - you had to be puddled to do it. Where exceptionally difficult conditions were encountered, a concrete core was employed.

The work at times was carried on under great difficulties, thunderstorms being the most dangerous. On the 9th August, 1849 there was a tremendous thunderstorm during which one man was killed by lightning and another drowned by an inrush of water into the cutting that he was excavating. Two months afterwards another storm did damage estimated at £2,550. On the 7th October 1849 the work on the reservoirs suffered a severe setback caused by flooding. The weir across Heyden Brook, which had been constructed to divert water down the valley while a dam was being built, gave way under the overwhelming pressure of a heavy flood made worse by a strong gale. About 2.00pm the weir collapsed and the water poured into the basin of the Woodhead reservoir, until at 5.30p.m. it reached the top of the embankment. Once it started to overflow, it rapidly cut a breach for the escape of all the impounded water. The water, once released, rushed down the valley, destroying fences, crops, bridges and buildings in its path for a distance of five miles.

There was a further scare in February, 1852 when after days of heavy rain the reservoirs were within a few hours of being completely filled. Mill owners started to remove valuable equipment and householders moved their furniture to a place of safety; the panic even spread as far as Glossop. Men on horseback were stationed at various points, ready to ride at a moments notice to give warning. Fortunately the weather cleared up and the danger abated. The heavy rains which caused this alarm were the same ones which led to the Bilberry Reservoir disaster in the Holme Valley and after the publicity which accompanied that terrible event in which around 80 people lost their lives, public concern was understandable. The Bilberry Reservoir dam collapsed because it had been built on top of a poorly sealed spring; under Bateman's supervision such shoddy procedures would never have been countenanced.

On the 4th July, 1868 James Nicholls was killed by a fall of earth. Four hundred navvies in white smocks walked at his funeral and each gave 1s towards the expenses of the funeral and relief of his parents.

Woodhead reservoir was the first on which work was commenced and the last to be finished in 1877. To anyone viewing the valley today, the massive dams look immovable, yet in the past there were genuine fears that one or more might give way releasing an unstoppable flood. If you look south from Woodhead Chapel across the reservoirs to the hillsides alongside the upper part of Torside Reservoir and the lower section of Woodhead Reservoir you will notice that there is considerable evidence of broken ground caused by landslips at various times in the past. The problem lay in the nature of the rocks to be found along the intended line of the Woodhead dam. On the geological section there are soft and hard shales, open jointed hard rock, silt, sand and gravel with particles of clay, and what is described as loose ground. Hardly the ideal materials on which to erect an impervious dam. The building of the Woodhead embankment was a lengthy saga to overcome the problem of seepage. Various methods were employed including sinking bore holes into the trouble spots and pouring ashes into them. The famous engineers Robert Stephenson and Isambard Kingdom Brunel visited Longdendale to inspect the Woodhead embankment and its problems. The seemingly intractable difficulty was finally solved by building a second embankment below the first where test boring had revealed a continuous strata of shale right across the valley.

The top three reservoirs are used to impound water for Manchester and the bottom two to supply compensation water to the River Etherow. Watercourses carry the water from the impounding reservoirs to Arnfield and then by Mottram Tunnel to Godley. Bottoms and Valehouse Reservoirs are lower than Arnfield. Although far larger reservoirs have been constructed during the intervening years, when completed the Longdendale Reservoirs had the largest total capacity of any artificial water storage in the world. Today the system is still North West Water's fifth largest resource.

In 1901, the Manchester Guardian stated that the full capacities of the reservoirs were: Hollingworth, 73,000,000 gallons; Bottoms, 407,000,000; Vale House, 343,000,000; Rhodes Wood, 500,000,000; Torside, 1,474,000,000; and Woodhead, 1,181,000,000. Despite the provision of settling pools, in time of flood some sand and peat is carried into the reservoirs and over the years must have reduced their original capacities.

Although the mill and houses at Valehouse were demolished and sold as building materials, the chimney was left standing when the valves were closed and water started to fill the reservoir in 1869. The odd sight of a chimney protruding from the waters of Valehouse Reservoir was a local curiosity until it was finally demolished in 1887. The Railway Company requested its removal because they feared that passengers rushing to one side of the train to see such a spectacle would destabilise the train and cause a derailment!

The mill owners opposing the building of the reservoirs and who demanded compensation water were those occupying Vale House; Tintwistle; Bottom's Lodge; Waterside; Best Hill; Broadbottom Mills and Hodge Printworks. Some of these were bought out. Those lower down the river were indirectly one of the causes of the floods which have plagued the Brookfield district every time there was heavy rain in Glossop-dale or Longdendale. According to the Glossop Borough Surveyor, Mr G. Faulds, the main cause of this flooding was the sluice gates on the Etherow owned by the Manchester Water Committee and he had been in constant communication with them with a view to the gates being removed. One problem was that the Rivers Catchment Board was an ad hoc authority and only the County Councils were members; hence Glossop could only act through the County Council.

A letter from the Catchment Board to Glossop Council in 1946:

"We promised to keep in touch with you regarding the proposals of the Catchment Board to alleviate the flooding in the Woolley Bridge area of Glossop. Having regard to the size of the expenditure estimated for the replacement of the existing Manchester Corporation sluice gates by a type of tilting gate which would prevent water backing up as it does now, investigations have been pursued with a view to removing the gates altogether as a cheaper means of attaining the same end.

The gates were erected under the powers reserved to the Manchester Corporation by their Waterworks Act, 1848, and appear to have been erected for the specific benefit of three mills. I have now obtained provisionally, the approval of the owners of these three mills to the removal of the gates. In addition, Manchester Corporation would raise no objection. (The three mills were Best Hill; Broadbottom and Hodge Printworks)

The removal of the gates would deprive the three mills concerned of a statutory right, and in one instance at least, alternative arrangements for water supply are likely to be required at the expense of the Catchment Board.

In addition to the three mills specifically mentioned in the Act, the Board has had notice from other mills that are interested, and the implication is that they will claim a prescriptive right to the water. I am not clear in my own mind what right these other mills have; and in any case, I am considering the point whether a statutory right can be surrendered by deed, or whether a Bill in Parliament will be required to relieve the Manchester Corporation of its obligations.

I anticipate that quite an amount of further negotiations will be required with various affected parties before the final agreement can be arrived at. But I feel satisfied that this line is the only one that can be adopted in view of the prohibitive cost of any alternative."

R H Adcock. Clerk to the Board.

Manchester coat of arms, Bottoms valve house.

Bottom's Fountain, which measures the compensation water.

This letter illustrates clearly the difficulties that face local authorities when trying to get to grips with problems. A sluice gate built for the benefit of local mill owners a century and a half earlier was creating trouble when water power was no longer in use and some of the mills had disappeared into the bargain. All grist to the mill of the legal profession. The eventual removal of the sluice gates below Woolley Bridge went a long way to solving the problems at Brookfield, but has definitely not eradicated it.

On the wall of the Valve House below Bottoms Reservoir is a marble plaque with the following inscription:

MANCHESTER CORPORATION WATERWORKS.

Authorised by Acts of Parliament obtained in the years 1847-1848-1863 & 1865. Works commenced in August 1848 and continued till the completion of this reservoir in 1877. During which period of 29 years they have been carried on under the immediate direction of the Water Works Committee annually appointed by the Council of which the following gentlemen have acted as Chairmen and Deputy Chairmen Viz.

Chairmen
Ald. Sir Elkanah Armitage Knight	1848-1865
Mr Ald Clark	1865-1867

Deputy Chairmen
Mr Ald. Hopkins	1848-49
Mr Ald. Pilling	1849-63
Mr Ald. Bowker	1863-65
Mr Ald. Grave	1865-67
Mr Ald. Patteson	1867

Sir Joseph Heron-Knight	Town Clerk
John Frederic Bateman	Engineer
George Henry Hill	Principal Ass. Engineer.

Here we have the names of the city fathers who were the motive force behind this great project; one can easily imagine their pride when pure water started to flow into Manchester homes. Note that the names of the aldermen come first, while mere technicians like Bateman and Hill who supervised the work and whose services would have been speedily disposed of if they had failed are put at the bottom.

There are still plenty of reminders of who was responsible for the works. At the Hadfield end of Tintwistle Bridge is a fountain and horse trough with the inscription "Manchester Corporation Waterworks 1879". Along Woolley Mill Lane is a well with MCWW clearly marked, and inset in the wall east of the Quiet Shepherd farm is a cast iron grating once again carrying the legend MW. As you walk around the reservoirs you can see the handiwork of the

View over Valehouse and Rhodeswood reservoirs.

stonemasons, puddlers, carpenters and navvies who actually built them under Bateman's guidance. The reservoirs may have inundated many farms, houses and mills, but today they certainly enhance the appearance of the valley. Now that concessionary paths give public access to much of the area without apparently damaging in any way the quality of the water, we can walk round most of the reservoirs and get a fine view of herons standing in the shallows watching for a fish to spear; huge flocks of Canada geese and lesser numbers of ducks and waders.

Frederick Bateman's career continued after the Longdendale reservoirs. The scheme had been designed to supply a population less than half that of Manchester in 1882, and it became clear that additional sources of supply must be sought. At Bateman's suggestion the corporation resolved to construct further works at Lake Thirlmere. A bill was passed in Parliament in 1879 and Bateman supervised the start of the new works in association once more with George Hill. Frederick Bateman was also responsible for waterworks in places from Warrington to Perth to Belfast amongst around thirty schemes.

As if this was not more than sufficient, in 1869 he proposed in a pamphlet entitled "Channel Railway" in conjunction with Julian John Revy, to construct a submarine railway between France and England in a cast-iron tube.

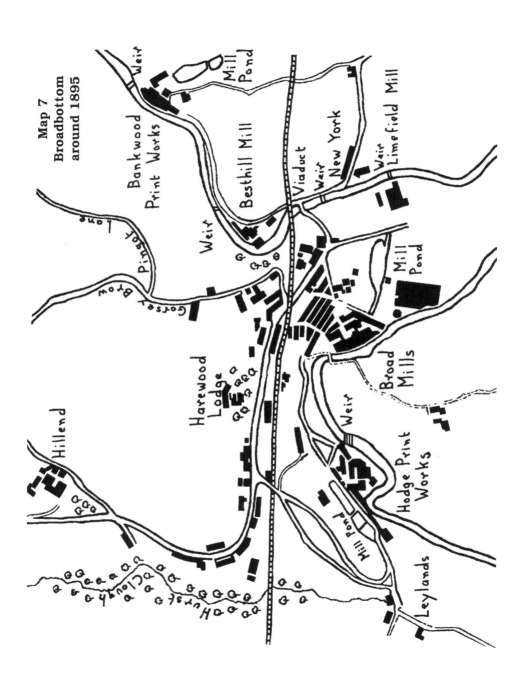

Map 7
Broadbottom
around 1895

CHAPTER EIGHT
THE TEXTILE INDUSTRY IN THE PAST

Henry VIII was not the first King of England to cast his eyes on the riches of the Church of Rome, he was just the first one with the brass neck to actually steal their possessions and share them out among his supporters. He even had the gall to suggest that once the state had got its hands on the riches of the Church, then no one would need to pay taxes again.

The doings of the high and mighty inevitably redound on those at lower levels of society and the suppression of the monasteries was no exception to this rule. The aristocracy could hardly wait to seize the property of the monasteries and were quick to put up the rents of their new tenants. The tenants were forced to work more efficiently or starve. The successful farmers were able to build themselves substantial new farmhouses because they were able to negotiate longer leases which made it worthwhile to improve the land and buildings. It is no coincidence that from the mid-1500's the older wood and wattle and daub cruck houses started to disappear to be replaced by farms built of stone.

The poorer farmers survived by turning to textile manufacture in their homes to raise the extra money, employing their families to spin the woollen thread while they wove it into cloth on a treadle loom in the home. This rural industry was to lead to the development of the local textile industries; firstly wool, then fustian and finally cotton. Soon men with a little capital set up as clothiers obtaining spun yarn from outlying farms and carrying it to the handloom weavers and later collecting the finished cloth and taking it to market in Manchester, Stockport or Huddersfield. William Radcliffe of Mellor, writing in 1828 left us the following description of the life of local people at that time:

"In the year 1770, the land in our township was occupied by between fifty to sixty farmers. Rents to the best of my recollection did not exceed 10 shillings per statute acre and out of these fifty or sixty farmers, there were only six or seven who raised their rents directly from the produce of their farms. All the rest got their rent partly in some branch of trade, such as spinning and weaving woollen, linen or cotton. The cottagers were employed entirely in this manner, except for a few weeks in the harvest. Being one of these cottagers, and intimately acquainted with all the rest, as well as every farmer, I am the better able to relate particularly how the change from the old style of land labour to the new one of machinery operated in raising the price of land. Cottage rents at that time, with a convenient loom shop and a small garden attached, were from one and a half to two guineas per annum. The father of a family would earn from 8 shillings to half a guinea at his loom, and his sons, if he had one, two, or three alongside of him, 6 or 8 shillings each per week. But the great sheet anchor of all cottages and small farms was the labour attached to the hand spinning wheel and when it is considered that it requires six to eight hands to prepare and spin yarn sufficient for the consumption of one weaver. This shows clearly the inexhaustible source there was for labour for every person from the age of seven to eighty years to earn their bread, say, 1 to 3 shillings per week without going to the parish."

An examination of the wills left at the time confirms the foregoing statements. The deceased often described themselves as websters (weavers), and the accompanying inventories listed such items as, looms, loom weights, cards, spinning wheels, cloth and spun yarn.

In his *Origin of Power Loom Weaving,* Radcliffe describes how his family at Mellor resorted to spinning and weaving to supplement their income, and how his mother taught him to card and spin cotton for his father and elder brothers to work on the loom. Later he learned weaving and in time set up in business in Stockport. He records how at the end of the eighteenth century there was "not a village within thirty miles of Manchester on the Derbyshire or Cheshire side in which some of us were not putting out cotton warps and taking in goods." He claimed to employ over a thousand weavers on his own behalf.

In addition to this, the cottagers were entirely employed in spinning and weaving and· Radcliffe describes how old barns, cart houses and outbuildings were repaired and fitted out as loom shops and new cottages built with such shops as part of the structure. Radcliffe may have exaggerated the prosperity of the hand loom weavers, but the steadily growing wealth as revealed in wills suggests that many families prospered before the introduction of the factory

Former weaver's cottage, Wedneshough.

system. This period of prosperity for the weavers was the time when the typical three storey weavers cottages were built. Not many survive in Longdendale when compared with the Saddleworth area.

The answer to the problem of the spinners being unable to provide the weavers with sufficient thread was found when local men invented spinning machinery. The clothiers who knew the local country with its fast running streams and reliable water supply put two and two together and started to build the first water powered spinning mills. The earliest mills were quite small, the small early spinning machinery did not require a huge waterwheel. Take the Padfield Brook which once had several mills along its length as an example. The water wheels were not mounted directly over the river since this would only allow for the use of a very inefficient undershot wheel and further could not be adapted to changes in the water level. The usual arrangement was to build a weir across the stream to hold back the water and then take a leat from the weir to feed a mill lodge where water could be stored. Water from the mill lodge could then be discharged at the desired rate to drive the water wheel. This allowed the power generated by the wheel to be controlled and also at times of low rainfall, the wheel could be stopped for periods while the lodge refilled.

The Factories Act of 1831 gives some indication of how important water power was at that date. It included legislation that time lost through want of water could be made up by starting at 5 am. and working until 10.00 in the evening, but not more than three hours a week to be made up. If any accident to machinery caused a stoppage then one hour per day was allowed for 10 days.

In the absence of written records we can never be certain as to exactly when some early mills were built. You can still come across signs of old weirs and leats along the courses of the smallest streams. A typical example of what was once a woollen mill is at SJ989959 near Mottram where beside the tiny stream is the ruin of Victoria Mill and what was once a mill lodge. The lodge dam was broken down long ago but thirty years ago you could still make out where the leat led the water to the dam from higher up the stream. Directly uphill from this ruin is Old Mill Farm on Edge Lane which presumably got its name from this mill.

Burdett's map of 1763-67 shows a water-powered mill just downstream of Tintwistle Bridge at a spot then known as Brookside, and also Woolley Mill on the Arnfield Brook. The first of these was probably a fulling mill. It may well have been there far earlier because water power had been used for fulling of woollen cloth since the Middle Ages. Fulling is a process whereby the woollen cloth is thickened. Originally this was done by trampling the wet cloth underfoot and adding cleaning agents such as Fuller's earth and wood ash. The fulling mill did away with this unpleasant human labour by substituting power driven mallets. The mapmaker's symbol for a mill was a tiny representation of a waterwheel which indicates the power source if not what process was carried out there.

Aikin's map, of 1797 shows many more mills in Longdendale: at Brookside, Turner's Factory is shown, and Cardwell's Factory of Woolley Lane. Sidebottoms Mill which was built around 1787 is shown at Millbrook on the Tintwistle side of the Hollingworth Brook. I wonder if the name Millbrook comes from the Woolley Mill a little further upstream? The building of Arnfield Reservoir cut off the flow of the Arnfield Brook so that the remains of Woolley Mill no longer have a water power source.

Along the Etherow, the earliest spinning mills appear to be those at Valehouse, Bottoms, and Waterside built by the pioneering cotton masters the Turners and Thornleys. Valehouse mill was built around 1795 by Robert and John Thornley. To house the workers a number of houses were built and a Wesleyan Chapel so a small hamlet grew up around the mill which in 1830 had a population of 600 people.

In 1826 Valehouse Mill was closed owing to the failure of the proprietors. The Manchester Guardian of 14.9.1827 carried the following advertisement:

SALE OF MILL by auction at the Norfolk Arms due to bankruptcy of Robert Thornley of Vale House. The larger factory is five stories high besides the attic and presents a front of 105 feet 9 inches, the width is 39 feet 6 inches. The smaller factory is three stories high, 117 feet long and 33 feet wide and both are capable of containing 15,000 spindles. The machinery is turned by a powerful water wheel of 18 feet diameter and four yards in width. The factories are heated by steam and lighted with gas. The fall of water is 19 feet 6 inches supplied by the River Etherow, a never failing stream; hands are plentiful and coal is obtained at a cheap rate in great abundance.

The sale of the machinery for the above mill was on 19th and 20th of September 1827 at Vale House. Amongst the machines on offer were two scutchers, one willow, 24 carding engines, two slubbing frames, three stretching frames, eighteen mules with 312 spindles each and one large factory clock with a copper face. The abundant supply of coal may have come from the pit at Deepclough a short distance upstream. Although this mill was powered by water, coal would still be required for heating and to increase humidity. A willow or blowing machine was for opening up the packed bales of cotton. It consisted of a large drum full of spikes to tear and loosen the cotton and to clean it. The manufacturer was Sir Francis Willow of Bury, hence the name. Later the Manchester Corporation were empowered to purchase lands and property which would be affected when the reservoirs were filled. Having purchased the mill and various properties the end came on the 17th October, 1867 when they were sold as building materials.

John Turner built Bottoms mill in 1795 and his son William sold the Waterside complex to the Sidebottoms in 1820. The Bottoms Lodge Mill was occupied in 1825 by John Turner, in 1836 by John Winterbottom and Co. (owners John Winterbottom and Samuel Lees). There were then two factories, the old factory being assessed at £192 15s and the new one at £61 10s. On the 16th October, 1867 the machinery was sold by the Manchester Corporation.

The Crowden Factory was shown on the Victorian Ordnance Survey maps and must have been typical of many small mills which failed to survive. It had various owners; in an 1835 directory Hadfield and Wilkinson are listed at Croden Brook and later it was Brown's Bleach Works. It stands to this day in a ruinous condition.

The fortunes of these early cotton masters varied considerably. Some prospered and gradually built up enormous factories employing hundreds of hands; others were carried away by early success and acquired expensive tastes

Ruins of Crowden factory.

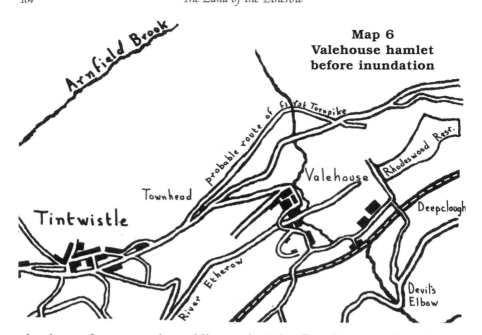

**Map 6
Valehouse hamlet
before inundation**

and a love of sports and gambling and at the first downturn in trade were broken. The pages of the Manchester Guardian in the early years of the 19th century feature whole lists of bankrupts.

To outline the history of every mill would require several volumes, but a brief history of the small Besthill Mill might serve as an example of the fate of some. Besthill Mill was built in 1784 by John Marsland on the Derbyshire side of the Etherow as a spinning mill. In 1799 it became known as Kelsall and Marsland. By 1809 John Marsland had installed spinning mules. In 1812, the factory suffered a setback when a mob of Luddites starting from Hollingworth smashed machinery and pulled out the boiler plugs. But by 1830 Samuel Marsland was employing 90 women and 30 men at an average wage of 10s 8d a week. The mill managed to survive the difficult times during the cotton famine but in 1884 the lease on the mill expired. There was a dispute between the lessees and Lord Howard about the right of way and as a result the lease was not renewed and the mill closed causing considerable hardship to folks in Broadbottom and Charlesworth. Many of the cotton masters had made considerable fortunes, and although they could not be compared in wealth with Lord Howard they had sufficient to tell him to "Go jump in the cut" and retire in comfort. As ever, the workers got the dirty end of the stick.

The successful cotton masters had the capital, foresight and knowledge of the trade to take advantage of machines such as the spinning mule and later the power loom. To accommodate these machines they built larger mills to a standard pattern. Mule spinning in particular required plenty of space for the process. Many of these mills have been destroyed by fire or deliberately demolished over the years but if you examine the construction of those left standing you will find find that the windows are spaced ten feet apart, that the columns inside are spaced at the same interval, and that the bays are twenty feet wide. Local mills were built from stone and the walls at the base were of considerable thickness. The cast iron columns were a standard item which could be slotted into each other and had integral brackets to support line shafting and timber beams. The method of building was such that each part helped to support others and the whole was very strong, but in the event of a fire the timber floors and roof would go first and the columns, if they did not collapse would be left standing drunkenly.

Building these mills and the rows of terraced houses for the workforce provided plenty of work for stonemasons and carpenters. In the case of the earlier mills, the stone would be provided by the little quarries or delphs that are so common in the area. When you look at a six storey mill and its chimney ponder for a moment and consider how the stone was raised into position by men working on wooden scaffolding lashed together with rope.

At the beginning of the nineteenth century there were still only about 300 Boulton and Watt steam engines in the whole of Britain. Manchester's first steam powered weaving mill was not opened until 1806 and as late as 1815 only a small proportion of Britain's workforce was employed in large factories. As larger and larger mills were constructed even the most powerful waterwheel was incapable of providing sufficient power and the cotton masters turned to steam engines.

The first were vertical beam engines which were slow moving with a huge flywheel. These were reliable and could run steadily for years. The engineer who looked after them was an important man, since if the engine stopped, the whole mill was brought to a halt. Initially, power was supplied to the machinery on each floor of the mill by a system of shafts and gearing. As mills grew ever larger, they were replaced by cotton driving ropes which drove the line shafts.

The cotton industry created work for others; hence we had cotton rope drives made at several small factories in Charlesworth, and belt fasteners for the leather belts used to drive the machinery from the overhead line shafts, made at Isaac Jackson's in Glossop. One of the many families of Booths at Charlesworth

Beam engine.

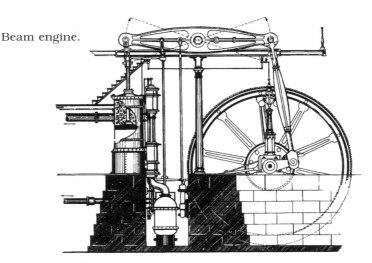

set up in business as "Machine Makers" supplying looms and other machines to local companies for years. At one time rope piecers from Charlesworth travelled all over industrial Lancashire fitting sets of rope drives.

This mention of driving belts reminds me of another aspect of life in local mills which does not usually get an airing. Leather belts, especially the wider ones were a desirable item being the very thing for repairing shoes in the days when boots and shoes had leather soles. So desirable was this material, that if a belt had to be removed for repairs it virtually needed an armed guard if it was not to disappear within minutes. A shoe last was a very handy piece of tackle to have around the place once upon a time.

Any scrap wood laying around the place was liable to be chopped up for firewood. A favourite trick was to insert a loom weight into the bundle so that the firewood carrier would have his work cut out. One of the victims of this little prank had a fair idea of who was to blame and said to them, "Thanks for putting that lump of cast iron in the bundle. You can do that every time if you like." It transpired later that he collected the cast iron weights until he had enough to weigh in at a local scrap iron merchants.

One boilerman used to sweep up the coal dust each day, mix it with a spot of cement and cast it into a small block. This he carried home in his butty bag each night and it made a nice kettle wedge.

The workers were not the only ones indulging in a spot of skullduggery; management had a few tricks up its sleeve. In one mill the engineer made a plug to fit into the main steam line. This plug was drilled with holes so that some steam could pass through but no matter how wide the valve was opened the flow was still restricted. When workers complained of the cold, the engineer would open the valve a couple of turns, but still use no more steam. In more recent times advantage was taken of the fact that the water which fills the sprinkler system does not pass through a meter. In two mills at least, advantage was taken of this to obtain a free supply. In one the water was just drawn off by a pipe attached to the sprinkler main. In the other a more elaborate scheme was adopted. An outlet was fitted to the sprinkler main and attached to a pipe which supplied the mill with water from a lodge on the hillside. Each night this valve was opened and the water used to fill the lodge. Next morning the valve was shut and the water drawn off from the lodge normally.

An inspection of older maps reveals a number of small mill lodges at various points on the hillsides. These once supplied mills which are long gone and in some cases the lodges have disappeared under housing estates or been filled in for reasons of safety.

Manchester Guardian 21.5.1831:

Fire Near Mottram - "Late on Saturday evening or early on Sunday morning last, the factory of Mr James Sidebottom, Hollingworth, near Mottram, took fire and the whole of the premises were consumed. At present the cause is unknown. The premises are insured nearly to their value; from two to three hundred hands, we are sorry to say, are thrown out of employ by the fire. On Wednesday the walls fell in, and the place now presents a complete destruction of the property; not an article of any value could be saved."

Fire was the bane of textile mills. Oil from the machines gradually soaked into the wooden floors. The air was full of cotton fluff which stuck to the oil so that a tiny spark was sufficient to send a flame racing through the building. The rope drives from the engine were a further hazard because they caused a draught which could carry a fire quickly to any floor of the building. Also access to the floors was gained by a stone staircase at one corner of the mill and later lift shafts. Both of these acted as chimneys providing a good draught once a fire had started and making it dangerous to exit by them. Hence the provision of cast iron fire escapes on the outside walls of mills.

Various modifications were incorporated in an attempt to produce a fire proof mill. Instead of wooden floors, brick arches filled with cement and rubble were used. The introduction of water sprinkler systems was a considerable improvement. A water tower provided a head of water where necessary and a system of pipes ran through every room fitted with sensor heads which were activated if the temperature rose above a determined point. The first sprinkler heads had a special low melting point solder plug, but as this tended to deteriorate with time and either fail to operate or allow the water to switch on without warning they were replaced with a glass phial containing a liquid which expanded and broke the glass at a predetermined temperature. Despite all these devices a truly fireproof mill seemed an impossible dream. In 1949 the greater part of the Broad Mills complex was ruined by fire. More recently Arrowscroft Mill in Hollingworth was destroyed. Albion Mill, a small mid 19th century mill, at Wedneshough is one of the few left standing and still in use.

The introduction of the factory system had a shattering effect on the lives of working people. When they worked in their own homes they did so at their own speed, not the speed of a steam engine which never tired. They could work at their looms or till their plots as the weather or their humour suited them. If the hunt passed by in pursuit of a hare they could abandon work and join in the sport. It is hardly surprising therefore, that there was widespread resistance to working in the new factories, or that the bulk of the workforce was made up of women and children who were less able to resist. Worst of all it led to the employment of pauper children from the workhouses of large cities who were exploited under the most ghastly conditions. Pauper children do not seem to have been employed in this valley but that does not mean that the local cotton masters were all well meaning philanthropists. With the passing of the first Factories Acts, a whole string of them were fined for a variety of offences such as employing children for excessive hours, or tampering with clocks so that people were deceived into working longer hours. The effects of these abuses was still evident fifty or sixty years ago in the shape of old people with twisted and rickety limbs.

An examination of the Quarter Sessions reports in the County Archives will reveal dozens of cases of Cotton Masters being fined for breaches of the Factories Act. On 7th December, 1830, Mr Turner of Waterside Mills was fined £20 for working children under sixteen years of age longer than the law allowed. In June 1835, Henry Lees of Woolley Bridge, fined 10s. and 4s. costs for employing someone under 18 years of age without surgeon's certificate and for working over 12 hours a day a further 5s. plus 4s. costs.

The cotton masters were generally able to get away with breaking the rules because there were few Factory Inspectors. In a return made to the House of Commons on the 10th March 1838, Mr Leonard Horner, the Factory Inspector, for the region stated that his inspectorship includes the whole of Lancashire, a considerable part of the North Riding and part of the West Riding of Yorkshire, and the counties of Westmoreland, Cumberland, Northumberland and Durham. He had four superintendents acting under his directions. He had about 1,700 factories under his charge and these varied in the number of persons employed from 600 to 1,400; they were situated for the most part, in groups in the towns, but a very considerable number were widely scattered over the country. His arrangements were that, besides his own visits, every factory should be visited by a superintendent three times a year, with the exception of some few of insignificant extent. Despite the shortcomings of the system, the Factory Inspectors slowly made an impression:

Manchester Guardian 24.10. 1835:

Factory Informations:- On Saturday last at the Stockport petit sessions, Mr Ralph Sidebotham, cotton manufacturer, of Millbrook, appeared to answer four informations laid against him by Mr Charles Trimmer, one of the superintendents of factories in this district. The first was for working 25 young persons before half past five in the morning on the 28th ult; the second for allowing them to work on the 21st ult, and four following days, more than 12 hours daily, and more than 60 hours in the preceding week; the third for making false entries in his time book No 2 on the above five days contrary to the regulations of the inspector; and the fourth for having on the above days neglected to keep the time book No 3.

Mr Trimmer rejected an offer to compromise the matter, as he said Mr Sidebotham had treated him improperly in his mill; and he called upon the defendant to tell the court why he had not produced the 25 young persons so worked.

Mr Law, for the defendant explained that the notice server had told Mr Sidebotham that it would not be necessary to produce them, if he would submit to one penalty, which he was ready to do. Mr Trimmer said he had never sanctioned any such statement; but he would withdraw one information if Mr Sidebotham would plead guilty to all the others, and submit to a penalty in each case. To this proposal Mr Sidebotham acceded, declaring that he had not wilfully violated the act or the regulations; that his mill clock had been one one occasion, three quarters of an hour forward, and as to the other irregularities, they were wholly caused by his servants, his orders having uniformly been to obey the law.

Mr Trimmer said the clock was 55 minutes forward: he withdrew the information for neglecting to keep the time book No 3; and the magistrates convicted the defendant in the full penalty of £20 for making false entries; and 20s. in each of the other two informations with costs. The amount of the penalties was directed to be applied in aid of the funds of the church and school at Tintwistle.

16.5.1874. BREACH OF THE FACTORY ACT AT BROOKFIELD

Samuel Whewell, manager for Messrs W. & J Shepley Brookfield, pleaded guilty to a contravention of the Factory Act by employing a half timer named William Hill after one

Albion Mill

Broad Mills

o'clock. The manager had been summoned and not the occupier because Mr. Shepley had done all in his power to carry out the Acts, and part of the defendants duty was to see that these acts were thoroughly enforced. The parents of the child were much to blame, but as it had been ascertained that they were too poor to pay a fine, they were excused on this occasion. After saying nothing in his defence the defendant was fined 20s and costs.

The factory owners were not the only ones to blame. Some parents regarded their children as economic assets and could not wait to get them into the mill. When I was a schoolboy in the 1930's it was still common to hear parents say, "E's 14 and we haven't 'ad a penny out of him."

Pigot's 1835 Directory lists the following cotton masters who had mills along the Etherow, or its tributary streams:

COTTON SPINNERS:
Hadfield and Wilkinson Croden Brook;
William Barber on Padfield Brook;
John Lees, Padfield Brook;
George Platt, Padfield;
William and Thomas Platt, Hadfield Lodge;
John and William Sidebottom and Co, Waterside;
Henry Lees, Woolley Bridge;
Samuel and Henry Marsland, Broadbottom Bridge (Besthill);

William Wardlow, Bank Wood Mill (Botany), Broadbottom;
Benjamin Harrison, Kinder Lee;
John Bowden, Holehouse;
Joseph Cooper, Holehouse;

COTTON BANDING MAKERS:
George Booth, Holehouse;
John Harrison, Woodseats;
James Rowbotham, Chew Wood;

It is interesting looking through the names of the early cotton masters to note that local surnames predominate; names which are just as common today. Most must have been men who had managed to amass sufficient capital to take the plunge and set up in business on their own behalf. All of them contributed to the growth of cotton textiles, but the family which had the greatest impact was the Sidebottoms. Theirs is a typical story of how a local family of relatively humble origins rose to considerable prominence and wealth in the course of a few generations because they had the foresight and drive to take advantage of the opportunities available.

Sidebottom has been a common surname in the parish of Mottram for centuries but our story starts when John Sidebottom, a nailer of Stalybridge, married Elizabeth Kelsall of Hollingworth at St. Michael and All Angels, Mottram on 10th May, 1759. Elizabeth was the sister of Henry Kelsall who built Best Hill Mill in 1784. At this remove we will almost certainly never know exactly why John Sidebottom decided to enter cotton textiles, he was not one of the pioneers of the industry along the Etherow like the Thornleys and the Turners, but the Sidebottoms were destined to achieve pre-eminence in the

Hadfield, Tintwistle and Broadbottom area.

John and Elizabeth Sidebottom had ten children; six sons and four daughters. One son John died when in his teens; two daughters Betty and Ann, never married; two sons, William and Thomas, also remained single, but were to contribute to the growth of the family businesses. By 1787 John Sidebottom had moved to the Manor House, Hollingworth and built Millbrook Mill. These early mills were small, nothing like the later huge buildings immortalised by L.S. Lowry. In 1820 he bought Waterside Mill and it was expanded by his sons, particularly James Sidebottom, who died in 1869 and lived in Mill House which was within the Waterside complex.

John Sidebottom was fortunate in the sense that he entered into business at an opportune time. There is a great deal of truth in the adage about being the right man in the right place at the right time. There was already a pool of skilled labour in the area and this was partly available because some of the earlier entrepreneurs had failed. By the end of the 1880's the Sidebottoms had enlarged their business until the Waterside and Bridge Mills complex was the biggest in in the area. There were 4,800 looms and 293,000 spindles making china cloths, shirtings, Indian and Levant goods.

The Sidebottoms, unlike some of their competitors were interested in bettering themselves socially as well as making a fortune. With their new wealth they were able to mix with a different strata of society and a century and a quarter later, two of John Sidebottoms great grandsons, were Members of Parliament for local constituencies. Tom Harrop

Sidebottom Memorials at Christ Church Tintwistle

Sidebottom who lived at Etherow House was MP for Stalybridge for 20 years and his brother William became the first MP for High Peak in 1885. Other family members were related through marriage to the Woods, Lees, and Chapmans, to form a local cotton aristocracy. Much of the Sidebottoms money and efforts were concentrated in Tintwistle where they were supporters of Christ Church, the Conservative Club, the Day School and the Brass band.

There was a saying in the Lancashire cotton trade about folks going from clogs to clogs in three generations. While this was not inevitable, there are plenty of examples. It seems that the first generation worked hard to establish the business and following their example the second built on this foundation, learning every aspect of the trade. By the time we reach the third generation we have people used to an easier way of life who think that the money will keep rolling in with little if any effort on their part. With time on their hands, they could indulge in a better education and enrich their lives by a study of the arts and literature. Unfortunately this often led to a neglect of the progress in the textile industry and the day to day running of the business being left in the hands of managers. There is something strange about a better education leading to the ruin of a thriving business!

With leading members of the family taking a greater interest in politics than cotton manufacture the company fell into decline. In 1896 the Sidebottoms went into liquidation and both Bridge and Waterside Mills were closed causing great distress in the area. At the death of Tom Harrop Sidebottom in 1908 Etherow House remained empty for some years. All that remains today is the lodge and grounds. Sidebottoms lived at Millbrook House until 1914; the mill itself was demolished by James Sidebottom in 1882.

John Gartside & Co, mill owners in Ashton-under-Lyne and Dukinfield took over the Waterside complex in 1899. They already owned the Albion and Arrowscroft Mills in Hollingworth. What remained of Waterside Mills was demolished in 1977. What a reversal of fortune from the days when Waterside Mills had 293,000 spindles and 4,800 looms;

BROAD MILLS

Waterside Mill was not the only Sidebottom enterprise. Broadbottom Mills, were established in 1801 by five sons of John Sidebottom of Millbrook, Hollingworth. William, James, Joseph, George and Thomas. In 1805 William and George paid land tax on the purchase of land from the Bostocks to build the mills. They also built houses for their workers nearby in Stonerow, Bottom,

Lymefield Mill, Broadbottom.

Summerbottom weavers' cottages.

Broad Mills water wheel.

Middle and Top Row and New Street. Before this time Broadbottom was largely uninhabited except for older buildings like Bothams and Broadbottom Halls and and a few scattered farms.

Top Row which consisted of ten houses was pulled down in the 1890's because of the sanitary arrangements. On average, there was only one privy shared between six houses. This sorry state of affairs was made even worse by the large numbers living in each house. These early houses like others built in the district around 1820 to 1850 were very basic and most have been demolished. Those remaining can be recognised by the low ceilings and doorways which have no fanlight, and by roofs of the local heavy stone slates. There were no damp courses, the floor was of stone flags and a stone slopstone served as a sink. Rising damp rotted the plaster for as much as three feet up the walls on the ground floor and despite the best efforts of the occupants there were constant problems with vermin, bed bugs being one of the worst. The saving grace of these dwellings was that being huddled together with fires burning much of the time they tended to be warm.

The Sidebottom Brothers lived in rather more palatial surroundings. William (1760-1826) lived at the Manor House in Hollingworth; Joseph (?-1849) built Harewood Lodge; while George (1769-1841) built Hill End House. The rapid manner in which many of the larger textile mills expanded gives a good indication of the profits made as do the splendid mansions the owners built for themselves.

When the Sidebottoms first started the business, it was as cotton spinners. The thread was then be delivered to the handloom weavers who worked in their own homes. At one time this work was carried out on the top floor of a three storey cottage and such cottages were widespread. Most have been demolished, but in Broadbottom there is still a row at Summerbottom. When viable power looms became available, the Sidebottoms expanded to become general cotton manufacturers. The weaving shed, erected in 1850, was of the usual single storey pattern with saw tooth shaped roof and windows facing north to give even lighting for the looms. By 1861 the mill employed 1,200.

The noise in a weaving shed was tremendous making normal conversation impossible; as a result the weavers became remarkably good at lip reading. There are still a few of the old weavers around and if you watch their lips when you are speaking to them you will notice that they tend to mime your words. The mill was on an excellent site with ample water power; the water wheel was about 24 feet wide. In early days coal could be obtained from small local coal pits in Mottram, Chisworth and on the Hague. When a steam engine was installed in 1838 these local pits would be hard put to supply its needs, but with the opening of the railway line in 1843, coal in any quantity could be delivered to Broadbottom, and unloaded directly into wagons by chute and carted downhill to the boiler house.

During the 1850's the gambling habits of John Sidebottom, (grandson of the founder) led to massive debts and the factory was only kept afloat with financial help from his mother. Once again we see the old Lancashire adage from clogs to clogs in three generations borne out. This problem was compounded in the 1860's by the Cotton Famine which led to the closure of Broadbottom Mills and the local community, almost totally dependent upon the cotton industry, was halved as people sought work elsewhere. Many moved to Yorkshire where the woollen trade benefited from cotton's problems.

The Broadbottom Mills reopened in 1874 as Broad Mills with John Hirst as Managing Director and by 1896 the mill was running with 60,000 spindles and 1,199 looms weaving shirting and prints. By the 1930's the number of machines had dwindled again until it finally closed as a weaving mill.

At its peak, Broad Mills could handle cotton from raw bale to finished cloth; it even had its own gasworks complete with gasometer. Before the gas mantle was invented in 1885 by an Austrian, Carl Aver, the light was provided by the naked flame of a fishtail burner. The gas was very crude and burned with a yellow flame which gave poor illumination and must have been a fire risk.

In the 1980's, the Tameside M.B.C. purchased the site and initiated a programme of landscaping and conservation. Only the foundations remain in most cases but there are some excellent illustrations of the beam engine and the water wheel which give a good impression of what they were like. The barring rack on the site of the former engine is a reminder of the days when the engine flywheel had to be turned into its starting position by muscle power. In 1999 Harewood Lodge was being converted into luxury apartments.

I was privileged, around 1954, to dismantle the last remnants of a beam engine which stood in the engine house at the west end of Wren Nest Mill so a short description of some of its features might be in order (before it is all forgotten). The foundations consisted of large ashlar blocks around three feet by three feet square and perhaps four feet long. There was no mortar between these blocks, instead a sort of damp clay or ganister on which the blocks were bedded. Holes about three inches in diameter had been accurately bored through the stone blocks before they were mounted in position and great wrought iron bolts passed through these to hold the engine cylinders in position. The lower ends of these bolts were secured with large cotter pins so that all the stone blocks were held tightly together and the engine was mounted on a foundation of stone blocks weighing tens of tons.

The engine house must have been built specially to house the engine because there was a huge cast iron beam incorporated into the structure on which the two heavy reciprocating beams swung. There was a platform with guard rail on the same level as the beams so that the engine minder could keep his eye on the mechanism and check the oil and bearings. The walkway was of stone flags which were cut exactly to size and fitted into a cast iron frame. The whole structure was a credit to the men who made and installed it.

When the oil and cotton fluff which had accumulated over the years was wiped away it was possible to make out the way it had been put together. Each section of cast iron was dovetailed carefully so that every piece fitted so closely that it was almost impossible to make out the join, and on the face of the cast iron was a pattern of roses, intertwined stems, and thorns which matched perfectly so that they seemed to flow on from one piece to the next as accurately as patterned wallpaper. It was a tragedy that such workmanship had to be broken up and melted down as scrap!

The line shafting in a cotton mill was a work of art, lengths of wrought iron shafting were bolted together with flanges and ran in brass bearings which were fitted with oiling rings. The bearings were mounted on brackets which were either fastened to the walls, or were an integral part of the cast iron columns. As the shafting ran the full length of the room, its component parts had to be in perfect alignment. If one bearing ran hot it might seize up, or start a fire, so the oiler and greaser had to keep an eye on the bearings, especially when a shaft was being started up for the first time. If a bearing started to overheat, various remedies were applied such as pouring castor oil over it. Everything possible was done to keep the shafting running as if it stopped every machine on the floor would be brought to a halt. Individual machines were driven from the line shafts with pulleys and leather belts.

It should be borne in mind that line shafts erected in say 1870 might still be giving service in 1948. I have seen one which had run for so long that the bottom brasses had worn through and the shaft was running on cast iron. The machinery in the maintenance workshop was of the same vintage. At Wren Nest Mill, and no doubt others, there were stocks and dies to cut screw threads of various forms and sizes that predated Sir Joseph Whitworth's standard screw threads which became the norm in Britain in the 1860's. Because of this crude tackle, at one time it was virtually impossible to bore a pulley so that it fitted exactly to a shaft. This is where the art of "staking a pulley" which the old millwrights took such a pride in came in. The pulley could be bored perhaps an inch larger than the shaft and the millwright would contrive to make it run true by carefully fitting four keys spaced equidistantly around the shaft.

The demise of the local textile industry could be attributed to a number of factors; competition from low wage countries being a popular explanation. The notion of Indians and Japanese toiling away on a bowl of rice might be believed by some but local textile workers were hardly living off the fat of the land. When the machinery in English mills were being sold off, the Japanese only bought the best equipment. One factor which is given less prominence is the notion of investing capital where it will show the greatest return. The textile unions with a largely female workforce were hardly the most militant and can hardly be blamed for the industry's troubles. Firms made efforts to modernise; the old steam engines were dismantled and individual electric motors fitted to looms and spinning machinery; money was invested in new machines and some specialist companies still flourished. One pertinent factor was that the industry was no longer perceived as having a glowing future and young people avoided it; another was that the children of the cotton masters preferred not to follow their forebears, instead becoming barristers, doctors or stockbrokers. So some of the blame at least can be laid at the door of the British educational system.

CHAPTER NINE
TROUBLES AT T'MILL

We have learned of the advances made by industry and the fortunes established by the most successful cotton masters, but large sections of the working population found their income declining until they were below the poverty line and this led to widespread unrest which manifested itself in machine breaking, plug drawing, food riots, agitation for shorter working hours and demands for a broader franchise.

Most modern governments try to hold the ring between the contesting sides of industry and aim for a consensus which satisfies each side in some degree. The government at the start of the nineteenth century thought that unrest was best put down by military force and tended to see the threat of imminent revolution when in fact such a threat did not really exist. They had of course the memory of the French Revolution only a few years previously to reinforce their fears. The country was still run by the landed classes and they had no intention of losing their privileged position. The very idea of a wider franchise was anathema to them since the working classes would easily outvote them. Ridicule was poured on the idea of a weaver becoming a Minister of the Crown.

The Luddite Outrages

The activities of the Luddites at the beginning of the nineteenth century is one of those pieces of history that has been generally ignored locally. The Luddites, many of them artisans in the cotton and woollen trades, were victims of technical progress. Having worked for centuries in their cottages and small village shops using machines that could usually be managed by one person, with perhaps the assistance of children, they suddenly saw new factories being erected, filled with machines which could out-produce them and powered by tireless water wheels and steam engines.

Government policies also helped to increase the amount of labour available and to force down wages by enclosing land which forced people into the new industrial towns and by encouraging the immigration of Irish labourers. It was made worse because there were no restrictions on employing women and children starting at ages as young as four or five, and these two groups soon became the largest section of the textile labour force.

If this was not bad enough, those who did have work still suffered. There were families of labourers earning around 12 shillings a week when the estimate of the cost of food of the simplest kind ranged from 12 to 14 shillings a week. Among the most impoverished were the handloom weavers whose average wages by the 1820's had fallen to 5 shillings a week, when there was work at all. Under such conditions the Luddites hit out at what they saw as their enemy; the machines that were taking away their livelihood.

The machine breaking started in Nottinghamshire and South-east Derbyshire among the stocking frame workers. All the Luddite activities were criminal, or were soon made criminal. Frame breaking was punishable by seven or fourteen years transportation to Australia; burglary, and the writing of threatening letters by death.

They operated ostensibly under the leadership of one General Ludd who wrote letters to manufacturers who persisted in using machinery, threatening dire consequences as a result of a visit by the General and his men. The manufacturers had every cause to heed these threats because machine breaking was widespread, indeed one of the factors which finally caused a diminution in the troubles was that there were few machines around Nottingham left to smash.

There never was such an individual as General Ludd, but where did the name Luddite originate. One explanation which appeared in the Nottingham Review was that once upon a time a boy named Ned Ludd who had been apprenticed to a knitter near Leicester was so reluctant to work that his master got a magistrate to order him whipped; whereupon the lad took a hammer and demolished his knitting frame, an act which gained such renown that when any machine was damaged people would say that Ned Ludd had been there.

At the beginning of the outbreak there was something of a Robin Hood character about proceedings. When some of the machine breakers stole valuables while about their work, General Ludd returned the items and wrote a letter to the victims to the effect that they had been taken without his knowledge and the perpetrators had already been punished. The Luddites made a point of only smashing machines and not harming any individual. On one occasion, soldiers guarding premises were disarmed by the Luddites who stood guard until the machines were wrecked. Then they discharged the muskets before handing them back and disappearing into the night.

The Luddites had considerable local support as they went about their work of demolition. Time and again the military were outwitted because they had been brought in from outside the area and were trying to catch the culprits on their home ground where there were plenty of folks keeping an eye out for the troops. It was not until a later stage when Luddites were shot by troops or men employed to guard factories that the Luddites resorted to violence against factory owners.

The Annals of Nottingham reported;

"Nothing could penetrate the mystery of Luddism, nor break the bond of union which bound its deluded and mischievous devotees together. In spite of all their errors, and all their crimes, it is impossible to withhold admiration from the stern integrity of purpose which thus led a number of poor men to withstand the tempting offer of bribes and thus betray the cause in which they had engaged." (There was also the real threat of physical harm to anyone who might be tempted to inform.)

At the time, law and order was maintained by local Justices of the Peace, assisted by village constables. This system had worked when everybody knew his neighbour and most crime was likely to be the work of strangers passing through. But with the growth of factories, large populations sprang up in what had been small villages and in the event of a riot, the constables could be overwhelmed. Magistrates were loth to call in the military since this was an admission of their own inability to deal with the problem. Instead they attempted to disperse mobs by reading the Riot Act. The Luddite outbreaks were far too serious for such methods and soon they had little option but to send for military assistance.

It would have created problems ordering the local militia to deal with unrest since they would hardly want to open fire on folks they knew. The usual policy was to bring in units from a distance or to use regular troops where available. Troops were poured into the industrial areas of Nottinghamshire and Derbyshire until the Luddites found it too dangerous to operate and the authorities began to congratulate themselves on having stamped out the problem. They could not have been wider of the mark. Within months there were further outbreaks of machine breaking in the woollen manufacturing districts of Yorkshire and the cotton manufacturing areas of the North-west.

Longdendale had its share of the trouble. Thomas Rhodes, woollen manufacturer of Bottoms Mill took an active part in putting down the Luddites. The information he gave to the authorities led to the arrest of many persons who had taken an active part in rioting and destroying mill machinery. Several were sentenced to death and others transported.

The general unrest also manifested itself in food riots as in the following eye witness account from nearby Gee Cross:

"I saw a large mob attacking the shop of Ralph Booth opposite our garden gate, and I saw the meal and flour brought out and distributed to the people, chiefly women, who received it into

Food riot at Stockport workhouse *(Illustrated London News)*

their aprons, handkerchiefs, caps, old stockings, or anything else in which they could carry it away. One old man called William Walker, for a frolic, had put a paper round his head with General Ludd written on it, but it cost him dear. He was arrested as a ringleader, tried for inciting a mob to disorder and tumult, and died on the ship transporting him to Australia."

Luddites were 'twisted' in by swearing the following oath:

I A.B. of my own voluntary will, do declare, and solemnly swear, that I will never reveal to any person or persons under the canopy of heaven, the names of persons who compose this Secret Committee. their proceedings, meeting, places of abode, dress, features, connections, or anything else that might lead to a discovery of the same, either by word or deed, or sign, under the penalty of being sent out of the world by the first brother who shall meet me, and my name and character blotted out of existence, and never to be remembered but with contempt and abhorrence; and I further do swear, that I will use my best endeavours to punish by death any traitor or traitors, should any rise up among us, wherever I can find him or them, and though he should fly to the verge of nature, I will pursue him with increasing vengence. So help me God, and bless me to keep this my oath inviolable.

An attempt to counteract this oath was made by the authorities, and placards to the following effect issued:-

"The villain who takes this oath deprives himself of that liberty which is the birth right of all Britons, deprives himself of trial by jury, and binds himself the willing slave of the vilest and most blood-thirsty assassins and incendiaries. He not only puts himself out of the protection of the laws, but he deprives other men of the power of assisting him: at least while he keeps his oath a secret, and refuses to reveal the purposes and objects of this detestable conspiracy. Thus all the deluded wicked wretches who are bound by this oath, are, at this moment, exposed to the greatest dangers, and are liable to be assassinated and put to death in the most cruel manner by any of their companions.

Again this oath is an offence against man, as it defeats the purpose of human justice, and enables the assassin and murderer to escape with impunity.....because the traitors who have taken this oath, weakly and wickedly suppose that it supersedes all moral and religious obligations, and think that such a compact which they have entered into, releases them from any duty which they owe to God, their King, and their country."

The Manchester Guardian did not begin publication until 1822, which is a great pity because as a firm supporter of the cotton masters and merchants it would have had a great deal to say about the riots. The Times of the day seems more concerned with parliamentary debates on the emancipation of Catholics; the murder of the Prime Minister Mr Perceval, and the distinct probability of war with the USA over the blockade which was keeping neutral goods out of Europe. All important topics of the time, and of course it could always report on the antics of the Prince Regent - rather like the tabloids today. I wonder who was interested in what the Prince Regent had for breakfast, or that he had five hours sleep the previous night? Nevertheless, despite such pressing matters there were reports on troubles in the provinces, the following being a selection of the more relevant:

The Times 17.4.1812:

Chester April 11: Two attempts have lately been made in Stockport, one in Spencer and Co's in Hillgate; it is a weaving factory of vast extent, where the work is wholly done by children. Part of a window was taken out, and several torches put in. The flames were beginning to spread when a woman gave the alarm.

Stockport April 11: We are extremely concerned to state that the discontents of the weavers in and about Stockport broke out in acts of violence on Tuesday last.......and a request for the assistance of the military from Manchester has been refused; Colonel Clay giving for answer, that he could not consistently with his duty in protecting Manchester, afford any.

20.4.1812: In the neighbourhood of Stockport a spirit of turbulence continued. The weavers still assembled in great numbers and proceeded in bodies to the houses of gentlemen and farmers from whom they extorted moneys and victuals. Many carried arms openly. Dr Mitchel's house was attacked on Wednesday night, and several bullets fired at him without any effect.

21.4.1812. Riot at Macclesfield: The instigators of the riot were about 300 in number, of these few were townsmen of Macclesfield, the majority being colliers and carters from Rainow and Bollington, or spinners from the hill country near Stockport. The total number of persons riotously assembled was at one period certainly 5,000. The boys at the bidding of their elders, took the more conspicuous part of breaking the windows; the leaders did the indoor work.

Now here we have one of the reasons why the culprits were so hard to arrest; the Luddites were so organised that they made their attacks on property and premises at a distance from their homes. This made it far less likely that they would be recognised and at the same time witnesses could state truthfully that they did not know any of the rioters.

In an effort to stamp out the insurrection the authorities moved all the troops they could find into the affected areas:

5.5.1812: During last week, not fewer than seven regiments proceeded towards Cheshire and Lancashire. Wednesday, the Bedfordshire Militia which has been for the last sixteen months quartered in Sussex marched for Northampton to which place it was ordered to proceed by forced marches. On the same day 600 of the Derbyshire Militia in 30 wagons passed through Oxford in haste for Warwickshire; and on Friday the first division of the Wilts entered that city on their route for Warrington. Four troops of the 15th Hussars have been sent to Nottingham. A detachment of the Horse Guards (blue) have been stationed at Glossop.

8.5.1812. Manchester May 5th: This town continues to enjoy a state of uninterrupted tranquillity. We have had a very considerable influx of soldiers. The Buckinghamshire Militia, 800 strong, with two field pieces attached, marched from Mansfield on Wednesday, and arrived here on Thursday evening; on Friday, The Berkshire, consisting of upwards of 600, reached here from Nottingham. the greatest part of the Manchester and Salford Local Militia, and the Newton and Failsworth, have been called out; and it is gratifying to state, that they have assembled with commendable alacrity. One hundred and fifty persons have already been sworn in under the Watch and Ward Act, for Salford, and upwards of 2000 for Manchester and the several other townships.

Considering the size of the mobs and the widespread activities of the Luddites, the vast majority were never caught, and when put on trial many were acquitted for lack of evidence.

1.6.1812: Trials of Rioters at Chester; Edward Redfern and Nancy Hurst; indicted for accompanying a large mob to the granary at Staley belonging to to the Huddersfield Canal Company and for breaking open and entering the same and stealing and destroying large quantities of flour. It appeared from the evidence that a mob of about 500 rioters attacked the granary. Both were found guilty. William Greenhough, Abraham Broadbent, and James

Crossland charged with destroying machinery and threatening the life of Robert Thorniley, a manufacturer of cotton at Tintwistle. Crossland was found guilty, Broadbent and Greenhough not guilty. Greenhough and John Hayward the younger were found guilty for a riot at Tintwistle.

2.6.1812: Chester May 30th; William Greenhough, for entering the shop of Alice Berry, at Tintwistle, and taking away a quantity of flour; James Crossland, for threatening the life of of Robert Thorniley, a cotton spinner at Tintwistle, and breaking and destroying his tools; John Temple, for breaking and entering the dwelling house of Samuel Wagstaff, and stealing five silver teaspoons and other articles, and John Haywood, for riotously assembling and breaking the factory of Messrs Sidebotham, and breaking and destroying a machine, received sentence of death. His Lordship held out not the smallest hope of mercy.

Execution of Rioters; Chester June 15th: This day Joseph Thompson and John Temples found guilty at the Special Commission held for this county on the 25th of May for the trial of the rioters, were executed pursuant to their sentences, at the New Drop behind the city gaol. About half past twelve o'clock, they left the Castle when the solemn procession, escorted by a party of the Oxford Blues, and accompanied by the proper officers proceeded through the city to the New Gaol, followed by an immense crowd of people. On the arrival of the convicts at the latter place, they were conducted to the chapel where they very devoutly joined the clergyman in prayer. At one o'clock they ascended the drop, and soon after were launched into eternity.

The executions of the others convicted at Chester were not reported in the Times but the Editor had to decide what to include and what to omit, and as these events coincided with Napoleon's invasion of Russia; the Battle of Salamanca, and the outbreak of war with the United States, he can hardly be blamed for not giving them pride of place in his columns.

In an effort to infiltrate the Luddite's organisation many spies were supplied by the deputy constable of Manchester, Joseph Nadin. Small secret service units of soldiers were formed on double pay operating under cover to infiltrate Luddite councils, identify oath givers and takers for local magistrates, and by any means see that enough men got arrested to instil fear in the rest. Despite the utmost efforts of the authorities paid agents to infiltrate the Luddites very few actual Luddites were ever arrested. The authorities went so far as to use their agents in an effort to encourage the Luddites to attack mills so that they could be arrested in the act. In the celebrated attack on Westhoughton mill in Lancashire, all those arrested turned out to be government spies; the real Luddites arrived the following week and burned the place to the ground!

Despite the secrecy of the Luddites, there were local arrests. On the night of Thursday 11th June 1812, Aaron Marwell of Hollingworth and Edward

Newton of Hadfield were arrested in the Prince Regent's Arms in Ancoats Lane by Joseph Nadin. They were committed to Lancaster assizes for having administered the abominable oath of "twisting in". Both were found not guilty.

The Derby Mercury contains the details of a letter sent to the Home Secretary from a Magistrate in the County of Cheshire:

"My Lord,

Yesterday several of the Luddites from the neighbourhood of Mottram, the most disturbed in Cheshire, came before me and took the oath of allegiance."

One can only wonder what had been going on in Mottram if it was the most disturbed area in Cheshire.

The taking of oaths of allegiance was due to an initiative on the part of Lord Sidmouth. A Royal Proclamation offered clemency to any wrongdoer who would step forward and name names. This affidavit before the Stockport magistrate Charles Prescott, is representative of the kind of results produced:

'The voluntary deposition of James Band of Hollingworth. Who saith, that on Sunday, in the month of March last, the day of the month he cannot recollect, he went to a place called Hobson Moor, in Hollingworth, accompanied by Peter Ashton of Hollingworth aforesaid, cotton-spinner, where they were met by two or three persons, whom examinant did not know, who proposed to him and his companions to take a certain oath, which they said would do them no harm: but if they did not take it they would be killed. That, thereupon, they consented, and one of the strangers produced a paper, and a book, which this examinant and Peter Ashton kissed, after repeating the words of the oath, read to them by the stranger. The precise words this examinant cannot recollect: but the purport of the oath was to bind the person taking the same to secrecy, and to put to death any traitors. At the same time, the stranger delivered to the examinant, a paper, containing the words of the oath which he had taken, and told him to twist in as many as he could.'

By October over a thousand men availed themselves of the clemency without a single criminal oath giver being turned in or tried. At least some of the men, including fifty eight from Manchester had apparently been twisted in by spies or agents of constable Nadin.

"It appears that the men who administered the oath to these people were either strangers or men who have left this part of the country." a Lancashire magistrate reported. Sidmouth's anti-Luddite plan for all its deceit turned out to be essentially useless.

A certain Captain Raines was serving with the Stirlingshire Militia which was stationed in Kent when the regiment was ordered north to deal with the Luddite riots. They proceeded by forced marches in wagons and Captain Raines found himself in command of a company based in Mottram. The roads were constantly patrolled and the mills watched, but much damage was done in the night when the soldiers were at a disadvantage, not knowing the neighbourhood. The public houses were closed at nine o'clock at night because they were suspected as being meeting places for the disaffected workers. Some landlords abused the soldiers and as a result Captain Raines reported them to the magistrates who suspended their licences.

Captain Raines later wrote a book on his experiences during the disturbances from which the following is an extract:

"Reports were frequently brought to me that the Luddites assembled every night within a short distance of our quarters for the purpose of drilling and holding their conferences, notwithstanding our piquets were constantly patrolling, they never had the good fortune to fall in with any of them. I afterwards learned they had spies continually watching our movements, who conveyed intelligence to the main body of the road the soldiers took. I proposed to Mr Lightfoot, the curate of the parish, who was well acquainted with the country, to accompany me and two soldiers for the purpose of ascertaining whether these people did actually assemble; he gladly accepted my proposal. We commenced our patrol about twelve o'clock at night, and after being out little more than an hour, we fell in with some of their look-out parties at the edge of a moor, about a mile and a half from Mottram, As we advanced we discovered them in great numbers, and though I had ordered my men to conceal their arms and turn their caps, it now appeared soldiers were discovered from the general flight which ensued. We followed them, running as fast as we could, the men now showing their arms and pretending to call for the piquet. It was with the greatest difficulty that I could keep the soldiers from firing; they were Highlanders, possessing all the ardour the natives of their country are remarkable for, zealous and hearty in the cause we were engaged in. I soon found it would be prudent to secure a retreat, whilst it was yet in our power, as from the numbers springing up in all directions, I saw we should shortly become the pursued instead of the pursuers; we therefore took refuge in a ditch, where we waited till the coast was clear."

But the heavy hand of the government did have an effect; from May on there were no more attacks on factory buildings for the rest of the year and even the night time arms raids tailed off in late summer.

The end of the Luddite riots was marked by the presentation of a piece of plate bearing the following inscription:

Presented November 4th, 1812, to Captain F. Raines, by the inhabitants of Mottram and its vicinity, as a testimony of their gratitude for the eminent services rendered them in his indefatigable and successful efforts to suppress the spirit of disaffection rapidly extending itself through that county.

The Old Hall, Mottram, was purchased in 1800 by Samuel Hadfield, who left it to his nephew George Hadfield, one of three brothers of Simmondley

Hall. George took a great interest in the forming of a Volunteer Corps in 1803. He was the Captain Commanding, and his brother Moses a Lieutenant. Being a wealthy man he had a Band in connection with the Corps, and when the Corps was disbanded after all fear of invasion had gone, he still supported the Band, which regularly visited his house at Mottram Old Hall, where they were always sure of a hearty welcome and plenty to eat and drink.

Despite his patriotic record, during the Luddite insurrections Mr George Hadfield became the object of the so-called "Newton Conspiracy". Chiefly through the Messrs Lees of Newton, reports had been circulated that Mr Hadfield had encouraged a lawless mob to destroy the machinery of his neighbours.

In a pamphlet entitled The Family Compact, or the Newton Conspiracy Mr Hadfield rebutted the charge and levelled a counter attack on his traducers. The following is an extract from this pamphlet:-

"I believe it was on the 21st of April last that an alarm was spread through the country that a mob was approaching, and apprehending that they might pay me a visit, it required some time to put my house in a state of defence. In the meantime they had passed through Mottram, and immediately afterwards I went to see in which direction; some said the great body were gone quite away, but they were soon undeceived, for they returned with accumulated numbers, and accounts exaggerated by terror represented them as having attempted to fire Messrs Sidebottom's mill and machinery, and that one of the Messrs Sidebottom had escaped with his life, and that at Mr Marsland's, of Broadbottom Bridge, they had brought out the blower for them to break, and had saved the mill and other machinery. These dreadful reports made me hesitate. I had with me no armed force, nor could be procured any civil authority whatever. But seeing them move in a body towards Wedneshough Green to attack Wood's factory, compassion for an honest and good neighbour induced me to approach them and try to save his premises and machinery. For that purpose I met them on the Green at a time when they were making a rapid charge upon the building and called for them to stop and not dare to break in the factory. I consulted in the hurry with Mr Wood, the proprietor, what was best to be done, and there appeared no other way to save the property than by bringing out the blower as others had done. This, however, could not be accomplished, and they got into the factory and broke the machine. Every person forming that body was a perfect stranger......... Returning home full of anxiety and regret that a country which had hitherto stood high for its loyalty and good order, should now become a scene of disorder and violence, I wrote immediately to the Secretary of State.

When some time ago, the common enemy had drawn his hostile bands to the opposite shores and threatened invasion; when the alarm was sounded through the nation and Government called upon every loyal man to defend his dearest interests; when all ranks of people flocked to the sacred standard of their country, or contributed pecuniary aid, and all united in displaying a degree of patriotism never exceeded by ancient Greece or Rome, where were the Messrs Lees.........They felt the electric shock it is true, but it had the effect of strong repulsion. They, like a well known creeping animal, at the slightest touch, shrunk, drew in their horns and retired to their shell while the storm was past, and until they could emerge in safety.....While they refused to contribute the smallest sum, I sacrificed at that time from conviction that it was my duty, upwards of £1,000, and have at all times never been afraid of my purse or my person, when either one or the other would be serviceable to my country."

Luddism lost as it was bound to, and all that it had tried to prevent won the day; the industrialisation of Britain continued at an even faster rate. Nevertheless the conditions of the workers did gradually improve and there was a considerable difference in conditions between the days of the Prince Regent and those of Prince Albert. The harsh way in which the Luddites were dealt with only served to teach the disenfranchised to go about the struggle by other more peaceful means. Local people do not seem to have been involved in the Radical Movement and Peterloo Massacre, or somewhat later during the Chartist agitation, to the same degree as say people just over the hill in Saddleworth, but there wa a great meeting of the Lancashire and Cheshire strikers on Mottram Moor on August 7th 1842, where it was resolved that "all labour should cease until the People's Charter became the law of the land". The attitude of local employers could have been a factor. They certainly played a leading role in building churches and chapels and the workers tended to follow them in religion. This did not mean there was no further agitation for better wages and working conditions. The ruling classes were learning the lesson that it was better to give way a little at a time rather than let pressures build up which might lead to a revolution.

With the threat of war no longer present, there was no need for a large standing army which parliament was determined to avoid at all costs both on the grounds of expense and as a danger to liberty. The local constable system was totally outmoded but something better had to be put in its place and hence Sir Robert Peel was able to introduce his New Police. It was not an easy task, local magistrates did not like the idea of giving up any of their powers and prestige, and there were fears of a police force on the continental model being established which would have a political agenda. This was why when police forces were set up they were based on the counties or large metropolitan boroughs.

Plug Drawing Riots

An Act of 1825 allowed the formation of Trade Unions and the spinners set about obtaining a uniform payment for 1,000 hanks as different cotton masters paid different rates even within the same district.. When this state of affairs was not remedied the spinners turned out.

Manchester Guardian Saturday, January 8th 1831:-

THE ASHTON TURN-OUT. DISGRACEFUL OUTRAGE NEAR MOTTRAM

A most daring and extraordinary outrage was committed on Tuesday last by a body of turn outs from Ashton and neighbourhood, at the factory of Messrs. John and William Sidebottom of Millbrook in Longdendale. On the forenoon of that day a meeting of spinners was held at a public house at Ashton and after it broke up, the persons composing it with others to the number of 500 to 600 left the town in small parties and assembled on the top of the hill near Hollingworth and then suddenly poured down upon the factory at Millbrook. The turn outs forced their way into the mill and dragged the spinners, who had returned to work, into the road. There they turned their coats inside out, tied them together with cords, inscribed the obnoxious price of 3s 9d on their backs with chalk, and then drove them along the turnpike road to Tintwistle, and over Tintwistle Bridge to Waterside, another factory belonging to the same firm, in which also a number of spinners had resumed their employment. Fortunately before the arrival of the turnouts, intelligence had been received of what had occurred at Millbrook, and the hands had all been sent away. Finding no one they left the place, still driving their captives before them down the Derbyshire side of the river to Woolley Bridge, which they crossed, and proceeded to Stalybridge, where they halted and loosed their prisoners, after having driven them five or six miles, and dismissed them, but first informing them that if they were found working again, until they had obtained their price (4s 2d) their lives would be forfeited. Notwithstanding the vicinity of Stalybridge to Millbrook not one of the offenders was known to Mr Sidebottom or to any of his work people. The strike was a failure and by 16th February the men had all returned to their work at the same prices as they were paid before they turned out.

Several of the rioters were later arrested and tried at Ashton-under-Lyne; when Samuel Lees, Joseph Hirst, Soloman Hampson, Rueben Slater, Michael Makinson, and James Thorpe were committed to Chester Assizes. A detachment of the 10th Hussars escorted them for 1½ miles out of the town to prevent them being rescued by the turn outs.

Among the mills which turned out was one not far from Hayfield, occupied by Messrs Ridgway and Thornton. Some of the hands, finding that their example was not followed by spinners in other neighbourhoods returned to their employment. These facts being communicated to to the committee of turn-outs at Ashton a party of 60 or 80 men chiefly from Mossley and the neighbourhood were despatched on Monday afternoon for the purpose of "Turning the knobsticks out."

The party passed through Mottram in a body between five and six o'clock, making no secret whatever of their intentions, except that they sometimes declared they were going to Ridgway and Thorntons and sometimes to George and Joseph Sidebottom's at Broadbottom. They arrived at Ridgeway and Thornton's about seven o'clock in the evening while the hands were all at work. Not knowing their way to the factory they enquired from locals, one of whom, guessing their object, ran across the fields to the factory and apprised the manager of their approach. The manager immediately ordered all the people out and had just got the factory cleared and the doors locked when the turn-outs arrived. On seeing the manager, one of them stepped out and presenting a pistol to his breast said he would "Blow at him." if he did not immediately open the door and turn out the spinners. The manager assured him that the hands were all gone but the turn-outs were not inclined to believe his word and they compelled him to open the door and a strong guard was posted outside the door armed with pistols while the remainder searched the factory.

Finding no one within they vented their disappointment on the manager whom they beat severely. On quitting the factory they set up a shout of triumph and discharged a number of pistols. Arrangements had been made by Mr White of Park Hall with the military at Glossop for intercepting them on their return but these failed in consequence of the rioters taking the road through Glossop instead of one that would have led directly to their homes and thus they escaped.

Manchester Guardian 13th August, 1842.

Plug Drawing. It appears that on Wednesday 10th August, parties of men went from Stalybridge to Glossop and stopped all the mills at that place.

24th August; Glossop. All the mills in this neighbourhood are still standing without the slightest approximation to an understanding between the workpeople and their employers. The printworks in the neighbourhood are in full operation.

17th September, Glossop: On Wednesday last the three prisoners who were wounded by Mr Shepley in the attack upon his mill, at Brookfield, near Glossop, on the 30th August were brought here from Manchester in the custody of Mr Beswick, escorted by a detachment of the 11th Hussars, for examination before the magistrates; on the charge of riot, conspiracy, and of beginning the attack on the mill and premises of Mr Shepley. Several witnesses were examined, whose evidence established the fact that the mob attacked the mill, beat at the doors, broke the windows, and that Mr Shepley and several of the special constables were repeatedly struck with stones, and one of them had his teeth knocked out, before Mr Shepley fired upon the mob. The prisoners were fully committed to the next Chester assizes for rioting, and beginning to demolish the premises. The prisoners received comparatively light sentences, the Judge taking into consideration their sufferings from their wounds.

29th September: At the Hyde Petty Sessions on the 26th Charles Rhodes was committed to the sessions on a charge of riot at Mr Joseph Cooper's mill at the Holehouse on the 18th August.

Hardly the actions of peaceful pickets. In addition to the opposition of the cotton masters, violence on the part of its supporters and fraudulent misuse of funds were two of the main problems confronting early trade unions.

The Struggle for Shorter Working Hours

The Ten Hours Bill was passed on 8th June 1847 and came into force on the 1st May 1848. Thousands of meetings had been held over a period of thirty-three years to achieve this eminently sensible reform. Locally, protest meetings were held on a piece of ground near Howard Street in Glossop which was known as the Ten Hours Ground for many years, and on Wedneshough. The effect of shorter hours was soon apparent in the improved health and greater output of those affected by it and in consequence another agitation was soon started for "Straight up and Down Time" that is to start at 6am and cease at 6pm. The employers reactions to all these agitations was predictable, they claimed any shortening of working hours would ruin them. The outcome was very different, the employers were motivated into installing more up to date equipment and better working practices and conditions.

One reaction of employees when times were bad was to emigrate to America where skilled labour were often in demand. This occurred during the Cotton Famine. Once established overseas, they would send for their families and write to their friends who often followed. At one time, there were restrictions on skilled textile workers moving to America because this would help foreign competition.

All the faults were not on the part of the employers! A good deal of petty pilfering was carried out by the workpeople, and the cotton masters formed a society for the prosecution of persons committing depredations within manufacturing firms in the Parishes of Mottram in Longdendale and Glossop. The articles of the association were signed on the 28th January, 1839 by J and W Sidebottom and Co., W.T and E. Platt, William Barber, Samuel Marsland, Samuel Shepley, Thomas and John Dalton, Robert Kershaw and Co., John Winterbottom, John Hollingworth, Ralph Sidebottom, James Rhodes, William Robinson, Hadfield and Wilkinson, John Kershaw, James Booth, John Wood, and Robert and James Shepley.

CHAPTER TEN
TINTWISTLE AND HOLLINGWORTH

According to Aikin's description; 'two miles from Mottram is the very ancient village of Tintwistle containing 35 houses and a Dissenting Chapel. It is essentially built of thick free-stone flags, got on the spot.' Clearly not a lot was happening thereabouts at the time. However, Tintwistle has had its moments.

Religious Matters

It is a long time since religious differences caused serious disagreement in Britain, but in the past it could lead to riots and broken heads. R.B. Robinson in his account of Longdendale written in 1863 tells the following story:

"There was once a non-conformist preacher at Tintwistle by the name of Andrew Grey, a Scotsman by birth. He preached in a barn there which was the first place of worship for the Independents of that Township, after the repeal of the laws against conventicles on the accession of William III. He was uncommonly zealous in the peculiar principles of Non-Conformity and was wont to apply to the white surplice of the Established Church, the epithet, "Rag of the Harlot of Babylon."

But all at once a great change came over the man - not a theological change, but a change of position; without warning, he conformed, and obtained the vacant living of Mottram. His old congregation, the Non-Conformists of Tintwistle were curious to see how he would look in the robe of the above mentioned lady and flocked to see him the first Sunday he preached at Mottram Church. He was reported to look "sheepish."

John Wesley met with more than his share of abuse as he travelled the country preaching to all who would listen. The following account of his adventures is from his diary for 1782:

"About seven in the morning I preached at Stockport, and where more and more heard the word of God and keep it. In the morning we took horse at five, but could find none to tell us which was the road to Leeds. So we rode to Mottram. Following the directions we received there, we rode up a mountain and our path ended. We made toward a large house, and the gentleman sent a servant, who pointed the way we were to take. But soon after it divided, and an honest man bidding us keep to the right (meaning the left) we did so till we got to the top of another mountain, among several old stone quarries. Here the road ended. However, we went straight forward till we came to the brow. With great difficulty we led our horses down and rode upon a path on the opposite mountain. But at the top this likewise ended. Still we thought it best to push forward, but my horse quickly became embogged. After he had thrown me on one side and scrambled out himself, we endeavoured to walk down the mountain. But such a walk I never had before for steepness, and bogs, and stones intermixed. That we got to the bottom without either hurt to man or beast, was little less than a miracle. But we were still at a loss till we met a sensible man, who directed us to Saddleworth. In our inn here we found one who had heard me preach at Builth, Brecknockshire, I fear to little purpose, for on my speaking a few words he ran away in haste. But the whole family seemed to fear God. So we did not repent our clambering up and down the mountains. At six we reached Leeds, sufficiently tired, but I soon forgot it as soon as I began to preach, and the spirit of the congregation comforted us over our labour."

Mr Wesley appears to have given a description of clambering over Tintwistle Knarr. One gains the impression that he was deliberately misled as to the proper route, unless he failed to understand the local dialect.

The exertions of Wesley and his followers certainly shook the Church of England out of its complacency and this eventually led to a programme of new church building to serve the rapidly growing industrial towns. Christ Church Tintwistle built in 1837 being one of these.

'Ow about 'Owt'?

Still on a religious topic but of a more frivolous nature is this tale of an unusual christening. There was once a couple in Tintwistle with a very large family and when yet another arrived they went along to Christ Church to have the child baptised. The parents had run out of ideas for a Christian name, so when the Vicar asked, "What shall I name this child?" the father said, "Call it Owt."

I presume, and certainly hope, that the Vicar managed to persuade them to think of a more suitable name; perhaps some genealogist poring over the records of Tintwistle Church for the 1930's may come up with the answer.

Great Conflagration In Longdendale

The destruction of the Bridge Mill by fire made a tremendous impression on local folks because whenever the old men started to reminisce the session seemed always to start with someone asking, "Dust' remember when't Bridge Mill were burnt down Joss?"

"Of course a do. It were in 1899, I remember it as if it were yesterday."

With that question solved they could then range over a whole variety of ancient topics. The only time I can remember Owd Joss being flummoxed was when someone asked, "Neh then Joss 'ow long is it since Dick Turpin was on the Market Ground?"

Joss cudgelled his brains but in the end was forced to admit that was one

Bridge Mill fire.

event of which he had no recollection. We will return to the nefarious Dick in due course, but first we must examine every aspect of the Bridge Mill fire.

Shortly before ten o'clock on Monday morning the 5th of June, 1899, the greatest mill fire which had ever devastated Longdendale broke out at the Bridge Mills, belonging to Messrs T H Sidebottom. The mills which worked in connection with the Waterside Mills, were situated on the Tintwistle side of the river, and employed around 1,500 hands.

Many of the workpeople had formerly been employed at Waterside Mills which had closed some years previously throwing operatives onto the Parish Relief. Work in the cotton trade was hard to come by at the time and the after effects of the fire were bound to affect shopkeepers and others. To make matters worse, the Bridge Mill paid higher rates than others in the area:

"Work commenced at 6.30am in the morning. After the usual breakfast half-hour, operations resumed at 8.30 and soon afterwards news was conveyed that a fire had broken out in the vicinity of the engine room of the mills. Nothing of a serious character was anticipated as several small fires at the mills had previously been extinguished without great loss and on the previous Monday an outbreak in the blowing room was quickly mastered. But this time the outbreak proved the preliminary to a tremendous conflagration. In a brief space of time one of the spinning departments at the top of the mill caught fire, and in a trice, the flames had fully commenced their work.

The engines were stopped and an alarm given to the people throughout the mill. The stopping of the large engines portended that some disaster was toward. Hurried and scared looks were exchanged, clothing and utensils hastily snatched up where time permitted, though in the panic numbers who were attired in their working garb had to leave their ordinary clothing behind as young and old rushed from the doomed mills to save their lives. Spinners and piecers were compelled to run from the Jenny Room dressed in shirts and drawers only and many lost money left behind. From all parts of the large block of buildings terrified workpeople streamed into the mill yard, to find to their dismay that the fire fiend was destroying the buildings where their daily bread was earned.

Emerging into the yard it was seen that the flames had got a hold of the top storey. The two highest blocks of buildings formed two sides of a square, and ensconced in the inner portion of these, fronting the main road from Hadfield to Tintwistle were the low weaving sheds, with their whitewashed roofs. It was on the side of the high block fronting Hollingworth that the fire had obtained a firm hold. Swiftly, the flames leaped along the spinning room comprising the upper storey. The windows began to crack, flames shot through and licked the adjacent walls, and it became obvious that a great part of the mill was doomed.

No more pitiable spectacle could be imagined than that of seeing a fine industrial concern in the process of destruction by fire; the workpeople helplessly gazing at the scene of ruin and disaster, conscious that it would mean suffering for them through lack of employment; women impelled to weeping by the knowledge that workless husbands and daughters meant privation at home. Strong men blanched at the sight.

Anxious enquiries as to the safety of the workpeople could be heard. Running to and fro were those desperate to catch a glimpse of relatives. Suddenly a chorus of horrified shrieks from the women broke out accompanied by cries of, "Come down, come down." The sight of an old man putting his head through one of the windows at the top of the building and calling for help. He was gasping for breath and momentarily stunned by the enormity of his danger.

Through the heroism of a young man, George Ashton, he was guided safely from the building, and on reaching terra firma testified to his thankfulness for his escape from what would have been an awful death.

When interviewed afterwards, Mr Etchells said; "I did not think the fire was so serious at first, as we have had several small fires at the mills. When the fire broke out two or three of us went into a small room at the end of the building, but the others decided to go. I stayed for a while and looked out of the window. The women sent up George Ashton, and as the fire was making headway I decided to leave the building. The room was full of smoke with the fire coming up the rope race like a chimney making a hissing sound. I had to creep out on my hands and knees to the fire escape. I told Ashton to go down the escape first as I did not think it would hold the two of us at once. I was greatly relieved on getting outside."

Another lad called James Avison displayed commendable presence of mind. Finding himself in one of the doomed rooms, with the flames advancing, he escaped by attaching a rim band to the headstock of a machine, and after throwing the band through one of the windows he slid down a good distance to the ground. His hands were badly burned by the friction. Another man, John Henry Hart, was fighting the fire on the top floor when he became trapped. With great courage he made his escape by sliding slowly down the spouting from the top of the mill.

Steps were taken to bring into play the fire apparatus at the mill, manned by members of the works fire brigade, and hurried orders were sent to Mersey Mills, lower down the valley, for the despatch of their fire brigade, but it was apparent that superhuman efforts would be needed to master the fire. At this time the wind was blowing gently from the west, and volumes of black smoke almost hid from view the weaving sheds or the intact portion of the mills and swept over Hadfield and up the valley.

Soon the Mersey Mills steam fire brigade arrived on the scene, and along with the manual pump belonging to Bridge Mills began to play on the burning building. The force of water was hardly sufficient to reach the top storey, where the fire was raging, so attention was turned to the lower spinning rooms, for despite the mill being deemed fireproof, it was feared that the weight of debris would crash through the flooring and ignite the lower rooms.

This large block consisted of three spinning departments occupying the upper storeys and underneath these a card room and a lower spinning room. The fear that the fire would spread to the lower rooms was well grounded. About half past ten a large portion of the roof fell in with a terrific crash, and all hopes of saving the building appeared to be fruitless. Yet the firemen laboured on under the broiling sun, making the best use of the appliances at their command.

Inspector Cooper of Hadfield took the "appliances" down to the scene, but as they consisted of hosepipes and stands and the hosepipes were too short to be attached to a hydrant they were of no earthly use.

Meanwhile other help had been sent for. Since the Bridge Mill was located in Cheshire, the Hyde engine, the famous "Maggie" steam appliance came in haste startling the inhabitants of Mottram and Hollingworth as the engine and horses dashed through. "Maggie" took up a position on the higher part of Tintwistle brow where the massive feed pipe was immediately connected to the Manchester Waterworks main and a 250 yard length of hose piping laid down to the mill below. There was concern at the time as to whether it was in order to draw water from the Manchester Waterworks main but this was done in the desperate circumstances. Later enquiries established that the mill management had the power to draw water from that source without permission. The engine was working at high pressure and the Hyde firemen brought the hose into play on the wing of the mill facing Tintwistle. In order to obtain greater effect with the water a number of the firemen mounted a wooden shed projecting from the premises. Repeatedly they were drenched by the water, but still they applied themselves to combating the flames and saving the adjoining buildings. The water supplies available were insufficient; a small pond in the grounds above the mill was emptied on the day of the fire, after which a supply was obtained from the river. There were hydrants on every landing for which water was drawn out of the river.

About 10.30a.m. a telephonic message was sent to the Glossop Borough Police Station requesting the members of the fire brigade to hold themselves in readiness to proceed to Hadfield. The horses were at once obtained from the Glossop Carriage Company's depot and the men got to hand. About ten minutes to eleven a demand arrived at Glossop for the services of the brigade, and six minutes later the brigade was dashing on its way by High St West, Brookfield, and Woolley Bridge to the scene.

When the building came into sight, flames were leaping all over the upper portion and the roof had fallen in. A position was taken up by the brigade on the edge of the river in the field adjoining the roadway leading to Tintwistle and the appliances got to work. The Chief Constable, Mr J G Hodgson, who was also Superintendent of the Fire Brigade, Sergeant Depledge, the firemen, and members of the police force from Glossop and Hadfield, were in the thick of the fight. The Chief and his men and other volunteers waded through the river, and got the hose turned on to the burning mass. The greatest force of water obtainable under the circumstances was poured on the Hadfield end of the building, where the flames, having swept from the other end right along the block, were burning furiously.

Gallantly the men fought against the conflagration, but owing to the river being so low, considerable force had to be expended to draw a supply, and this diminished the quantity of water poured on the flames, so that from the outset it was impossible to throw water on to the top two storeys. This was greatly remedied by the intrepidity of the Chief Constable and his men. Risking their lives they clambered onto a building abutting this wing of the mill, which now glowed like a furnace, and standing under the towering mass, Mr Hodgson effectively manipulated the hose and poured in a good supply of water. The position was one of great jeopardy for the Chief and his men, who were working like Trojans. Repeatedly as the hissing and cracking sounds were heard, fears were expressed that the building was coming down, but the plucky men steadily maintained their ground until at length compelled to fall back by the relentless flames.

Soon afterwards, the fire manual "The Deluge", from Messrs F Sumner arrived and as quickly as possible the appliances were got into order and a stream of water discharged on the building. At such a time of disaster all classes of men pressed themselves into service, and pumping at this manual could be seen, the Vicar of Tintwistle, Rev J W Fairhurst, with his coat thrown on one side.

On the Hollingworth side of the buildings the smart little steam engine from Mersey Mills, drawing water from the river hard by, was playing upon the building, aided by the Bridge Mills manual, which was vigorously worked by a good staff of men. Despite all efforts the flames continued to make headway carrying all before them.

From the side of the hill in the fields on the Cheshire side there could be obtained a vivid view of the progress of the flames. Here some hundreds of people congregated. They had left the Tintwistle roadway because the view of the fire was concealed by the dense volumes of black smoke emitted. On the west side a perfectly clear view could be obtained of the flames from as far as Woolley Bridge. Hundreds began to arrive from all parts of the district, augmenting the large gathering who surrounded the mill. Numbers came over the hill from Glossop, whilst others hearing the startling news, came by cycle and vehicle to the scene of the disaster. The fire was witnessed by Mr T H Sidebottom; Mr Weetman, Managing Director at Messrs Sumner's; Councillor H Partington of Glossop; and Councillor W Sargentson.

At ten minutes past twelve a high portion of the walls on the Hollingworth side fell with a terrific crash and this appeared to give fresh impetus to the fire. Shortly afterwards a mass of stone fell with a crash inside the building and the fire forced its way into the room below, the third room from the top. Flames were seen sweeping along this room, but for a brief time the windows remained intact. A crackling sound, as the windows gave way announced that this room was now in the clutches of the flames. Firemen mounted the weaving sheds abutting, and poured on water where the blaze was greatest. An explosion, followed by wreaths of bluish white smoke indicated that steam pipes had burst and that it was impossible to save any substantial portion of the building.

Despite the great hold which the fire had obtained, the firemen persisted, the enormity of their task only spurred them on to renewed efforts with a desire to confine the fire to this part of the mill and thus save the adjoining weaving sheds. Throughout the two large wings of the mill, the fire proceeded on its course. The lower storeys caught fire, and although the windows were broken and water poured in, the rooms were utterly gutted. During the whole of the afternoon and well into the evening the jets continued to play on the fire, which was gradually extinguished. All that remained was the contorted machinery and the blackened walls, grim monuments of the destruction which had been wrought.

When the flames had spent their fury, danger was not at an end. The firemen were engaged in damping down the smouldering material and preventing burning debris damaging the weaving premises adjoining. If they had been unable to cope with the magnitude of the blaze, which had destroyed the two highest blocks, they were at any rate able to check the progress of the flames to the sheds adjoining. By four o'clock the flames were abating, but for long afterwards the building was a glowing mass of red hot material.

A large fissure extending from the top of the building downwards, on the Woodhead side, showed the force which had been exerted by the fire, and a glimpse of the fiery furnace which the interior of the mill presented. From the top of the sheds, the firemen were for several hours discharging water on to the smouldering pile, which frequently broke out afresh in various places.

As evening approached the fire was suppressed. The Hyde engine and its firemen bearing grimy traces of the days exertions, left the mill about eight o'clock, leaving behind the Glossop Borough manual, Wren Nest Mills manual and the steam engine from Mersey Mills to complete the work of extinguishing the smouldering remains. The Glossop Borough manual, with firemen Bamford, Beard, Shaw, Bowden, and others remained at the scene of the fire throughout Monday night, together with the Mersey Mills steam engine.

The Borough Fire Brigade left the scene at 11 o'clock on Tuesday morning, when all real danger had been overcome, but it was deemed expedient that the Mersey Mills engine should remain on the spot for some time, and throughout Tuesday they continued to pour water on various parts of the mill. This compact little engine left the place about six o'clock on Tuesday evening; those who had manipulated her, dirty and worn out as they were, having rendered great service under the circumstances.

As the news spread that the mill had been destroyed, sightseers came from miles around. Cyclists from Hyde and Ashton, Stalybridge, Glossop and as far as Manchester, hurried to the scene. People resident within a mile or two, flocked to the spot, the crowd was so large that the main thoroughfare was blocked, and the fields in the vicinity covered with a swaying human mass. The police had all they could do to keep the vast concourse at a safe distance from the ruin. The walls from the outside seemed as though they would scarcely hold together, and from some portions stones and slates came crashing down outside the structure.

Inside the walls, the bottom floor was stacked with a shapeless heap of masonry, woodwork, slates, steel and iron, the machinery of the upper stories having crashed through the floors one after another. In some places shafting and gearing hung suspended, looking as though a touch would send them plunging into the chaos below. The weaving sheds were not unscathed, in several parts the falling stones had smashed in the slates and damaged the looms, and water had penetrated in places and damaged cloth. The parts of the building left standing stood out like a giant spectre against the sky.

While the fire was at its height a shocking accident occurred to one of the mill firemen. George Lund, an overlooker at the mill, was standing on the roof of a shed manipulating one of the hose pipes. In order to make his foothold secure and so that he could place his foot upon a beam, Lund attempted to break one of the skylights. In doing this his foot slipped through the window and he received a gash on his shin. The deep cut had penetrated to the bone, and severed an artery. On jumping to the ground blood streamed over his shoe. The injured man was attended to by Superintendent Cooper of the Dukinfield Division police who was present. Dr Whelan quickly arrived followed by Dr Wylde of Hollingworth, and a tourniquet applied. He was later conveyed home in a spring cart. A youth named McCommon also injured his fingers badly whilst at one of the manuals. The wonder was that there were no greater incidents during the day.

From later enquiries, it appears that the fire broke out on the ground floor in the Engine House due to friction, at about a quarter to ten. It was carried rapidly to the top floor by the thirteen cotton driving ropes of the steam engine. Questioned later the management denied that the engines had continued to run for twenty minutes after the fire started and insisted that they were stopped after five to seven minutes. This may have been true, but in Hadfield there are still those who tell the story that on the occasion of a previous fire, when the engineer promptly stopped the engines, he received a good roasting from the manager and was told not to stop the engines in future without his express permission. The next time there was a fire he obeyed these instructions and the mill was burned down. As is usual after such events there were rumours to the effect that the fire buckets were empty, but these were emphatically denied by the works firemen involved in combating the blaze.

Mr Hodgson when interviewed later was to state that if they had been equipped with a fire engine and been called to the fire as soon as it commenced they might have been able to contain the fire. Their manual was sufficient to deal with a cottage fire but was totally inadequate for a fire in a large building. Some other interesting facts also emerged; there was not a single hydrant on the Tintwistle side of the river, so the manual had to be connected to a hydrant 200 yards away on the Hadfield side of the Etherow which greatly reduced the pressure available.

The water jets could not reach higher than the third storey. The shortage of hydrants was not caused by negligence on the part of the mill owners, but owing to difficulties in procuring water from Lord Howard who had only engaged to provide water for domestic purposes in Hadfield. At the same date there were 204 fire hydrants in Glossop with an ample supply located around each of the big mills. In the Chief Constable's opinion, manuals were a relic of the past, when for £500 a suitable engine could be purchased. The Glossop manual was a toy compared with the Hyde steam appliance.

The Chief Constable's remarks must have dented the Council's civic pride because in 1900 a new fire engine was purchased at a cost of £531 8s 1d.

Chief Constable Hodgson was described as the biggest man you ever saw. Miscreants who received the cat o' nine tails from Mr Hodgson did not go back for a second helping. So big was he that when he mounted his horse, its stomach hardly cleared the ground. There is still a story current that on the occasion of a later fire at Wood's Mill, the New Mills Brigade arrived before Glossop and Mr Hodgson rode onto the scene to tell them to keep the fire going until his men could arrive!

The steam power at the Bridge Mill included seven Lancashire boilers, three Green's patent fuel economisers, compound horizontal and beam condensing engines representing 1,232 horse power. The machinery included 42,746 self acting weft and 47,888 twist mule spindles and about 2,000 looms. The weekly wage bill exclusive of management averaged £950. Both large blocks destroyed were five stories high; one was 16 windows, and the other 25 windows long.

Afterwards it was estimated that the damage amounted to £45,000 which was covered by insurance. The workpeople in many cases lost clothing and their prized watches. Over 1,500 persons were thrown out of work and had to move to find employment. As a result whole streets in Hadfield and Tintwistle were emptied. The Tintwistle Parish Council decided to form a Relief Committee to meet cases of distress. Although no human lives were lost during the fire, two of the horses which had drawn the "Maggie" in its furious dash from Hyde, died shortly afterwards.

Before dismissing the efforts of the police and firemen of the time, it should not be forgotten that when the Jubilee Mill in September 1994 and Wren Nest Mill in June 1996 caught fire. Even with up to date equipment it still proved impossible to save the oil soaked buildings.

Dick Turpin Rides Again

Dick Turpin eluding his pursuers.

There have been plenty of romantic stories written about Dick Turpin, despite the undoubted fact that he was an utter scoundrel. Many of these stories have a basis in truth because highwaymen were fond of such actions as giving some of their ill gotten gains to the poor, or acting the part of a wealthy young blood by mixing with the gentry at race meetings and similar public outings. Their generosity to the poor was motivated by a need to keep mouths tight shut rather than any altruistic feelings. The turnpike road from Manchester to Saltersbrook might have been constructed in 1732 with Dick in mind because in 1737 he was forced to flee the London area with a price of £200 on his head and then set up in business as a crooked horse dealer in Yorkshire. Under the name of John Palmer he operated profitably for some time by stealing horses in various parts of the country and then selling them cheaply at a safe distance.

Stories passed down through the generations are considerably improved at each telling but for all that they must have had a reason for coming into being in the first place. Children are among the best at passing on these stories even though they tend to forget most of them as they grow up. Tintwistle seems to be the centre of these legends concerning Dick Turpin; one gentleman has an old anvil which he claims was used by an ancestor to shoe Dick's horse. The operation was carried out at the point of a pistol and the shoes were put on the wrong way round to deceive any pursuers. These were certainly the tricks that highwaymen employed. The problem with these stirring tales is that Dick Turpin never operated as a highwaymen in the district so the forces of law and order had no reason to pursue him. Dick could well have had his horse shod on the anvil in question but I cannot imagine that he would want to draw attention to himself by pointing a loaded pistol at the blacksmith.

As if the presence of this anvil in Tintwistle was not sufficiently exciting, another local resident has the hammer used to knock the nails in. With all these mementos associated with Dick Turpin turning up, I am beginning to wonder about the origins of the horse shoe which was once nailed to our coal house door. More seriously, small boys in Tintwistle could cheerfully point out the building where Dick used to stable his horse. It used to stand on the corner of Woodhead Road and Bank Brow, the cobbled lane up to the Stocks,

Dick's career as a horse trader was of short duration, John Palmer's true identity was revealed when he was imprisoned for shooting a cockerel which belonged to his landlord, and in due course he was hanged on the Knavesmire at York on 7th April 1739.

To return to the vexed question of when Dick was last seen on the Market Ground, I am sure you can all recall when he had a pot stall next to the man who sold hot pies and stuck his thumb in to make a hole through which to pour the gravy. On the other side of him was the fellow who sold mushy peas and stirred the pot with his wooden leg. I wonder why Owd Joss couldn't remember him?

Reports of suicides seem surprisingly common in the local newspapers of the late 1800's. No doubt life was very hard for many folks when the mills were on short time and cash in short supply. It was not at all uncommon for desperate folks to throw themselves in the mill pond or reservoir. If they chose to end it all in the Longdendale reservoirs then it could be a matter of luck as to whether they were discovered by the Tintwistle or Glossop police. Although there may be no written record of the police pushing the body over the county boundary and then notifying their opposite numbers of the tragedy there are plenty of stories of exactly this happening.

Hollingworth certainly appears in Domesday Book as "Holisvrde" but its does not merit a mention on Burdett's map of 1763-7. Instead we have Wedenshaw Green. When we move on to Aikin's map of 1795, the spot we think of as Hollingworth is named as Wednesough Green and the road through it as Treacle Street.

It is generally agreed that the first part of the name Wedneshough is derived from the Saxon God Woden; the last part could be from hough or haugh which could denote an enclosure, or flat land by a river. Bearing in mind the fact that the local dialect has many words which do not appear in any dictionary and that these words have persisted through the centuries, there could be other equally valid speculations. Just suppose the place was Woden's sough. Sough is not in my dictionary but "gone down the sough" still means gone down the drain for all that. Yet again it could be Woden's Shaw, a shaw coming from sceaga, Old English for a small wood.

Plaque on cottage at Wedneshough.

Before we leave these ancient times, what of Arrowscroft? We tend to associate it with the cotton mill that once stood on the site, but the name comes from the fact that it was once the field where the local archers practised at the butts. In 1414, the year before the battle of Agincourt, the archers of Longdendale were practising at the butts on the Arrowscroft when a tremendous deluge flooded the field and they were forced to flee.

The popular notion of the English Civil War is that it was fought between the Cavaliers who supported King Charles, and the Roundheads who were on the side of Parliament and that everybody supported one side or the other. A large section of the population wanted no part of the war, and some, such as the Moorlanders in Staffordshire were prepared to resist by force the demands of both sides for as long as they were able. As usual, ordinary folks were required to do most of the actual fighting, while the wealthy landowners who made up most the leadership of the forces of King and Parliament were the ones with the best chance of making a fortune. Much of the country was not directly involved apart from the demands of the combatants for cash and silver to finance their war efforts and as there were no great manor houses or castles in the area, Longdendale missed most of the action. But local people would support the Parliamentarians as Manchester and Stockport were among their strongholds.

There is in existence an interesting document which lists the amounts paid towards the support of the Parliamentary Army by several of the more substantial inhabitants of the township of Hollingworth in the year 1645:

2nd August 1645

Accompts made and sworne unto by Several Inhabitants of the Townshippe of Hollingworth in the parish of Mottram in Longdendale, and County of Chester, as follows:-

	li s. d.
Imprimis. John Hollingworth of Hollingworth, above written Esq. paid to Collonell Robert Duckenfeild, in pposieon money..........	8 0 0
Item. lent one horse to the said Collonel att the value of...................	8 0 0
Item. dampnified in quarteringe ten men and nineteene horses of & belonginge to Major Rich 18 dayes...............................	10 0 0
Item. damnified one man & one horse of Major Rich his company4 weekes.	1 8 0
Item. one man of and one horse under the Comand of the said Major Rich ij weekes	0 14 0
Item. Eight men & eight horse under the Comand of the Major Rich one night...	0 8 0
Item. when Sir William Brereton Kt marched with his fforces towards Yorke here was quartered with mee Seaven score menand seaven score horse whereby I was dampnified...	8 0 0
Item. Twenty six men and 26 horse one night......	1 6 0
Item. ffourteene men and 14 horse one night...............	14 0
Item. Sixe men and sixe horse one night..	0 6 0
Item. In the maintenance of 2 souldrs..	31 0 0
sum.....	70 16 0

Neither spelling nor simple addition seem to have been strong points in 1645!

Amounts for wealthier inhabitants are listed below, The poorer folks would have little or no money but no doubt the soldiers would help themselves to the odd chicken and anything else that was not nailed down:

Alexander Hollingworth	82	6	8
John Booth of Woolley	31	12	4
John Booth of the Bancke	20	5	0
John Bretland de ffeilds in Hollingworth	20	5	0
Thomas Hollingworth	20	5	0

There were similar entries for George Bower, John Woolley, Robert Hadfield, Reginald Tinker, John Beeley, and John Roberts. At the end are the accounts made by the Constables of Hollingworth from 1640 to 1645 from which the following items of interest have been selected:

For setting forth an impressed souldier with cloathes £1 10s is charged. For furnishing the High Constable, Mr George Parker with 9 horse loads of victualls to the value of £4 10s. The unfortunate constable adds, "when I brought the said victualls, the Commissary tooke five sacks from me and then promised to restore them again but never did yet, which sackes were well worth 10 shillings."

A dragooner's horse cost £5 and a dragooner's saddle, bridle, stirrups, boots, spurs, sword, girdle and other furniture for a rider to the said horse cost £4. In 1644 there was a charge for the provision to Sandbach for the Scottish Army £1 12s. and towards the collection for the British Army £4 16s.

Despite all this Parliamentary activity, a party of Royalists on their march into Yorkshire before the battle of Marston Moor, stayed one night at Carr House on the Hague. The name of their leader, Captain Joseph Oldfield of Spalding, with that of King Charles, and the date (1644), remained for many years inscribed in Latin with a diamond ring on a window pane of this old house. I wonder what impositions they made on local folks?

CHAPTER ELEVEN
HADFIELD AND PADFIELD

It is time now for a look at the opposite side of the river. Padfield and Hadfield, despite the similarity of their names, are very different. Padfield was formerly a large Township with a total area of 6464 acres, most of it desolate moorland, which stretched from the Padfield Brook to the Yorkshire border at Far Small Clough close to Saltersbrook; and from the old course of the Etherow to the top of Bleaklow. Hadfield, by contrast consisted of only 425 acres, but with no moorland and a far greater concentration of industry. Hadfield can also claim the distinction of having Paradise within its boundaries. The boundary between Hadfield and Dinting is not obvious on the ground, being designated long before today's roads were built and not following a stream or ridge. Much of Mouselow lay within the Township of Dinting and the boundary started where the old tracks divide at SK030957, followed Shaw Lane westwards for some distance before passing across what are now the grounds of the Comprehensive School, then across Newshaw Lane, down the path which ends in Shepley Street at Brookfield, finally crossing the road to end on meeting the Glossop Brook.

Much of the best farming land in Padfield is now submerged under the reservoirs, but before they were constructed the valley bottom was noted for fruit growing, plums being a speciality. There was even a local celebration called the Plum Wakes which took place when they were ripe, and visitors came from all quarters to buy the fruit and generally enjoy themselves. Plums were not the only fruit grown in the locality, on the Hague is Pear Tree Farm scene of the Pear Wakes. Formerly there were farms located further up the valley, some lie beneath the water, some are in ruins and yet others have disappeared without trace. For example within living memory there was a farm on the site now occupied by the Torside Information Centre.

From the records of the Howard Estates we learn that on the 16th April, 1660 the following persons were living in Hadfield and Padfield, occupying land and paying annual rents:

Thomas Blood; Thomas Bower; Nichollas Bramhall; Nichollas, and John Darnalley; Robert Dewsnappe; Thomas Doxon; Thomas Garlique; Reginald Gee; James, Thomas, Ralph, William, and Reginald Goddard; Nichollas, Thurston, William, George, Guy, Alexander, Hugh, Thomas and Ellen Hadfield; Thomas Haigh; Thomas Newton; Thomas Phillips; William, Nichollas and Anthony Sicke, (Sykes).

These folks are worthy of inclusion as their surnames are still common and we can be certain that their ancestors were farming the same lands in the days of the Abbots of Basingwerke and probably long before that. Indeed we can confirm this from the wills kept at the Lichfield Joint Record Office. Here are just a few selected at random:-

John Doghson was at the Heath in 1576; Ralph Bower gives his occupation as yeoman of Gamesley in 1558; John Derneley was farming in Glossop in 1536; John Hadfeelde was a husbandman in Padfield in 1586; William Newton was at the Heath in 1554; John Hagh was at Mousley Bottom in 1554; Thomas Blud, husbandman of Hadfelde left a will in 1589; Thomas Garlicke was a currier in Hadfeld in 1592; John Goddart was living in Padfeld before 1559; Robert Bramhall in Hadfield in 1568; and Nicholas Sykes left a will at Thorside dated 1570.

Padfield being the largest hamlet, had the largest farms and the farmers were among the wealthiest in the parish. In the ancient government of the parish, Padfield men often took the principal part, partly owing to the farmers being more numerous. The Churchwardens from Padfield between 1703 and 1802 have included James Braddock; 1705, William Hadfield; 1711, John Hadfield, 1717, Benjamin Fielding; 1721, William Hollingworth; 1733, George Hadfield; 1740, Joseph Dernley, 1743, William Sykes, 1764, John Garlick, 1768, William Cresswick; 1781, Nathaniel Barber, 1800, George Sydall; 1802, Robert Lees.

The Old Hall in Hadfield was built in 1646 by one of the Hadfields. Butterworth, writing in 1827, says of Hadfield Hall:

"At the top of the village stands an ancient building which formerly went by the name of Hadfield Hall. It appears by the initials in front thereof IHAT 1646, that it was built two years prior to the death of Charles I, during the great Rebellion. The villagers say it was erected by the ancestors of the present George Hadfield of Old Hall near Mottram, a relation of John Wood who resides in a very neat and respectable house in this village."

The Old Hall stands in what once was the centre of the village and around it are some of the oldest houses in the area. The local cross must have stood around the centre of what is still called Hadfield Cross. The base of the street lamp opposite the Old Hall is reputed to be the base of this cross. Note that the village centre was carefully sited in regard to the possibility of flooding.

In the garden of number 54 Hadfield Cross once stood a seat inscribed with the lines:

"This seat was erected in 1862 the time when I had nothing to do, the cotton was dear all nearly stopped, money was scarce and credit spent up." Psalm CXXXVIv2 "we hanged our harps upon the willows in the midst thereof." J Sherrif.

The 'Kiss' on the Padfield-Glossop township boundary.

Hadfield Old Hall.

Alas, vandals have done away with this memento of the Cotton Famine.

Romantic stories have been written about battles between the Romans and a Celtic Prince called Alman who had his stronghold on top of Mouselow. To add some credence to such tales we have Redgate which is supposed to have gained its name from the blood which ran down this way as a result of a battle. One thing is certain, the Romans would not have tolerated a British camp overlooking their fort at Edrotalia and would soon have evicted any tribesmen. In his report on Edrotalia, Robert Hamnett mentions numbers of British querns for grinding flour which were unearthed during the excavations at Edrotalia in the 1890's. He was of the opinion that the Romans had carried them away as useful loot from Mouselow. Another point of interest is that there is a farm marked on present day maps as Alman's Heath (SK038959) and on some older maps the area is marked as Alman's Death. Hence the story that it was here the legendary Alman met his end. All very neat, but one thing that troubles me is that when you are transcribing old wills one of the difficulties in deciphering some scripts is to tell the difference between "h" and "d."

In 1811 there were 78 houses and 450 inhabitants dwelling within Padfield and by 1891 these numbers had risen to 557 houses and 2573 inhabitants. In Hadfield in 1811 there were 88 houses and 479 inhabitants and in 1891, 1024 houses and 4772 inhabitants. This growth was mainly due to the cotton industry. But for the Padfield Brook forming the boundary between Hadfield and Padfield the cotton industry would hardly have become established in Padfield. The contribution of the Sidebottoms has already been dealt with; Waterside Mill bestraddled the township boundary between Hadfield and Padfield and after filling the mill ponds there, the Padfield Brook disappeared under the mill to re-emerge where it entered the Etherow.

Hadfield and Padfield had their fair share of cotton masters. William Rhodes was once a woollen manufacturer in Tintwistle. One of his sons, Thomas, born in 1815, married Mary, the eldest daughter of William Shepley of Brookfield, and commenced business with a few looms in his father-in-law's mill. He afterwards occupied Arrowscroft Mill in Hollingworth and stayed there until 1859 while he finished building Mersey Mills. Thomas Rhodes succeeded in business and built Mersey Bank House in 1862. William Shepley Rhodes was his eldest son by his first wife; by his second wife Amelia, he had further children, Thomas, George, Herbert, Mary, Emily, and Edith.

When the first elections for the new Glossop Borough Council took place on 21st December 1866, Edward Platt, Thomas Platt, Thomas Rhodes, William

Shepley, James Sidebottom, and Robert John Lees were all elected. They all gave their occupations as Cotton Manufacturers or Mill Manager except for James Sidebottom who distinguished himself by the title of gentleman. A few days later at the first meeting of the council William Shepley and James Sidebottom were elected aldermen. Many of these worthies were not happy about Hadfield being in some degree subordinate to Glossop and would have preferred to have the former place run its own affairs. They had a point because there are definite advantages in knowing your local councillor and being able to approach him.

William Shepley Rhodes was elected a councillor for Hadfield Ward in 1874, and represented it until 1883. He was again elected in 1884, and was made an Alderman in 1893. He was the Mayor of Glossop 1891-93. Herbert Rhodes, the fourth son of Mr Thomas Rhodes, was elected a Liberal councillor for Hadfield Ward in 1885. On March 25th 1895 he was elected an Alderman. He left issue, William Herbert Rhodes, of the "Woodlands", Stalybridge, and Thomas Stanley Rhodes. Herbert Rhodes, with Sir Edward Partington, built the Victoria Hall and Library as a Jubilee gift to the Borough of Glossop.

The family were once well known as owners of Mersey Mills, which was known as Rhodes' Bottom Mill, and Hadfield Mill, better known as Rhodes' Top Mill, where there is still a building once used as a smithy with an unusual stone chimney and the road leading up to the mill is lined with stones which were once used as engine beds. In 1790 there was a cloudburst which altered the course of the Etherow where Mersey Mills were built. As a result the county boundary was moved so that part of the mills are in Hadfield thus losing Hollingworth income in rates. On the 24th of October, 1896 one of the engines at Rhodes' Top Mill ran away; the flywheel being smashed to pieces, and portions went through the roof of two cottages.

Another Padfield cotton master was Robert Lees, who built Padfield Brook Mill and handed it on to his sons. He also built Padfield Brook House and the row of cottages known as Lees Row. The mill was later occupied by the Platts and demolished in the early 1970's after standing empty for years.

A significant number of the people who worked in the cotton mills came into the area from some distance seeking employment. Many came from Yorkshire and Lancashire, but others came from further afield. From distant Cornwall for instance, and the West of Scotland where hand loom weavers were facing competition from power looms. The Sidebottoms from 1830 to 1840 had agents in Ireland who were recruiting labour. However, in an age of large

Padfield from top of Redgate.

Old Smithy chimney at Rhodes Top Mill.

families it was not necessary to bring in large numbers from outside the area.

Folks naturally tended to congregate in areas where there were others they knew. At Waterside for example, there were blocks of small terraced houses right next to the mill and a large number of the tenants came from Ireland. The doors and windows of these houses can still be made out in the wall which lines the main road. There was an off-licence at each end of the row and drink often led to riotous proceedings which were settled most efficiently by the Catholic Priest, the arrival of the police being calculated to turn a rumpus into a riot. Indeed on occasion the contending parties combined to rout the police.

Since World War II a number of people have moved into the area, some were displaced persons from Eastern Europe, others from Italy and Ireland. By dint of hard work many of them managed to buy their own properties and some caused a minor sensation by painting the stonework of their houses in bright colours. Time and climate has destroyed this handiwork, but think for a moment of the effect of a mid-terraced house painted in bright reds and blues contrasted with its drab neighbours. One of the most surprising things about these relatively recent arrivals, is how quickly they became assimilated into the local population. In the case of their children, in most cases it is not until you know their names that you realise their origins.

There were other industries in the area during the early years of the Industrial Revolution. Mr John Boyer had a paper mill at Tor Side in 1811. It passed through various hands during the next forty years, finally becoming empty. Shortly afterwards part of it became a beerhouse, the navvies working at the waterworks being the principal customers.

Some years after the main line to Sheffield was constructed, a branch line was taken off at Gamesley, and over Glossop Road by a level crossing, the gateposts of which are still standing. It then ran behind the Dinting Printworks which had its own siding, crossed the A57 road by a bridge close to the Spring Tavern, went on over Woolley Bridge Road at a level crossing near the Pear Tree Inn to service the River Etherow Bleach Works and Mersey Mills, and finally on to Waterside and Bridge Mills. It was opened on 10th October, 1879 and the last train passed along the line on 18th February, 1964. Maconochie's made good use of this branch line to bring in potatoes, carrots, fish, dates and many of the other ingredients required for their products. The finished goods could equally well be carried away by the same route. There was a further branch line to Rhodes Top Mill at Hadfield.

The bridge over the A57 close to the Spring Tavern was demolished in

1966. An object which which is a matter of conjecture is a standing stone with a vertical line down the centre immediately opposite the Spring Tavern. There is no inscription on the face of the stone but as it is exactly two miles from Glossop Town centre I will make a good guess and suggest that it once served as a milestone on the turnpike road.

With the decline of the cotton industry it was vital to the area that other employers move into the region. One of these companies was Maconochies the food firm, famous at one time for its canned Meat and Veg, Kep Sauce, and Pan Yan Pickle. If old soldiers are to be believed, they subsisted entirely on Maconochie's Meat and Veg. for the duration of the War. There were even two ladies employed by the company who were known as Minnie Kep and Pan Yan Mary. These stalwarts had been moved on the hoof, as it were, when the company moved from London. The company has been "taken over" several times since, but has provided employment for thousands of local folks.

On leaving school at fifteen, I joined the company for approximately six months, and very educational it was too. I always enjoyed sitting with the older men at break time and listening to their stories, largely winding up some of the more easily provoked with stories of how they had seen the most marvellous crop of outdoor tomatoes growing in Tintwistle, or arguing about the relative efficacy of dog fat and goose grease. There were those who held firmly to the view that dog fat was an absolute cure-all with remarkable penetrative properties. This wonder product if left in a hollow on one side of a granite sett would penetrate through to the opposite side overnight!

A favourite story tells of one old chap who sat on one of the old tippler lavatories and after lighting his pipe, threw the match down the toilet, Unfortunately for him the toilet was filled with paper and seconds later a searing flame caused him to leap from his perch at an unaccustomed speed. If this was not bad enough, in his rapid rise, he cracked his head against a beam and fell back semi-conscious and received a serious burn to a tender part of his anatomy.

There were some remarkable characters employed there at the time, among whom was Zac, of whom it was said that he could not pass a public house without his tongue hanging half way down his chest. Whilst never having seen him in this condition I remember one occasion when Zac's beer funds were running low. His answer to these dire financial straits was to pick up a frozen side of beef, throw it over his shoulder and set off in search of a customer along the aforementioned railway line. The foreman in the kitchen was a gentleman by the name of Johnny Mays who was no doubt well aware of the capabilities of his staff. Zac's disappearance was spotted in a short time and Mr Mays was soon dashing about in an effort to discover his whereabouts. Strangely, nobody had the slightest idea where he was, but they all seemed to have seen him only minutes before and were certain he could not be far away.

Others were not so fortunate in their misdeeds. The security officer was an ex-Glossop policeman, Bobby Ruck, a strapping chap who had felt a few collars in his time. One day, a lorry driver having delivered his load, decided to help himself to a 56 lb box of dates. Bobby Ruck caught him in the very act and lifted him up dates and all and shook him about somewhat. The driver got an awful fright which probably did a lot more good than prosecuting him.

The boilerman, besides stoking the flames, had a little sideline doing a spot of hairdressing during the dinner hour, (lunch had not been invented in those days). One day his customer was a certain Stone Jud Mellor who had formerly worked as a quarryman and liked to perform feats of strength for a bet. He is perhaps best remembered for carrying an iron-framed piano on his back up Collier Brow. However, I digress. The boilerman was half way through cutting Stone Jud's hair when the hooter sounded for work to recommence. The boilerman downed his hairdressing tools at once and said, "Tha'll afert come back tomorrow Jud." Jud didn't even blink at this turn of events and carried on till the next day with half a haircut.

Another incident which provided some entertainment for the onlookers, if not the principals in the drama, occurred when the Works Manager brought his car down to the Maintenance Department for some repairs. He parked it at the bottom of a ramp where the Engineering Foreman was working on a company van. The Foreman failed to see the parked car and proceeded to back off the ramp making a nasty mess of the Works Manager's car in the process. The Foreman's face was a study as the Works Manager raged up and down clenching and unclenching his fists. The Under Foreman seemed happy with the unexpected turn of events and went round with a beaming smile. He was even heard to remark, "I never expected promotion so soon!"

Marley Brow now goes under the name of Park Road for some reason or other. A sweep was hard at work on Marley Brow one day and prior to climbing onto the house roof he carefully sealed off the fireplace below with sacks to prevent the egress of soot into the house. In the house next door a lady was quietly sitting by the fire when the sweep pushed his brush down the wrong chimney and a great puther of filthy soot filled her best parlour. The first intimation the sweep received that anything was wrong was when she rushed out into the street covered from head to foot in soot and screaming at the top of her voice. Naturally the police were sent for, but they could not stop laughing at such a ludicrous situation.

An Unusual Funeral

A sensation was caused in 1850 by the circumstances surrounding the funeral of James Wood of Padfield. Being the son of Jonathon Wood he was better known as Jam o'Jonathon's. He was an infidel with no time for the Church. James might be an unbeliever, but when he died on July 15th, at the age of 78, he still had to have a funeral, and that meant a trip to the Parish Church in Old Glossop before burial since the foundation stones of Saint Andrews Church were not laid until Saint Andrew's Day 1872.

He left instructions in his will that the mourners who attended his funeral were to have as much to drink as they wanted. Not surprisingly this attracted a bunch of characters who turned up eagerly at the prospect of a free drink. James did not leave matters to chance, his instructions were clear, the funeral procession was to stop at the Willow Grove Inn, where the coffin lid was to be removed and the corpse filled with as much ale as it could hold! The Willow Grove Inn still stands on Wimberry Hill and is now called Willow Grove House; in 1850 it was owned by Mrs Ellen Hadfield. When the cortege arrived, James' instructions were carried out to the letter. A tundish was obtained, placed in his mouth and ale poured in till the body could hold no more. The huge assembly of mourners were meanwhile making the most of the free drink, getting themselves into a disgraceful condition in the process.

At last the undertaker was able to get the hearse on its way once more with a drunken rabble following as it made its way along Church Street. The Curate at the Parish Church, Rev John

Willow Grove House.

Stone, on finding the Church filled with a disgusting mob, shouting and singing lustily, promptly ordered them out for their lack of reverence and refused to inter the corpse.

The corpse was left in the Church and buried the following day, 19th July, without any mourners in attendance, there being no free ale on offer. Unfortunately the Vicar was thus deprived of the burial fees.

Padfield is not over endowed with public houses. In 1846 Mr Joseph Wood was the landlord of the Temple Inn, which gave the name to Temple Street, where it was situated. It is now the Peels Arms. The change of name was owing to a dispute between two lodges of Oddfellows. The inn was built by a lodge of oddfellows who had borrowed money from the other, and when pressed to repay the borrowed money they did so, but rechristened their property after Sir Robert Peel, at that time the Prime Minister of the day.

The Volunteer

The outbreak of the Boer War caused tremendous excitement throughout the country and Hadfield was no exception. The surprisingly strong resistance put up by the Boer farmers had come as a nasty shock and Britain was forced to raise extra forces. Small groups of regular soldiers went about the country accompanied by military bands and pieces of artillery in a scheme to encourage young men to sign on with the colours.

The sight and sound of a military band and smartly turned out soldiers marching by brought folks scurrying out of the side streets. The horse drawn artillery was perhaps the biggest draw. Small boys fell in behind the marching men making the most of the occasion. Frequenters of local taverns spilled out onto the pavement to savour the moment. A number of local young men were carried away with the sight of the soldiers in their smart uniforms and decided to enlist, and amongst these would-be heroes was a Hadfield man whom we will call Danny Dolittle. Word soon got abroad that Danny was off to take the King's shilling and a collection was started in Hadfield to give him a grand send off. As soon as Danny got his hands on the cash he threw a riotous going away party in a local pub. Indeed, the party went so well that he decided to have another the following night; and another, and another until the cash had disappeared completely. Soon folks were asking when is he going off to join his regiment? Finally Danny had to admit that he had changed his mind and was going back to his job in the mill. Hadfield folks never forget his failure to enlist, or his parties - and they never got their money back either.

Last Night At The Arundel Arms

People talk about the number of public houses there once were in the locality. Most streets had more than their quota, mainly long gone. Whatever became of them all? Some of the buildings which were once used as hostelries are now double fronted shops or houses. The Arundel Arms, better known to most as the "Deadman's" because it was situated next door to Glossop Cemetery, did a good trade when it was first built alongside what was the main turnpike road, but

The former Arundel Arms, Cemetery Road.

when a new road was built through Brookfield it lost much of its custom. One thing is certain, from an examination of old copies of the local newspaper, it was frequently raided for serving drink out of licensed hours. There is a story that one Chief Constable was in the Deadman's drinking after hours when the police decided to raid it. He managed to avoid detection by hiding in a cupboard.

There has been a tremendous change in public attitudes to drinking and driving. A hundred years ago it was commonplace for some of the leading business men to drink themselves legless in a hostelry and after being hoisted into their trap depend on the horse to find its way home. One of these thirsty fellows went so far as to leave a sum of money with the Landlord at the Deadman's with instructions to leave a pint of ale on top of his gravestone every Saturday night after his own funeral. His instructions were duly carried out and legend has it that the glass was always empty next morning. The attitude of the police was also somewhat ambivalent where drink was concerned. Wealthy householders would secrete a bottle of beer in their grounds to ensure that the beat constable had a walk around the place during the night, and if some drunk came staggering along with bottles stuffed in his pockets, they might just relieve him of a couple to make sure he did not come to any harm.

Situated well away from other inhabited property, the Deadman's had for some years operated a self granted special licence which permitted the unusual opening time of 10.30 pm coinciding with the closing time of other establishments. Some referred to it as 'The Club' and spoke of it keeping 'Club Hours'. As the crucial time approached, the cognoscenti would be observed emerging from their evening drinking haunts and heading up the hill. The place was frequently raided by the local gendarmes, but usually it was an exercise in futility. They would storm through the doors, only to find the place empty but for the landlord playing patience on top of the bar. Just how everyone knew a raid was imminent is a matter for speculation. But if the bar was empty shortly after half past ten, then something was amiss and a rapid retreat was in order!

Not any Tom, Dick, and Harry frequented the Deadman's after closing time; no indeed. It was rumoured that on a good night there were more councillors packed around the bar than required for a quorum at a council meeting. If all the stories are true, then the place resembled a sort of local "who's who" as prominent citizens jostled shoulders with off-duty police.

Despite its seeming popularity, the brewers were not satisfied with their returns and it became only a matter of time before the place was closed. Word of impending closure spread like wildfire and when the dread day arrived, a tremendous crowd assembled by any mode of transport available to them. I am reliably informed by one gentleman who was malingering in bed at death's door with rheumatic fever at the time, that the Deadman's was closed in November 1957. He remembers the occasion very well because several of these roisterers tried to get him to join them by throwing stones at his door and windows.

The tone for the evening was set when one early arrival, already well mellowed, roared onto the car park and proceeded to demolish a pair of garage doors instead of parking in a normal fashion. In the rush to join the boisterous crowd inside, cars were abandoned rather than parked neatly and soon the small car park was overflowing and the road on either side of the pub lined with cars. The road is narrow enough in the first place but when, later on, people started double parking, the road was blocked and when the last bus from Hadfield came trundling up Marley Brow it was unable to get through, and soon unable to back out either with vehicles left by their owners behind as well as if front. The patrons of the Deadman's might be having a great time, but the bus driver and his few passengers were not amused. Their wrath had not abated by the time they had tramped to the town centre and made a complaint at the Police Station. With irate citizens thumping the counter and waving umbrellas the local force had to act and a police car was soon on its way. At least that was their intention; on arriving at the Deadman's, or at least as close as they could get, they were greeted with the liveliest night the place had ever known. Music was blaring out, a long line was weaving its way through the cars outside to the beat of the conga, and when they eventually managed to make their way inside, it was to find they were out numbered by off-duty colleagues.

The newcomers could hardly arrest members of the public without carting off colleagues who were in little better state. With members of the Watch Committee crowding round the bar it was time for some tactful police work. But what was to be done? Threatening to shut the place and take away its licence was hardly an option. One drunken chump was daft enough to point this out to the police sergeant in charge. He was soon informed by the sergeant that he would have no difficulty in finding some offence for which to book him. Most of the drinkers were in no state to be allowed near a vehicle so asking them to move their cars was out of the question. The only bright spot was that there were no neighbours in a position to complain about the racket.

The day, or perhaps night, was saved by something which had never happened at the Deadman's before; the drink ran out. Disappointed patrons were persuaded to hand over their car keys and the police managed to move sufficient vehicles to release the bus and clear the road. The bus driver was persuaded to use his vehicle to carry a load of inebriates to the town centre with the intention of returning for the rest later.

Shortly after the pub had closed, it became a place where folks could leave their pets to be cared for when going away on holiday. A Glossop man who had been living in the South of England while all these aforementioned events were taking place, returned to the area after a domestic upheaval. He was walking along Cemetery Road on his way back to Glossop from Padfield after visiting relatives when he decided it was time for a drink. He started hammering on the door knowing the pub's reputation for opening when it felt like it. He eventually roused the inmates who demanded to know what he wanted. "A drink of course, what do you think I want? It's only ten o'clock"

CHAPTER TWELVE
MOTTRAM AND BROADBOTTOM

Mottram does not appear in the Domesday Survey, yet it is generally agreed that it was in existence long before that date. Even if not a scintilla of evidence could be found to support this view I would still tend to support it because it seems impossible to travel anywhere in the region without passing through Mottram as it is a natural cross roads. It must have always been like this; the Roman soldiers would have to pass through en route to Stockport, Manchester or the fort at Castleshaw, doubtless glad to have reached the shoulder of Shaw Moor after a steep climb.

Later trains of packhorses would pass through; the Packhorse Inn did not get the name for nothing. It once had extensive stables and barns to cater for the horse trade, demolished to make a car park as recently as the 1960's. With the advent of the Turnpike Roads, carts and stagecoaches would struggle up the Moor with passengers walking alongside until the summit was reached.

With all this traffic passing through it is hardly surprising that Mottram was a sizeable village with plenty of inns. A glance at Aikin's map of 1794 suggests that Mottram was comparable in size with Ashton-u-Lyne and bigger than Glossop, while Hyde was similar in size to Hollingworth or Tintwistle. Hattersley and Godley townships were also once part of the parish of Mottram. Dr J. Aikin's map has been mentioned frequently when describing past places and events. This map first appeared in a book published in 1794 entitled *A Description of the Country from Thirty To Forty Miles Round Manchester*. The book was published at the suggestion of a local man, John Stockdale, who had become a successful bookseller in London. Mr Stockdale paid Dr Aikin to write the book and his original intention was that it should give an "account of the township of Mottram in Longdendale and the singular country around it." Fortunately for posterity, Dr Aikin went beyond these terms of reference and we have an invaluable source of information at our disposal. From Dr Aikin's book we gain an impression of the place 200 years ago:

"Mottram contains 127 houses, which for the most part are built of a thick flag stone, and covered with a heavy slate, of nearly the same quality, no other covering being able to endure the strong winds which occasionally occur. Of late many houses in the skirts of the town are built with brick, there are also eight public houses, which with twenty eight more in the vicinity, are certainly many more than can be wanted, and form no small nuisance by the

Packhorse Inn, Mottram.

Old Post Office Farm, Mottram.

encouragement they afford to tippling and idleness. Within a small circuit of this neighbourhood there are 12 large cotton machines worked by water, besides a great number of smaller ones, turned by horses, or by small streams. Coals of an indifferent quality are occasionally got at Mottram, and on the Derbyshire side in different places.

Salmon swims a great way up the Mersey, and their young, called brood, run up the rivulets among the moors to an incredible height, and are easily caught in the shallow water by persons skilled in groping. Trout are also plentiful in these streams, and is occasionally sold at 6d per lb. These and a few eels are the only fish in this part of the Mersey."

Mottram Church

Mottram Church is situated at a vantage point with fine views in nearly every direction and one can only wonder why some medieval baron did not erect a castle here. There is a popular notion that all churches dedicated to Saint Michael are situated on hill tops; Saint Michael and All Angels certainly meets this criterion.

The earliest definite reference to a church in Mottram was in 1291 in the Taxation Mode by Pope Nicholas. The first church was almost certainly built of wood and the existing stone church built in the 15th century, although there are traces of 14th century work inside. The tower was probably built around 1488 because Sir Edmund Shaa, in his will dated March 20th 1487-8, made the following reference; *"I bequeath to be spent of my goods upon the making of the steeple of the church of Mottram, if it be not made at my decease, and also upon other works or ornaments such as are necessary to be had for the said church 40 marks."* Sir Edmund Shaa died on April 20th, 1487, a month after signing his will. The church is built of a coarse stone full of small pebbles which is believed to have come from quarries on Tintwistle Moor.

In 1850 the church was reported to be in "a very dangerous and unsafe condition, with some walls being as much as a foot out of true" by Mr. Shellard, the church architect. Extensive repair work was put in hand and completed in 1856. We are often informed that the church is popularly known as the "Cathedral of East Cheshire'. I have never heard a single soul refer to it in this way. It is certainly in an imposing position, but to describe it as a cathedral is taking things a little too far.

Mottram church has known turbulent times. At some date before 1532 Peter Vannes was the Rector but he never even visited Mottram, one of his over sixty livings. He was Assistant Secretary to Henry VIII, Secretary

Stone on the Black Bull's Head below Mottram Church.

to Wolsey, Latin Secretary to Henry VIII and Edward VI. Envoy to Rome where he solicited divorce for Henry at the Vatican. Archdeacon of Worcester, Dean of Salisbury, Rector of Tredington; he died in Venice in 1563. The reigns of Henry VIII through to Elizabeth I were times of religious upheaval and clergy would have to conform to the changes if they wished to keep their livings, and more importantly their heads.

The English Civil Wars were another period of unrest. Gerard Browne became Vicar of Mottram in 1637; he was described as "a painful and godly orthodox Minister, and a man of pious life and conversation." He was not to be left in peace and was ejected in 1643 under the Solemn League and Covenant, introduced by the Long Parliament. The support of Scotland was secured by Parliament in return for the abolition of episcopacy in England. The National Covenant was required to be accepted by all clergy and parishioners throughout the land. Naturally many refused, amongst them Gerard Browne. By all accounts he was willing to go peaceably, so long as he was proceeded against legally in due course. It was not to be. According to the court records, two hot-headed Puritan clergy were accused of inciting a band of "several disordered persons" armed with swords, muskets and other weapons to force their way into Mottram Church to apprehend Gerard Browne. These clergymen were Robert Worthington and William Broadhead, who was at this time minister at Saddleworth. Their attempt failed because Gerard fled to the home of John

Etchells with whom he was lodging. The mob arrived outside the house threatening to pull it down with mattocks, shovels and spades.

Even after this episode, Gerard did not immediately leave the area, for he was supported by John Bretland, an attorney living at Thorncliffe Hall. Gerard Browne's successor was a Mr Walker who was first invited to preach at Mottram by Robert Worthington. However, when John Bretland heard the news he threatened that his arrival would be met with bloodshed, So alarmed was Robert Worthington that he told the Churchwardens, who that Sunday had the church doors locked. "And that day the said Mr Walker did not come, nor was there any preaching at Mottram."

Mr Walker was succeeded around 1655 by Francis Shelmerdine. Despite his Puritan leanings, he came from the Anglican ranks for he was curate at Cheadle from 1636-41. When the Civil War started, he sided firmly with Parliament and left to become private chaplain to Col. Henry Bradshawe, serving in his regiment in Bradshawe's own company. The war over he was fortunate to secure the living at Mottram, no doubt with the assistance of his republican associates. In 1662 he was ejected in his turn from the living for non-conformity.

Mottram Grammar School

There was a school master at Mottram as long ago as 1557. John Thornell taught there in 1563 and Reynold Bretland in 1597. In 1612 Robert Garsett a Norwich Alderman, left £100 towards the maintenance of a free school at Mottram on condition that the Lord of the Manor or another gentleman did likewise. Richard Wilbraham, then Lord of the Manor, raised £100 through voluntary contributions and in 1619 he and Garsett's son paid £100 apiece to the school's trustees who in 1632 used the money to buy land in Haughton near Woodhey. The school continued to receive benefactions through the 17th century. Nicholas Dearnley left £30 in 1677 and Robert Hyde £5 a year in 1684. By the early 18th century the master had an annual salary of £16 10s of which £14 came from land in Bunbury. (Bunbury is situated between Crewe and Chester near the village of Haughton Moss) The school's benefactors required "a religious, honest and learned person" to teach the children of the parish reading, writing, and the Greek, Latin and English languages.

In 1766 the bishop nominated the church usher Wardleworth as master at the parishioners request. He was not a success in the position. By 1788 there were only 30 pupils and the vicar reported that the parishioners were anxious

Motto over door Mottram Grammar school master's house.

for his removal. By 1789 the school was 'woefully neglected'. Wardleworth's inadequacy eventually obliged the parishioners to build another school.

Wardleworth may not have been a success as a school master but he tried to leave his mark as a stone mason. As part of the coronation celebrations for George III he erected the sundial near Mottram church. This sundial replaced an older pillar which was probably the remains of the old cross which predated the church. The interesting thing about the sundial erected by Mr Wardleworth is that the base consisted of an old millstone which came from Woolley Mill. A millstone would not be required in a spinning mill and 1760 is too early in any event. This can only mean that Woolley Mill is of some antiquity and may have been a corn mill. Millstones were also used for grinding bones and sand so there are a number of possibilities. The sundial was restored in 1897 to mark Queen Victoria's Diamond Jubilee and stands there today.

In 1643 during the English Civil War, an Act of Parliament was passed ordering the removal and destruction of crosses in public places. Many were hidden away in the walls of buildings or buried until such intolerance had died down. Some were replaced later and many of the sundials which stand in churchyards near the south door were made from the shafts of damaged crosses.

Near the sundial is a path which skirts the primary school and then runs down the field. At one time this path was flagged and at the bottom stood "Daniel's Well" which supplied local villagers. Once piped tap water became available the old wells soon fell into disuse.

The Church Inn and sun dial.

There was some improvement under Wardleworth's successor, James Turner, vicar of Mottram, and in 1811 there were 130 pupils. By the 1830's under William Johnson the roll had fallen again to fewer than 20. It was run by an assistant who was paid 14s a week while Johnson received £65 a year but only performed nominal duties. The school gradually fell into abeyance until in 1858 George Woodhead restored the old building at a cost of £200 and reopened it in 1860. In 1912 it passed fully under the control of the county as a public elementary school.

Sir Ralph de Stavelegh

There is a local legend connected with Ralph de Stavelegh of Staley Hall and his unusual return from the crusades. In the usual version, Sir Ralph broke his wedding ring in half before leaving for the crusades and after swearing fidelity till death he and his wife each retained half of the ring. Sir Ralph was eventually taken prisoners by the Saracens. One night, while a prisoner he dreamt of some evil about to overtake his wife and kindred at home, which depressed him so much that when he awoke he fell on his knees and prayed to God to restore him to his home. He fell asleep once more and awoke to find himself back in England with the road to Staley Hall in front of him. As a memorial to this remarkable event a stone was set up at the very point where he awoke and stands there to this very day. We know it as the White Stone at Roe Cross.

The rest of the story has appeared in similar forms so often as to be not worth the repetition. Suffice it to say that an unwelcome suitor was trying to force Sir Ralph's wife into marriage to get his hands on the estate. These evil machinations were foiled when the two halves of the ring matched perfectly, the suitor was sent packing, and the couple lived happily ever afterwards. There could be a basis of truth in much of the story. There have always been scoundrels ready to steal a man's property in his absence. The bit about travelling from the Holy Land to England while asleep is less easily accepted.

Mottram Cutting

The name Roe Cross poses a question; should it be Roads Cross or was there once a cross at this point? There could well have been because it would have stood as a way marker at the summit in the days before the Mottram Cutting was made. This would have put it close to the present position of the White Stone.

Now for an oddity. Try drawing a line connecting the White Stone at Roe Cross, Mottram sundial, Charlesworth Cross and Edale Cross. Goodness gracious is there something in this ley line business after all. Before the building of the executive estate at Four Lanes there was a pond which was exactly on the line between the White Stone and Mottram Cross and Alfred Watkins suggested that such ponds were used to reflect light from beacons placed at vantage points along a ley line. To spoil this theory, Hollingworth Cross and the Abbot's Chair on Monks Road are well off the line, and if we head in the opposite direction, so is Ashtonhill Cross. Perhaps some ley line enthusiast might like to investigate further to see if there are any other ancient features conveniently located along the route.

Mottram Cutting is a local landmark. Originally traffic between Stalybridge and Mottram had to use the Old Road which

The White Stone.

was part of the Manchester to Saltersbrook Turnpike. The toll gate stood at the Stalybridge end of the cutting to control the side roads entering at this point. This turnpike road was replaced by the straighter Mottram Road at the beginning of the 19th century. These improvements involved the excavation of the Cutting which may have taken as long as twelve years to complete. It was opened around 1825-6 and presumably the embankment which stretches from the Roe Cross Inn almost to the point where the road meets the Old Road once more, was built from the spoil excavated. The wall on the north side of the cutting was something of a local wonder being one of the highest dry stone walls ever built. This wall has been pointed up relatively recently, no doubt because of the tremendous growth in the amount of heavy traffic using the cutting and threatening to loosen the stonework.

Another feature of the wall is the so called 'Frog Stone'. The story behind this curiosity is that when the cutting was being made, a workman split the stone and a frog, some say toad, jumped out. The stone retained a perfect impression of the creature so it was built into the wall as a memento. For many years it has been the practice to whitewash round the imprint to make it stand out. Originally the shape of the creature was quite clear, but the stone has weathered over the years.

Frogs and toads can immerse themselves deep in mud to survive the winter cold without food and one can easily imagine the creatures being buried deeper by some flash flood only to be discovered millions of years later when the rock formed from the mud is finally broken open. But to live for such a period under the pressures involved in forming the rock is asking rather too much of our credulity. To find a fossilised toad is one thing, but for one to leap out of a rock when it is split open is another. The odd thing about these finds is that the shape of the animal is often left in the rock as if to suggest that it was in a plastic state when the toad entered it.

At the International Exhibition in London in 1862 a piece of coal with the shape of a frog in it was on show together with a live frog which was claimed to have been discovered inside. Naturally this exhibit drew the crowds and led to a letter to The Times being published on 12th September of that year. The author claimed that the whole thing was a disgraceful fraud and should be withdrawn from the exhibition forthwith. For days afterwards replies flowed in, all supporting the notion that creatures had been found embedded in rocks and coal. One gentleman wrote to say that at Chillingham Castle in Northumberland, a damp patch in a marble slab which formed one side of a

The frog stone.

chimney piece caused the marble to be sawn open to find the cause and a live toad was discovered within. Another made reference to a Mr Seguin in France, who encased 20 toads in a block of plaster of Paris and found after 12 years that four were still alive. Here is a greatly abbreviated example of one letter:

The Battle of the Frogs

Sir,

I am surprised and grieved to find that any living person still exists who is so sceptical as to doubt the possibility of the occurrence of living toads and frogs in solid blocks of coal or stone. Such a disbeliever would assuredly not be entitled to Christian burial at least in consecrated ground.

Many years ago my grandmother, informed me that one evening, as she was dozing in an armchair before the fire, she was startled by a loud noise. She instantly rose, and was somewhat terrified to observe a fine fat frog drop from her lap. The servant had just put a large lump of coal on the fire, and the sudden splitting of this had produced the sound. She was perfectly convinced that the frog had been embedded in the lump of coal.

The second instance, I present on the authority of Mr Timothy Gosling, a quarryman, whom I have known for 30 years. Mr Gosling was employed a few years ago in blasting the rock near Birmingham. On breaking one of the large fragments of rock with a sledgehammer a toad suddenly appeared.

The trouble with these letters is that they all seem to refer to someone else who has seen the marvel, or to experiments in other lands. Nevertheless it would be rather pleasant if these stories turned out to be true. It would certainly give scientists something to think about.

Lawrence Earnshaw

In the Gentleman's Magazine of 1787, Josiah Beckwith tells us that Lawrence Earnshaw was born at Mottram Moor around 1707 and his father was a weaver. William Chadwick writes that Earnshaw was born in a house about a hundred yards from the Mottram Moor Turnpike Gate on the road to Hollingworth. There is no record of his birth in the parish registers at Mottram but the surname Earnshaw was exceptionally common in the area at that time. It is not unusual for entries to be missing from parish registers especially prior to 1750 so I think Josiah Beckwith is almost certainly correct. With his marriage we are on firmer ground; Laurence Earnshaw married Mary Lees of Mottram parish at Saint Michael's and All Angels on 22nd January 1734-5. There were three children of the marriage, Joshua, John and Lydia. Mary Earnshaw died in 1755.

Not a great deal is known of Lawrence Earnshaw from contemporary records but it appears that he showed an interest in clocks as a boy and after serving four years apprenticeship with a tailor and seven with a woollen manufacturer, he spent a month with Mr Shepley a Stockport clockmaker before taking up the trade.

Josiah Beckwith lists chemistry, metallurgy and mathematics among Earnshaw's skills together with engraving, gilding and painting. He made sundials, optical instruments, cast bells and worked in metals. He taught music and also repaired musical instruments. Earnshaw left an inventory with his will which among other items lists a virginals frame, and books which were still something of a rarity. In his workshop the following items were listed:

....a vice, anvil, clock ingeon, balance weights, wooden lathe, grindle stone, hand saw, tenon saw, dovetail saw, turn saw, 26 files, 13 chisels, two pairs of compasses, drills, a bow, 34 planes and two hammers. The whole being valued at £20.

In 1753 he invented a machine to open and reel cotton in one operation, which he destroyed after showing to neighbours because of apprehensions that it would harm working people. Lawrence is alleged to have said, "He would not be the means of taking bread out of the mouths of the poor." His reluctance to

Earnshaw Memorial.

develop his inventions together with a wife who was often sick was probably the reason he died in relative poverty on May 12th 1767. The entry in the burial register at Mottram reads "Lawrence Earnshaw, ingenious man of Mottram."

William Chadwick also informs us that Earnshaw made a mechanism for raising water from a coal mine at the Hague, but that the mine failed to produce a profit, or he might have benefited financially. Earnshaw certainly knew James Brindley who used a water wheel powered by the River Irwell to pump water out of a coal mine at Clifton in Lancashire so it could well be that Brindley was his source of inspiration in this venture. Lawrence Earnshaw is best remembered for his elaborate astronomical clocks of which four were built. One of these is on display in the Henry Ford Museum, and a second is held by Exeter University.

As a result of an article written by William Chadwick in the Ashton Reporter in March 1867 commemorating the 100th anniversary of his death a monument was erected in Mottram churchyard at public expense.

Recent Events

I moved to Mottram in November 1962 on a bitterly cold day which heralded a severe winter which easily earned the title of the worst since 1947. Folks have long claimed that the climate is a top coat colder in Mottram than anywhere else around and I would be the last to dispute such an assertion. Situated on a saddle between Harrop Edge and Warhill, Mottram suffers more than its share of high winds and the bus stop at the top of Stalybridge Road is not known as "pneumonia corner" for nothing. The howling gales have one redeeming feature, there is no need to have the windows cleaned, the wind and rain do a first class job for free.

Mottram like any other village had its share of characters. When I lived there my next door neighbour for some years was a gentleman called Adam Hill. Adam had worked for the Stalybridge firm of Goodbrands and travelled all over the world installing their products. He arrived in Mottram at the age of three years and over seventy years later he was quite rightly still regarded as a foreigner. "Mind, you, when I take a look round at some of the locals, I wonder if I wasn't lucky to be born further afield." he would say.

He was very well spoken and without a doubt his cultivated manner of speech was a constant reminder that he was an incomer. Adam could tell more than his fair share of stories, to which he added any embellishment that came into his extremely fertile imagination. The only thing that made one doubt the veracity of his tales was that they seemed to improve with every telling.

"Limping a bit this morning Adam. Rheumatics playing up?" "No, its the old trouble with the wound in my leg, I don't know if I ever told you about it. It happened in the 1920's when I was working for the company in Chicago. Of course that was in the days of prohibition and the gangsters were bringing bootleg liquor over the border from Canada and gun battles were a regular occurrence. One night I went out on the town with a group of Americans I was working with and before we knew what was happening we were caught up in a shoot out between gangsters and police. Looking back I suppose I was lucky to receive nothing worse than a slug in the leg."

Adam needed no prompting to launch into one of his stories. Without any encouragement he would roll up his sleeve and show you the small scar on his left forearm which he attributed to an Indian arrow which struck him when he was sailing down the Orinoco. Or was it a Pygmy spear in darkest Africa? The one thing all these exploits had in common was that they had occurred in distant lands.

In Mottram there were two brothers called Buckley, both skilled workers in the building trade who built their own houses in Stalybridge Road, still in good order today. One of them, Harry, was particularly talented as a wood carver and there were three houses with double gates which were fine examples of his handiwork. On each he had carved representations of Aesop's fables, complete with storks, frogs, crows, and foxes. One set of gates was outside his own house at 33a Stalybridge Road, another was along Hobson Moor Road, just past Landslow Green, and the third was somewhere on the way up to the Mudd. The other brother, Edgar, was 'a character and seven eighths', and it is difficult to know which of the stories attributed to him are the plain truth. Modesty was not listed among his faults.

"I wasn't one of the hammer and nail brigade. I could set out a spiral staircase, or anything like that, not that there's much call for that class of work these days." I am always amazed by these old time craftsmen who often had very little schooling but nevertheless mastered some extremely intricate techniques.

Certainly he was interviewed as a suspect at the time of the unsolved Gorse Hall murder, but was soon released. It seems he was arrested on the strength of owning a gun and being thought capable of shooting someone, or anyone come to that. When asked about it years afterwards he would say, "No I didn't shoot the miserable beggar, but the one who did deserves a medal, because he was a tight fisted old sod."

Edgar's house overlooked a field which before the building of an executive estate was full of rabbits and he would cheerfully shoot a few over the back fence and send his dog to retrieve them. This arrangement came to an end when the dog instead of bringing a rabbit back, decided to eat it. Without hesitation Edgar shot the dog. "It were no use to me, doing tricks like that." he explained.

Edgar kept a gruesome memento in a matchbox; a pair of shrivelled human ears. His explanation was that when he was engaged in fighting near Salonika during the First World War, an Austrian soldier shot Edgar's officer, so Edgar bayonetted him and cut his ears off. A reporter from a Manchester newspaper once visited Edgar having been advised that he had some interesting stories to impart. The reporter staggered out of Edgar's house some time later with a face as white as a sheet. "We couldn't even think of printing such bloodthirsty antics." he was heard to mutter.

It was not for these desperate doings that Edgar was most famous, but for his skill at growing tomatoes. Nearly every year he took the first prize at Mottram Show which he richly deserved if the effort he put into the job was any criterion. Each year he would remove all the soil from his greenhouse and then wheel barrow load after barrow load of pig manure round to make a fresh mix of soil before laying a new tomato bed. One year all his efforts came to nought, and yet his tomatoes still won first prize. It happened this way:

Edgar set off to the Showground with some marvellous specimens and on seeing Adam Hill leaning over his garden gate could not resist the opportunity of showing them off. Adam praised them so highly that Edgar gave him a few and went on his way. As soon as Edgar had gone, Adam raced through his back garden and across the fields, arriving at the show well before Edgar and promptly entered the tomatoes as his own exhibit and carried off first prize. Edgar was miffed when he only came second, but when he realised what Adam had done he danced up and down with rage. For years afterwards every time the subject of tomatoes was raised, one only had to make a casual remark such as, "I believe Adam used to grow some fine tomatoes," to set him off once more.

Edgar was never known to touch alcohol, which in view of what he was reputed to be capable of when cold sober was perhaps just as well. For a man nearly eighty years of age he was remarkably supple; he would cheerfully demonstrate his ability at doing high kicks against a lamp post and could clap his hands behind his back as easily as most folks can in front.

Edgar performed one very useful service; because he had lived in Mottram for all his life apart from service in the forces, he knew all the public rights of way and made it his business to keep them open. One developer persistently tried to block one with barbed wire, but Edgar was just as persistent and went every day without fail and cut the wire away with a pair of pliers. Another wealthy industrialist built himself a fine house and thought he could block off the footpath which ran through his front garden. Edgar thought otherwise and would talk a daily walk through this garden and spend a few minutes staring in through the front window of the house. The owner was most unappreciative and bought a Doberman dog which he let have free run of the property. This proved to be a bad move because when the dog made for Edgar he cracked it over the head with the knob end of his stick. "It turned away like a Christian." said Edgar afterwards and he continued his daily walks almost until the day he died.

A little further down Stalybridge Road at The Elms, lived L.S. Lowry, the artist famous for his paintings of cotton town scenes. Edgar used to do a spot of gardening for Mr. Lowry and to listen to their conversation was quite something as neither appeared to be listening to a word that the other was saying. "Yond' Lowry's bloody crackers," Edgar would confide to me afterwards. Perhaps I should have asked Lowry what he thought of Edgar. What a pity he did not immortalise Edgar on canvas, now that would have been a masterpiece worth having. Mr Lowry had a bee in his bonnet about the bus stop across the way from his house and was engaged in a long running battle with the bus companies. I never got to the bottom of what was troubling him, perhaps it was just the idea of folks peering into his house from the top deck of the bus.

The earlier mention of the new executive estate reminds me of another problem. When construction started, the builders had a dump of building sand in the middle of the site which was also the highest point in the field. This spot ended up as somebody's front lawn which might have been a satisfactory state of affairs if the entire local mole population for some distance around had not taken a liking to it. The owner used considerable imagination in an effort to dislodge these pests; I was particularly impressed when he attached a pipe to the exhaust of his car and tried to gas them. When trapping and poisoning had all been tried without success, the owner finally came up with the ideal solution; he had a load of large rocks delivered and built a rockery. A truly fine example of working with nature instead of against her.

In Market Street Mottram there stands a shop which was once occupied by Greenwood's bakers. Mrs Greenwood's pies were widely recognised, particularly among building trade workers, as the best in the Northern Union, wherever that may be. Any weekday around noon the place was besieged with a mob of hungry fellows eager to make short work of these celebrated pies and energetic work with shoulders and elbows was necessary in order to reach the counter. The story that mounted police were required to control the unruly mob is, however, a gross exaggeration. Mrs Greenwood absolutely refused to serve anyone she took a dislike to so it behove customers to behave once through the shop door. Besides baking these wonderful pies, Mrs Greenwood catered for weddings and parties; at least if she liked you she did. On the other hand if she did not approve, then she would not provide a spread for all the tea in China.

The Savoy Cinema

Mottram was once graced by a cinema which rejoiced in the name of the Savoy, It stood on Mottram Moor just above the old police station at the junction of Mottram Moor and the Back Moor.

The manager, before it closed around 1956, was a Mr Lamb, known as Larry the Lamb after the character in the TV programme Toytown. Despite its splendid name it consisted of a large wood and asbestos board hut. Amongst its clientele the Savoy was variously known as the "flea pit" or the "bug house" and ridiculous stories about the place abounded - "Don't cheer too loudly or the bugs will fall off the rafters." being typical. There were only two types of seating accommodation, the best seats were at the back on a small platform which was raised perhaps a couple of feet and cordoned off with a wooden rail from the rest of the audience who sat in the "spit and whistle."

Despite these shortcomings, the Savoy was popular because it was cheap and one could often see a film which had been missed at one of the larger cinemas in Hyde or Stalybridge. There was even a "bouncer" in the shape of a stocky little man with piercing blue eyes who used to walk up and down the queue outside glowering at the youngsters in the vain hope of keeping them quiet. I don't suppose for a moment this gentleman realised it, but his threatening performances were all part of the entertainment.

BROADBOTTOM

Broadbottom was once part of Mottram Township and before the building of the mills consisted only of isolated farms. So small was its population that Aikin did not consider it merited inclusion on his map. There were packhorse routes which passed through coming from Chisworth via Stirrup Farms and crossing the Etherow near where the sewage works stands today. Then past Leylands Farm which was once an inn called The Cuckoo in the Nest, no doubt stopping for a rest and drink on the way. Then up Hurst Clough Brook to Hill End Lane and the Mudd and Mottram Church, while others went up the Gibble Gabble to Bankgate then along Pingot Lane to Woolley Bridge. The packhorse routes were not suitable for the new industries and a new road with an easier gradient was made connecting the Crown Pole at Mottram with Hill End Lane and then sweeping in a crescent to Broadbottom.

The former pre-eminence of Mottram is illustrated by the fact that when the railway was built, the station at Broadbottom was officially known as Mottram and later as Broadbottom for Mottram.

Hodge Printworks was established in 1805 by a Manchester calico printer called Samuel Matley. He took over a small woollen mill and built a weir on the river to direct the water to his mill. Grey cloth was brought in, bleached with lime, dried on the south facing croft and then dyed in large stone vats. Part of the mill was excavated in 1986 and the vats were exposed revealing traces of lime and indigo. These vats are easily examined today and we can ponder on the methods used in the past to manoeuvre the heavy stone slabs into position and seal the joints to make them watertight. With the scant regard for the workers safety at the time, one can only wonder if anyone was so unfortunate as to slip into a vat of dye.

Broadbottom has suffered from sudden flash floods on many occasions.

Hodge Dye Vats, Broadbottom.

On the 11th July, 1932, the village, which was already in the grip of the depression in trade, received the worst the storm had on offer. About five o'clock, big drops of rain fell, and as people rushed for shelter, a deluge descended, accompanied by thunder and lightning. A cloud seemed to burst in the vicinity of Nine Rows and in an incredibly brief space of time the water was rushing down from Gibble-Gabble, out at King Street and Gorsey Brow, sweeping down stone walls and tearing up paved and macadam roads as if they were mere sand.

The wall of Broad Mills was swept away, and the mass of masonry fell with a crash like thunder into the mill yard. The scene was indescribable as the floods gained in volume, and residents were greatly alarmed for the safety of many houses. The most thrilling escapes were at Hodge Fold, where the accumulated waters from the higher ground poured down the hillside, uprooting large trees and carrying them bodily downstream. Hencotes were swirled along by the rushing waters, immense stones were dislodged, and thousands of tons of debris were piled up at the rear of Hodge Fold houses. The brook running at the rear of these houses, had its course completely diverted, and a fourteen feet waterfall entirely disappeared, the bed of the stream being filled to that depth by the wreckage which was piled higher by the minute. Despite the frantic efforts of the little community of souls at Hodge Fold, the rapidly rising waters gained on them, and in an amazingly short period of time a terrific roaring torrent swept through these four houses. The experiences of the residents were terrifying, and soon they were struggling in water three feet deep.

At one moment they were looking out of the windows on the scene of devastation, but felt that the water would not overflow the high banks in front of the house. Then to their horror, they saw almost the whole of the land in front of their home disappear. It was washed away in a second, and the house was left standing perilously on the very edge of the turbulent waters, threatened any every second with demolition. At that moment, the water from the hillside invaded the house, and in a frantic dash for safety with her children, Mrs Griffiths managed to snatch a few articles of bedding, and seek refuge higher up the hillside. Even when the storm abated the house was not considered safe for habitation again.

The Joys of a Tanner Trip

The inner districts of Manchester between and before the World Wars were hardly the most salubrious places to live. Much of Gorton, Openshaw, Ardwick and Ancoats consisted of row upon row of terraced houses without any front garden and only a small backyard just big enough to hold a coal house, an outside toilet and a dust bin. Access to the back of the properties was by a long ginnel which served two rows of houses.

Some older properties were even more basic, being crumbling brick back to back houses with only one door opening directly onto the street, with a common toilet for several families. Children had the cobbled street as a playground and the only open spaces were a few public parks. These were the places to go to see a blade of grass or a tree. It was hardly surprising in the circumstances that many children had never seen a sheep or cow in their lives and were happy to believe that milk came from the condensed milk trees where it grew in tins. The blitz destroyed whole rows of these tiny terrace properties and after the rubble had been cleared, the open spaces provided somewhere for children to kick a ball about. Manchester folks had not forgotten their rural origins because these spaces were known as "crofts".

Coming from such a crowded environment, the denizens of these dreadful districts naturally seized on the opportunity to get into the surrounding countryside on one of the special excursion trains available at sixpence return during the Summer months. Hayfield, Broadbottom and Glossop were prime destinations for these outings of the huddled masses.

The simple country souls who inhabited such remote regions eagerly awaited their arrival. The gable ends of houses had great whitewashed signs; 'Hot Water', 'Fresh Eggs', 'Real Farm Teas', and the like to entice the hungry trippers. Imagine if you will, a group of hopefuls arriving at Broadbottom Station on a glorious Summer's morning. The station is surrounded with high trees, the birds are singing, the path down through the wood to the river in the valley bottom is lined with masses of wild flowers. Compared to Ancoats they might well have been transported to paradise.

Then they reach the bridge high above the swift running Etherow. What excitement when someone spots a kingfisher disturbed by all the racket, darting across the water. The only open water to be seen in Manchester was the murky canal; most of the rivers running through the city were culverted or hidden behind buildings - just as well since they were so loaded with industrial effluents that folks claimed it was possible to walk across them. Irk, Irwell, and Medlock; no limpid streams these; more like slow moving sewers in whose dismal depths no living creature could exist.

Once over the bridge and onto the path leading up to Charlesworth, signs appeared on either side of the route inviting the visitors to the delights of the region. COME TO BRADSHAW'S TEAROOMS, 200 YARDS ON LEFT. A little further along another sign beckoned. DON'T GO TO BRADSHAW'S. COME TO HARRIS'S. FREE SWINGS. Here was free enterprise at work, no one worried about knocking copy, neither could they complain that their creature comforts were not catered for.

At the end of a long hot day the happy excursionists would straggle back to the station, well fed but utterly exhausted after a memorable day in the fresh air, clutching a bedraggled bunch of wild flowers as a memento. An expedition to be savoured for months to come.

Some Mancunians enjoyed these excursions so much that they set themselves up with little weekend bungalows. These were generally very simple consisting perhaps of a an old railway carriage which had been converted and set up in a farmer's field. There were once several along the lane from Hodge Fold to Bottom's Hall, and others near Hobson Moor Road. Most have gone, destroyed by the ravages of time, vandalism, or because their sites were suitable for building.

CHAPTER THIRTEEN
ANCIENT STRONGHOLDS

The Roman invasion of Britain occurred in AD 43, when they landed in force in Kent. By AD 48 they had successfully overrun the lowland south and midlands and had advanced at least to the Rivers Severn and Humber. To subdue the uplands was to take them another 40 years. It would appear that the more civilised south adapted more easily to Roman ways since that is where the majority of Roman villas are to be found whereas the uplands of Britain are the place to seek Roman forts. The Roman legions were strategically placed to deal with uprisings; the Second Legion at Caerlon to overawe the Welsh tribes; the Sixth at York to control the north; while the Twentieth Legion at Chester could intervene in either area. The smaller forts were occupied by cohorts of auxiliary troops which might be drawn from any part of the Roman Empire.

Like all empires the Roman Empire was continually having trouble on its boundaries with less civilised tribes and nations. These tribes were well aware of the comparative riches of Rome since they traded with them and imitated them. There was no simple solution to the problem, since if the Romans defeated a troublesome tribe they might easily add to their own difficulties by lengthening frontiers and thus come into contact with other tribes who might be even more turbulent. One solution was to use a client tribe to defend the boundaries of empire with the promise of Roman support.

The north of England at the time was occupied by a numerous and warlike tribe known as the Brigantes. These people were less civilised than those the Romans had already conquered and although the aristocracy of the tribe boasted an Iron Age civilisation, the bulk of them were still in the Bronze Age. The ruler of the Brigantes was Queen Cartimandua who was an ally of the Romans although there had been some fighting previously. This suited the Romans who had their hands full subduing Wales where the British chief Caratacus was conducting a skilful guerrilla campaign. Eventually Caratacus was defeated but managed to escape and fled to the court of Cartimandua hoping for refuge and support. Instead Cartimandua had him handed over to the Romans in chains and he was taken to Rome.

At first the Romans had no wish to occupy the north and wanted only to safeguard their frontier by alliance with a friendly state. However, sometime before AD 57 Queen Cartimandua quarrelled with her consort Venutius, from who she had been divorced, and the Brigantian state based on marriage alliances broke up. Cartimandua promptly captured the relatives of Venutius who retaliated by invading her territory. Venutius was anti-Roman and Cartimandua called on her allies to intervene, which they did successfully.

Later when the Roman world was in the midst of civil strife, Venutius took the opportunity to pay off old scores. Cartimandua had married her former husband's armour bearer, Vellocatus, and Venutius came out openly against the pro-Roman party. He invaded Cartimandua's territory and once again the legions had to intervene, rescuing the Queen with difficulty but leaving the rest of Brigantia under Venutius' control.

Under Venutius, the Brigantes had a powerful army in the field which the Romans would have to destroy if there was to be peace in the south. There was no alternative but to conquer the north. The Romans advanced up each side of the Pennines to Carlisle and Newcastle, building roads and forts as they did so. In addition to building roads, the Romans used their ships to supply forces - there is nothing new about combined operations. The Brigantes were eventually crushed between the arms of the pincers. The Roman fort at Gamesley came into existence around this time, the exact date a matter of conjecture with guesstimates ranging from AD 77 to 84, with AD 79-80 perhaps most likely.

The very fact that the Romans found it necessary to build so many forts and station three legions in Britain on a permanent basis gives a clear indication of how seriously they rated the opposition, and that the area was never really pacified.

The site of Edrotalia is typical of other Roman forts, situated on slightly elevated ground, at the junction of the Etherow and Glossop Brook which formed a natural defence on two sides of the fort, aided also by the steep ascent from the river to the fosse of the fort. The fort was sited so as to control the entrances to two valleys giving access to the north Derbyshire hills.

Roman forts tended to be of a uniform pattern which makes it somewhat easier to understand what Edrotalia was like in its heyday. When a Roman general decided that a fort must be established, it was staked out according to the general plan adopted by all detachments of troops. One portion was set to dig out the fosse to the usual depth and width, whilst others cut down the timber required for the soldiers huts, residences of the officers, other necessary buildings, the gates, plus sharp pointed stakes for the inner slope of the fosse.

The rounded corners of the fort and the absence of barbicans at the gates and intermediate towers are a feature of all early Roman forts. In the first century the Romans depended for defence mainly on the strength of their garrisons and not on the strength of their forts. In later times, intermediate towers were erected between each gateway and the corner observation towers, also a barbican on each side of each gateway.

The Roman fort at Gamesley was first identified as a Roman Station in July 1771 when Rev John Watson, Rector of Stockport visited the site and wrote a report to the secretary of the Society of Antiquaries describing his discoveries which were read to the Society on 10th December 1772. Mr Watson states that the country people called the interior the "Castle Yard," and eleven fields adjoining the "Castle Carrs." The name Melandra seems to have been invented by someone in the past, possibly Mr Watson, but there is absolutely no evidence that the Romans knew it by that name. A fair amount of learned guesswork has

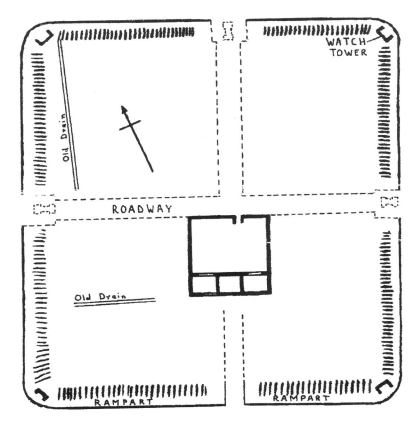

Roman Fort at Gamesley.

been written concerning the origin of the name Melandra, but other than to give academics an opportunity to air their knowledge of Latin and Greek nothing useful has emerged. There are reasons for believing that the Roman name was Ardotalia or Edrotalia from the River Etherow in the same manner as the Roman fort at Derventio took its name from the River Derwent. Anyway I prefer Edrotalia.

Mr Watson's report is of particular value because at the time of writing he was able to say: "The plough had not then defaced it, and its form could not be mistaken."

The form of the fort was an oblong with the corners rounded off; its extent 122 yards by 112 yards; and the walls were 12 feet thick. There were four entrances, and probably an inscribed stone over each, as one was found by a farmer Sammy Cooper of Lower Gamesley when he was digging out stone on the land a few years before Mr Watson's visit. The farmer had built the stone into the wall over the doorway of his house, where it remained until 1842 when the farmhouse was pulled down and re-erected, the stone again being built into a wall over a doorway exposed to the weather. This stone is now in the museum at Buxton together with many other items which were formerly kept in the Victoria Hall in Glossop.

The inscription on the stone is "C(o)ho(rs) i Frisiavo(num) (Centuria) Val(erii) Vitalis". Watson's translation of the inscription on the stone was "Valerius Vitalis, commanding a century, or company of the first Cohort of the Frisians, was stationed here."

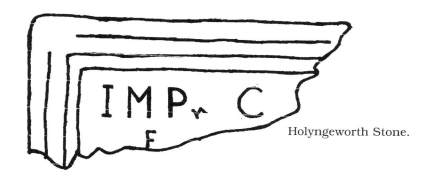

Holyngeworth Stone.

In 1832 a portion of a larger inscribed stone was found and passed into the hands of Captain de Holyngworthe of Hollingworth Hall who purchased it for 2s. 6d. from the finder. The stone has since been lost but fortunately a sketch was made. This stone was almost certainly of greater importance than the existing one, the "IMP" suggesting that the missing portions would reveal the name of the reigning Emperor. Prior to the reservoir belonging to Manchester Corporation being made at the Hague on the Cheshire side, the River Etherow was undermining its banks and a retaining wall was built to prevent further encroachments. The work was carried out with stone from the site of the fort, amongst which was another inscribed stone. One of the workmen having no notion of the historical value of the stone built it into the interior of the wall. A bystander seeing what he was doing said, "Thart puttin' summat in neaw ut ull be wanted some day."

A few days later, Mr Bennett Woodcroft, a gentleman visiting the neighbourhood and hearing of the matter, went to the site and offered £5 if workmen would recover the stone, but the clerk of works would not permit the wall to be taken down. Who knows? Perhaps at some future date the wall may be demolished and the stone recovered. The rest of the Holyngworthe stone is as yet undiscovered, but could well be buried in some barn, or drystone wall.

Since Mr Watson's day, and probably from long before that time, the site was used extensively as a quarry for dressed stone by the farmers in the vicinity, for most of the farm houses, barns, outbuildings, and fence walls contain considerable quantities of stone obtained from the fort. The nature of the stones and the peculiar manner in which they were dressed makes them easily distinguishable.

The first serious attempt to excavate the site and make a search for antiquities was carried out from 1899 to 1900 and we are indebted to Mr Robert Hamnett for making a report on their discoveries. The Manchester Classical Association made a report on the site around 1906 and Mr Hamnett and his associates made later excavations in 1906-7.

Amongst the items unearthed at Edrotalia were; whet stones with the marks made when knives or weapons were sharpened on them; Roman weights of bronze and lead; a few iron spear heads, a hatchet, a Roman soldiers iron signet ring, an intaglio of glass with the design of a ram on the seal, the remains of oak posts which were found resting on flag stones; the crown of an altar and querns. The Roman soldiers were evidently gamblers since lead dice were found. Among the miscellaneous items found around the same time and grouped with the items from Edrotalia was an iron horseshoe from the old track along Doctor's Gate. It looks very similar to a modern horseshoe. One is left wondering if Dick Turpin passed this way as well!

NVM·AVG
GENIO·COHO
I·FRISIAVO
A·C·PRAEF

Roman Altar from Edrotalia.

The coins found and identified with certainty were: Silver Denarius, Emperor Galba, A.D. 69; Silver Denarius, Emperor Domitian, A.D. 95-6; Silver Denarius, Emperor Trajan, A.D. 100; another one A.D. 109; (bronze coin of a Jewish ruler of Jerusalem, Simon Bar-Cohab, A.D. 132-135. This is one of the most interesting in the collection, as Bar-Cohab revolted against the Romans); Bronze Denarius, Carausius, A.D. 286-293; Bronze Magnus Maximus, A.D. 383-388. All these were placed in the Museum in the Victoria Hall, as well as a Bronze Denarius, Emperor Posthumus, A.D. 259, found in the Hague. These give a clear indication of the length of time that the Romans were in occupation at Edrotalia.

Odd items turn up from time to time which provide further evidence of the Roman occupation. When Mr Samuel Shepley was making a goyt for his mill reservoir at Brookfield in 1841, he discovered a stone coffin in which had been buried a Roman soldier, one of the garrison at the adjoining Roman fort. In the coffin was a silver coin of the Roman Emperor Domitian A.D. 81-96.

I have to add a rather disappointing note to the efforts of Mr Hamnett and his energetic colleagues. During the excavations of 1889-1900 photographs of the important finds were taken by Mr T. W. Sharpe and copies were sent to "The National Photographic Record Association" who deposited, with full details, a copy of each at the British Museum. Alas, the Museum say they have no record of these photographs and the Derbyshire Archaeological Society has no knowledge of them either.

Where did the materials come from to build the fort? The timber would be felled locally, but what of the stone and tiles? Mr Hamnett was of the opinion that the stone used in the building of the fort came from Hargate Hill Quarry, and at the time of the excavations tells us that a very good example of a Roman road led from 'Melandra' to the Quarry. This road could well be the first section of the road that went via Monk's Road to Buxton.

Another suggestion is that the stone came from Tintwistle Quarry and was floated on rafts down the Etherow. This notion has its merits because the river was much larger at that time and the Romans would have tackled such a project with ease, probably by building a series of weirs across the river where extra depth was required.

Yet another report prepared by the Manchester Classical Association contains the following information:

"Large numbers of round boulders of convenient size have been found ....which were probably used for throwing from the ballista. One of these stones was found which had been artificially shaped. The stone in question was from Cown Edge, where the quarries from which the walls of Edrotalia were built may still be seen."

So there we have three expert opinions on where the stone to build Edrotalia was quarried. Robert Hamnett was probably on the right track because Hargate Hill is the nearest quarry to the fort being only a mile distant while Tintwistle and Cown Edge are roughly twice that distance. The notion of transporting the stone by floating it down the Etherow on rafts also has considerable merit and could well have been the easiest way. I suspect the matter could have best been settled by getting one of the old stone masons to spend some time with a hammer and chisel on a few pieces of the stone. These chaps have a feel for their materials and some claim to be able to tell stone from Mouselow, Lees Hall, or wherever by the way it works.

This reference to ballista stones reminds me that at one time in the front garden of a house in Saint Mary's Road, just below the intersection with Princess street, there were three large stones, eighteen inches or more in diameter which were reputed to be catapult stones from Edrotalia. If these were truly Roman missiles, then it would have required considerable strength to man-handle the stones and a very powerful machine to propel them through the air. I have succeeded in causing confusion in museums by asking how big Roman catapult stones were. The staff have always been most helpful, but in the end come back with the same answer, "We don't know." All the catapult stones in museums which I have seen to date have been much smaller than the stones in Saint Mary's Road, the largest being about 8" in diameter. The ballista stones unearthed at Navio were 3.5", 4", and 6" in diameter.

The excavations carried out by the Manchester Classical Association were intended mainly to find remains of roads, but led them to the conclusion that the camp was undoubtedly of two dates. It was noteworthy that the coins previously found divided themselves into two well marked periods; A.D. 68-100 and A.D. 286-388. This coupled with the evidence provided by the two levels of roads seemed to point to two separate occupations, the earlier in the first, and the later towards the close of the third century. Another interesting find was the iron shoes of the south gate which were found on the stone sockets of the gateway. The eastern entrance was cleared to the foundations which were found to be perfect, with a guard chamber on the left, and a small tower on the right, having their lower courses of stone still remaining. The gateway was a double arched one, and many of the arch stones were found in the debris which enabled a portion of one of the pillars of the arch to be restored with the original stones found at its base. A stone flagged conduit was uncovered for over sixty yards which was probably the main drain for the camp, and outside the station, near the west tower was found a gravel road nine feet wide, leading to a plateau in an adjoining field which may have been used as a parade ground.

The foundation of the wall at Edrotalia is of gritstone flags, resting on boulders embedded in clay, the first course of pick dressed stones being set back a few inches. The height of the walls can only be conjectured, but would be at least shoulders high above the rampart, and perhaps castellated. The rampart at the top would be sufficiently wide to allow the sentries to pass. At each of the four corners was a tower with the outer face rounded, the entrance probably being from the rampart as no trace of an entrance from the interior of the fort was found. This would enable the lower room to be used as prisons or store rooms, the sentries being responsible for the safe custody of their contents.

The gateways were double, with a portcullis in front. In the recesses between the entrances stood the sentries, a small guard room being in one of the lower rooms. Over the centre of the outer arch was an inscribed stone. Between the western and eastern entrances was a gravelled road called the Via Principalis. Some of the kerb stones lining the road were still in situ in 1900. This road divided the fort into two unequal parts, the southerly part, the smallest, containing the Praetorium, granary, and altars. The other contained the soldiers huts, streets, and workshops. The floor of the granary was paved with square tiles. Floor tiles, wall tiles, and fragments of hypocaust tiles were also found. Some of them have the letter R on them, some VV, which is an abbreviation of Valiant and Victorious, the motto of the 20th Legion.

The residence of the officers contained three lower rooms, how many above, no one knows. The centre one had a floor of broken tiles, the other two of hard beaten clay. Just outside the north wall of the centre room was the foundation of a platform where the officer could stand and orate to the soldiers, or the Governor of the district could address the chiefs of the district.

Ovens were plentiful, and were very simply made. Stones were placed in a circle, leaving an opening for the door, fire clay was then placed on the bottom, willows or some other suitable material were then stuck in the ground; and a beehive shaped construction was plaited; this was plastered over with clay, a charcoal fire was then made inside, and by the time the willows were burned through the clay was sufficiently hardened to retain its shape.

There is evidence that the fort was destroyed by fire, many of the stones bore signs of having been subjected to intense heat, and charcoal was found close to the inner walls of the three rooms in the Praetorium and other places. This may well have occurred when the Picts and Scots came over the Roman Wall in the 367, burning, looting, and slaying. This incursion was extremely serious with the invaders capturing the Roman commander in the north and killing the Count of the Saxon Shore.

There have been some minor excavations at the site in more recent times by students from Manchester University, but nothing of note has been published on the subject. Very little remains visible of Edrotalia today, just the earthen banks delineating where the walls once stood. It is surprising how rapidly a site can deteriorate; around 1941 there were still a few stones standing as the remains of walls. With a large housing estate nearby it is hardly surprising that the site has become a playground and any sizeable stone not cemented into place, has been rolled down the nearest slope. A good idea of its original appearance might best be gained by a trip to the Roman fort at Hardknott in Cumbria where a considerable portion of the walls remain.

There must have been roads to connect the various Roman forts and

Hardknott Fort in Cumbria.

stations. Mr. Peter Wroe has left us an account of his efforts to trace several of these roads in a book entitled "Roman Roads In The Peak District." We have already examined one possible route up Longdendale heading towards Penistone and going round clockwise Mr Wroe has traced the line of the roads to Brough and Buxton and has dug sections at intervals along both to verify the methods of construction. At one time it was confidently stated the Doctor's Gate was of Roman origin and the paved portion over Coldharbour Moor cited as a classical example of Roman work. Mr Wroe's efforts certainly cast doubts on this view and some are of the opinion that Doctor's Gate is a medieval track. Some weight is added to this view by the fact that the paved section mentioned has very definitely deteriorated over the last sixty years. Of course there could be yet another explanation. Both routes could have been made by the Romans, after all they were occupying the country for long enough.

On the exact route of other roads we have less evidence. The Edrotalia to Buxton road furnishes a good example of how easily traces of antiquities can be lost. At SK024909 the Roman road to Buxton was crossed by the minor road which leads on to Cown Edge and Robin Hood's Picking Rods and on the south side of this road the aggar or embankment of the Roman road was indicated clearly by the manner in which the stones in the wall curved over it. Sometime during 1998-9 this wall was rebuilt; the dry stone waller has done a first class job, but in so doing has completely hidden any indication of the aggar because he has laid his stone in relatively horizontal courses.

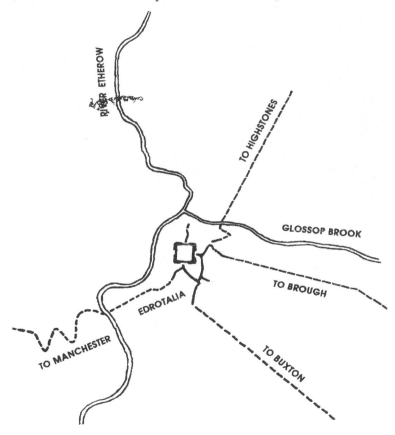

Map 8. Roman roads from Edrotalia.

Mr Watson in his report mentions seeing a gravel road leading from Edrotalia and pointing towards Stockport, and another passing through the Hague and Mottram and on to where it joined the great military road from Manchester to York. The Victorian Ordnance Survey map and the 1910 map of

Mouselow from Cemetery Road.

the Roe Cross area both indicate a Roman Road heading North from Gallows Clough in direction of Castleshaw. Presumably after leaving Edrotalia and crossing the Etherow this road made for the low point at Roe Cross farm between Shaw Moor and Harrop Edge following the line of the Coach Road, and once this obstacle had been by-passed, turned North. Roads to Manchester and Stockport would set off in the same way and separate later. The 6 inch map for Hattersley 100 years ago has the straight stretch of road passing through the estate marked as a Roman Road - certainly the right route for Stockport.

Mouselow is definitely a puzzle. One has only to stand on the summit to realise that it has commanding views in all directions and it hardly surprising that traces of early earthworks are still to be seen. The puzzle is to discover who actually built them. Romantic tales of battles between Romans and Britons have been written and the name Redgate for the steep road on the north eastern side could well be a folk memory of a bloody battle on the site. Other suggestions are that Mouselow Castle dates from Anglo-Saxon times or that later was the site of a castle during the disturbed times of Stephen and Matilda.

Once again we are indebted to the Rev. John Watson for his description of the site as he found it in 1775:

"The next remains which I discovered in this neighbourhood is that of a large Saxon fortification called Mouselow Castle, on the top of a very large hill, in the Parish of Glossop, in the County of Derby, near the banks of that river which some call the Mersey, and others the Etherow. Its name seems to be derived from the Anglo-Saxon Mope, an heap of anything answering nearly to Mow Cop, a large round topped hill between Cheshire and Derbyshire. This etymology tends to show what I am describing as a Saxon work, and the form of it corresponds with the ideas we have of the military taste of that people.

On the top of it there was strong fort surrounded by a wall, the whole encompassed by three large ditches. The ascent being small towards the south-west, the strongest works were raised on that side, on all other parts the hill is exceedingly high and steep, a circumstance in which the Saxons differed from the Romans, who seldom or ever out of choice, fixed on such elevated stations as this, even the very hill was rejected by them when they settled at what is now called Melandra Castle, within a computed mile of Mouselow, on the banks of the same stream. This military settlement of our Saxon ancestors was considerable, for the fortified ground took in some acres. The earth on the top of the hill is exceedingly irregular, and has been robbed of most of its stone to build houses, and make fence walls. There are good springs of water within the compass of it."

The Rev. Watson's comments on the derivation of the name may be wide of the mark but at least he makes it clear that in his day there was still a wall in existence as evidence of its previous fortification. An examination of the walls at the top of Redgate will reveal a number of regularly shaped stones which give the impression of having been taken from some building.

Robert Hamnett writing in May 1914, adds the following:

"Soon after Watson's visit the hill was planted with trees. We have undoubted evidence that before the Saxons or Danes built Mouselow Castle that it was a British fortress, and captured by the Romans, who took the British querns away along with other loot. Some of these are in the Glossop Museum, along with the carved stones found at Mouselow by the Rev George Marsden in 1846, whilst digging for stone to build himself a house. He built these stones in the gable end of a house, and they were removed by the Lord of the Manor, and are now in safe custody. They are very interesting and it is a pity that we have no funds available to explore this interesting ancient site."

Unfortunately Mr Hamnett does not tell us how he knew that the querns found at Edrotalia had come from Mouselow. Possibly he found some at Mouselow as well, or maybe he assumed they had come from there as the most likely source. And there we have it; perhaps we shall never know for certain who constructed a defensive position on top of Mouselow..

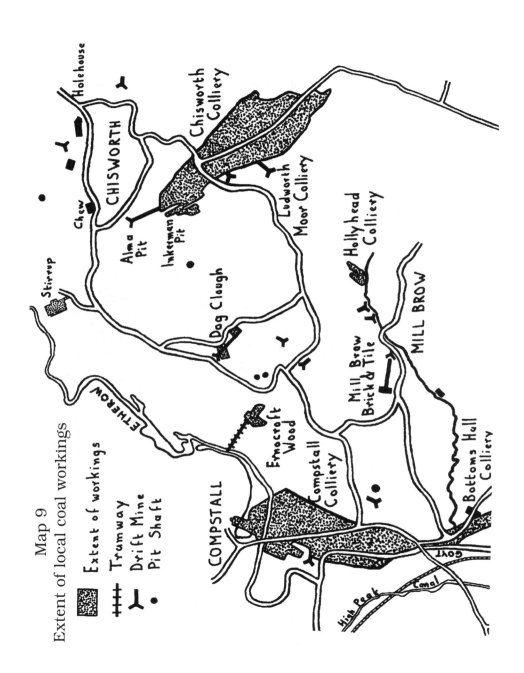

Map 9
Extent of local coal workings

Extent of workings
Tramway
Drift Mine
Pit Shaft

CHAPTER FOURTEEN
CHARLESWORTH, CHISWORTH and LUDWORTH

These three ancient townships are all linked by the Glossop to Marple Bridge Road, much of which was turnpiked in 1803-4. This road started at the Charlestown Bar which stood near to the Drover's Inn at the bottom of Chunal. The toll house stood on the triangular piece of land which now serves as a car park so that it could take tolls from traffic using the Chapel-en-le-Frith turnpike or those by-passing Glossop via Turn Lee Road and Primrose Lane. The next toll gate was at the bottom of Simmondley Lane where it could control goods coming from Simmondley, and the next on the opposite side of Glossop Road to the Plough. The branch road from the Plough to connect with the existing road at the Spread Eagle was built at the same time. The toll house at Dinting is still standing as is the next one at the end of Woodseats Lane. The Dinting and Holehouse toll houses are today private dwellings, whereas the Woodseats one is just a stone shed. The last toll bar stood at Rose Brow close to the Windsor Castle Hotel where the road met the turnpike to Stockport which was also controlled with a bar.

Holehouse Toll House.

Manchester Guardian. Sat 5.5.1821.

Notice Is Hereby Given

That the Tolls arising at the several Toll gates or Bars hereunder mentioned erected upon and across the Turnpike Road leading from GLOSSOP to MARPLE BRIDGE with its branches will be put up to be let by auction to the best bidder for the Term of one Year commencing on the 15th day of June now next at the house of Mr John Wagstaffe in Glossop aforesaid on Thursday the 17th of May now next at the hour of Two in the afternoon at which time and place will also be held the next meeting of the Trustees of the same Road.

    The said tolls were let the last year for the several undermentioned sums and will be put up at these or such other sums respectively as shall be declared immediately preceding the putting up and whoever happens to be the best bidder must at the same time be prepared to give security with sufficient sureties to the satisfaction of the Trustees then present for the due payment of the sum agreed for at such times and in such proportions as they shall direct and no person's bidding will be accepted, whose sureties are not present at the meeting.

Rose Brow Bar	£165	Holehouse Bar	£260
Dinting Bar	£167	Woolley Bridge Bar	£122
Glossop Mill Bar	£100	Glossop Bar	£90

Matthew Ellison Clerk to the said Trustees, Glossop Hall, April 16th 1821.

The Woodseats Lane toll bar must have been erected at a later date to control the movement of coal from Woodseats Pit.

Before the road was turnpiked it would be a track used by packhorses; clothiers carried woollen and cotton goods in various states of manufacture between spinners and weavers and finished cloth to markets in Manchester and Stockport; drovers moved cows, sheep and geese; farmers carried goods to market; coal was carried for use in the textile mills which were springing up.

The completed turnpike was $12\frac{1}{4}$ miles long, all in the Parish of Glossop. In 1840, the interest paid to bondholders was £514 15s. at the rate of 5%.

The Glossop Road was the scene of a feat of athleticism in the early years of the 20th century when Harvey Oldfield, a Whitfield butcher, won a wager by covering the distance between the Norfolk Arms in Marple Bridge and its namesake in Glossop in under an hour pushing a wheelbarrow.

We have a reminder of the Turnpike era in the delightfully named Mouse Mill Cottage at Holehouse. This building is of interest; although it is now used as a private dwelling it has been a small textile mill and an inn in its long existence. In 1811 it belonged to John Booth, cotton manufacturer; in 1812 to Robert Booth; in 1837 to John and George Booth. On the 17th of February, 1841 George Booth aged 31 accidentally shot himself dead with a pistol while cleaning it. By 1866 it was in the possession of Ralph Booth. George Booth kept a diary in a school exercise book. Here are a couple of extracts:

Oct. 24th 1833; Thomas Burdekin and two others sent to Derby Tread Mill for being catched poaching in Chew Wood. The gang consisted of six or seven but the others are not took yet.

Feb. 18th 1833; My father agreed with Luke Wilson last week to make a new water wheel and to alter the gearing and to put it in a proper condition to work for £45 taking the old wheel in at the bargain, but Luke refused that bargain and today my father agreed to give him £54 without the old wheel.

He also noted the murders at Bill's o'Jack's near Saddleworth in April

1832, which shows of how quickly news spread by word of mouth when newspapers were read only by a minority and only published weekly.

Also recorded were details of charges for goods moved by horse and cart and instances of families 'flitting'. When working folks got into financial difficulties and fell behind with the rent they could load their few sticks of furniture onto a cart and do a "moonlight flit".

At first glance Mouse Mill Cottage appears to be a two storey building but a closer examination reveals a cellar which has been formed due to road "improvements" which have raised the road level. In this cellar was the bar in the days when the cottage was an inn and it has features which give an insight into the sort of tough customers who must have frequented the place. Instead of the ornate bars of the modern public house, the Mouse Mill had a slot in the wall just large enough for a glass of ale to be passed through after the customer had handed over his money. There was no chance of anyone putting their hand into the till or getting a drink without paying. Another interesting feature in the cellar is the manner in which the lead water pipes have been joined. The joints are spherical in shape, what were known as onion joints. These were made by pouring molten solder from a ladle over the pipes and wiping then with a moleskin cloth. This was the method employed before the invention of the paraffin blowlamp and the more familiar long wiped joint, which gives some indication of how long ago the joints were made. Nowadays you would be hard put to find a plumber prepared to tackle a wiped joint in a lead pipe!

The little stream that runs by Mouse Mill Cottage forms the boundary between Charlesworth and Chisworth Townships. A closer inspection of this stream above Mouse Mill Cottage will reveal a small weir and the leat which once led water to the water wheel. Many years ago when repairs were being carried out, the oak paddles of the water wheel were discovered under the cottage floor. So much history in one house, one can only wonder how much has been lost elsewhere.

Before leaving the Holehouse area I must tell a story told by a local resident of how the place got its name. "There used to be a very old house on the other side of the brook in that hollow and years ago it was pulled down and the stone carted off to build a wall. It was known as the "house in the hole" because of where it was built and hence we got the name Holehouse." A delightful story, but Thomas Bouth of Hollhouse left a will in May 1588 which suggests that the name is rather older. That is not to say that my informant was wrong; just that the event may have occurred even earlier than he imagined.

Charlesworth, Holehouse and Fattinghey are almost within a stone's throw of one another and yet locals claim that at one time it was a simple matter to differentiate between the inhabitants of each by their different dialects.

At the top of the hill from Chisworth to Charlesworth stands a large house, once a public house called the Wagon and Horses of which the landlady was a certain Nan Garlick. Nan certainly had an eye to business because she had a large water trough installed outside so the horses could stop for a drink; hopefully the carters would come inside for a drop of something stronger. The overflow from the trough was used to flush the toilets. The trough still stands there, cracked in places but making a fine flower bed.

A former corn mill in Ludworth has been mentioned in various histories, the assumption being that it was located on the River Etherow and statements made to the effect that no trace of the site remains. However, Burdett's map of 1763-7 shows a water powered mill at Ludworth situated on the stream which flows down from Mill Brow to Marple Bridge. There would hardly be two corn mills in such a spot as Ludworth. By comparing Burdett's map with more recent maps it would appear to have been approximately in the same position as, or slightly upstream of Clough Mill. Considering how many small mills and mill ponds have been built along this stream since Burdett's day it is hardly surprising that no one has stumbled on any traces of an old corn mill.

Charlesworth, Chisworth and Ludworth had their share of cotton mills along the streams feeding the Etherow, but none of these tributaries were capable of driving a large water wheel like the one at Broad Mills. These mills were ruined by the Cotton Famine. By this time the steam engine had replaced water power anyway but the railway was not conveniently located for the transport of cheap coal to Charlesworth and Chisworth. That is not to say that the district did not play an important part in the local economy. After the Lee Valley Mill was washed away when the dam burst in October 1831, it was rebuilt by Mr John Harrison and during the First World War it was used for making gun cotton until it was destroyed by fire. Not far away, Chew Mill was a dyeworks making khaki cloth for the troops.

The surname Booth is very common in the area, so common that it is difficult to separate the various branches of the family. One Booth family were involved in the cotton business but without striking success. Another branch became involved in engineering. James Booth who died on the 14th February 1843 at the age of 67 was a clever mechanic. On the 1st of December, 1819 he obtained a lease of 1,638 square yards of land in the "Tom Riding" and "Little

Field", and on it he built a machine shop. In 1802 he married Martha Hall and they had five sons; James, John, George, Joseph, and Robert, who all assisted him in his business. James' stated occupation was that of "Loom Manufacturer". The company made loom parts to the specification of John Wood at Howardtown Mills and other cotton masters. In 1838 Mr Booth took a further 1,037 square yards of land and erected a foundry.

Coal Mining

You could walk through the district today totally unaware that the ground under your feet is honeycombed with old mine workings, yet a hundred and fifty years ago there were small collieries throughout the locality. In his book *Stone upon Stone,* Rev Purcell, Vicar at Saint John's, mentions the sight of the many coal pits on the skyline when he arrived in 1845. At the beginning of the 19th century, coal mining must have been a thriving business because the mines paid more in rates than all the cotton mills put together. A further indication can be gained by examining the 1851 census and the registers of the Non-Conformist Chapels and Glossop Parish Church to discover the number of men who described themselves as colliers. In 1851, approximately 160 men were employed in mining, around 3% of the male workforce.

When coal mining started in the area is unknown, but farmers who had an outcrop on their land must surely have put it to good use. The first recorded mining on the site of Ludworth Moor Colliery took place in the 1920's when a local farmer, Eric Humphreys, worked an outcrop "bell pit" with the help of his wife and father, using a motor cycle engine to pump out the water and milk churns to move the coal to their farm.

Roderick Thackray in "Ludworth Moor Colliery, the Mine and the Men," tells how he found coal sledges dated to the 17th century below Compstall Bridge where outcrops of the White Ash Seam had been worked. He also noted that the workings of 300 years earlier looked identical to those at Ludworth.

A walk down the little valley by Lee Valley Mill gives a peep into the past. The size of the derelict mill gives a good impression of the number of folks who worked here and of the capital that was invested in building and equipping it. At one time the little valley must have been a hive of industry; mill lodges still remain and here and there the vestiges of walls, culverts and drains.

Several of the collieries were on the boundary between Chisworth and Charlesworth around Holehouse. Rose Grove, Woodseats New Pit, Holehouse Engine Pit, Bot Wood Tunnel Pit and the oddly named Owd Nick's Pit. This last was worked by a collier who got such a quantity of coal that it was said he had sold his soul to the Devil, and was situated between Holehouse Mill and Lee Valley Mill. None of these small pits had a steam engine; the Engine Pit got its name because it was close to Holehouse Mill and the vibrations of the mill engine could be felt in the pit.

Other pits in Chisworth and Ludworth were known as Sandy Lane Pit, Alma Pit, Tunnel Pit, Stirrup Benches Pit, Inkerman Shaft, Hollyhead, Dog Clough and Peep o'Day Pit. This is by no means an exhaustive list; locating and naming the old pits is a confusing business because as the tunnels extended so far that it became too laborious to move the coal, new entrances would be excavated to give easier access, each with a fresh name, even though they were working the original seam.

The local pits were an extension of the Lancashire coalfield, being the last seams to be exposed before the Derbyshire Dome. The coal seams are duplicated on either side of the Pennines, but those on the eastern side are generally thicker and easier to work. These coal seams occur in a series of rocks known as the Lower Coal Measures. The coal measures consist of layers of sandstone and shales with intermittent seams of coal which are arranged in a particular order but which vary in thickness and in places are missing or too thin to be viable. Usually bluish-grey shales known as mudstone overlie the coal seams and this is the rock we see in spoil heaps.

The coal seams worked in the district in descending order were; Big Smut; Red Ash; White Ash; Ganister Coal; Yard Coal (used as coking coal); 6 inch Mine; and Simmondley Coal. These seams were sometimes known locally by other names such as Big Mine or Little Mine. The names are derived from the burning characteristics of the different seams, the thickness, and in the case of Ganister coal because it was found next to a useful bed of ganister. The Simmondley seam got its name because it was the lowest and thus the last to come to the surface on the eastern edge of the coalfield around Simmondley.

The miners could tell which seam they were working by the texture and appearance of the coal. Mr Alfred Gee who worked the last drift mine in the area on Ludworth Moor, when asked about the Simmondley Seam, said, "Oh yes, it was about so thick with a band of muck running through it," at the same time indicating with his hands that it was about 15 inches deep.

The Ludworth Moor Colliery, which closed as recently as 1980, worked the Big Smut, also known as the Compstall Two Feet Seam but beneath lay the old workings of the Alma Pit which mined the Yard seam. The Big Smut is a type of coal once known as cannel because it burns like a candle. On Ludworth Moor the full thickness of the coal was two feet six inches which included a dirt band near the base of the coal. Ludworth Moor Colliery was a mine in which naked lights could be used and smoking allowed as no methane was ever discovered in it.

The local coal was very sulphurous and noted chiefly for the difficulty in lighting it. There is a story of a young married couple purchasing some of this coal just before they were going away for a week's visit. The husband laid the fire, put the kettle on, struck a match, applied it to the paper and sticks, and then began to get himself ready, expecting the fire would be lit and the kettle boiling by the time he was ready. But it was not the case, and the couple went off on their visit without a cup of tea. When they returned, they were astonished to find during their absence the fire had lit up, and the kettle was just beginning to boil - or so the tale goes. An exaggeration no doubt, but it was a common saying that the coal "took a week to light and a fortnight to go out."

The methods of working over the years have varied with the position and thickness of the seams and with the technology available. Where the coal outcropped, a sloping tunnel could be dug into the hillside and the coal dragged out in baskets. This method is known as drift mining. As the tunnel extended deeper into the ground problems arose with ventilation and the distance the coal had to be transported. To create a flow of air and thus prevent the accumulation of black damp air shafts had to be provided at intervals. These airshafts were sunk from the surface and accurately sited so as to meet the tunnel below by means of a magnetic compass. Drift mines were also known as adit or day-eye. The name day-eye comes from the appearance of the tunnel mouth where daylight was visible as an eye of light.

As steel rails became available a track could be laid along the main tunnel and the coal pushed out in tubs by men or drawn out by pit ponies or by a winch at the pit entrance. The men who owned these small mines had no great amounts of capital and they used anything that came to hand to get the coal. Tubs were purchased from mines which had gone out of business and bed frames pressed into service to make a track for the tubs.

Mr Douglas Brereton of Holehouse gave me a clear description of the way a drift mine was worked. A tunnel would be driven into the hillside, often from a point lower down than the seam so that the water could drain away, and then the coal on the higher side of the tunnel extracted. All the coal could not be removed since some had to be left in situ to support the earth above. The main tunnel would be driven through the coal and then other tunnels at right angles to it on the side where the seam sloped upwards. When these side tunnels had been driven as far was economic or possible from the main roadway, blocks of coal were removed from the solid remaining between these side tunnels leaving rectangular pillars of coal to support the roof. The colliers would have to work on their sides and throw back the coal towards the main tunnels. This method was known as the pillar and stall system.

When this part of the seam had been worked out there could be as much coal remaining on the lower side of the main tunnel. Water was the chief problem so a drain would be made lower down the hill to let the water escape and then the coal extracted. Once completed the drain exit would be partially blocked with a stone arch and a pipe built in, sufficient to let the water out but prevent children getting in. These outlets can be found throughout the area but over the years they have been hidden by foliage and earth. If the sources of small streams are traced many will be found to come from these drains.

Sir Humphrey Davy did not invent his safety lamp until 1815 and it would take some time for this life saving device to find its way into every pit. Before that time the danger of sufficient gas collecting to cause an explosion was detected by the change in colour of the tallow or mutton fat candle flames used for lighting. When this occurred, the men would try to get the air moving by 'batting' it with their shirts.

All the coal would be cut by hand with pick, shovel and crowbar, and gunpowder used to blast through solid rock to reach a seam. Any extra shale, rock or clay removed to make access easier had to be moved physically out of the mine, and so the roadways along which the coal was moved would be no higher than was absolutely necessary, often little over three feet in height.

An example of the primitive equipment used to relatively recent times was revealed by the tragedy at the Ludworth Moor Mine when Eric Mullineux of Chisworth lost his life, and his father, Ebor was injured. The Mullineux family commenced working the the Ludworth outcrop coal a few years before the War. They supplied coal to local factories and when Marple Gasworks was short during the War they supplied 20 tons of coal weekly. Early in 1946 when the coal petered out and water became a problem they decided to sink a shaft that would tap the seam at a more profitable point when disaster struck.

Water was pumped from the pit shaft with the aid of a pump driven by an old car engine. The tragedy was discovered by another son, Joseph when he went to the mine with a can of petrol for the pump. He found his father unconscious on a ledge down the shaft where the water pump was mounted but could see no sign of his brother Eric. With assistance from a nearby farm his father was hauled to the surface and taken to Stockport Infirmary, where he remained unconscious until night time. Eric's body was found when the police used grappling irons in the sump at the bottom of the shaft.

The existence of old pit shafts can be discovered in unexpected ways. These pits were dug long before the National Coal Board was dreamed of and consequently there are no plans or other records for later users of the land. When the old shafts were worked out, they might be filled with material removed from a new shaft, but often the entrance would be blocked off with oak branches and rocks and then covered with earth. This might last for years, but not for ever. One farmer bringing in a load of hay in Ludworth, got a surprise when his cart suddenly lurched as the ground gave way; fortunately the cart did not fall into the reopened shaft. During the summer of 1996 a cow stumbled into a disused mine on Ludworth Moor. The farmer was unable to rescue the beast and eventually the Marple Fire Brigade was called out. They successfully raised the animal with the aid of slings.

In the days when sons followed fathers the knowledge of the sites of worked out pits would be passed on but this will soon be gone forever. In one case, an old woman from a mining family warned her relatives not to have anything to do with a new property because there had once been a pit in the field. A few years after the house had been completed, the occupants received a shock one morning when they awoke to find a chasm in the front lawn.

When water wheels were replaced by steam engines, the local pits were adequate to supply the needs of the small mills but could hardly cope with the requirements of establishments like Waterside or Broadbottom Mills. The local industry had problems from its earliest days. With no roads the coal could only be transported by packhorse. Later the turnpikes would help, coinciding as they did with the growth of the cotton industry, but the thin seams and poor quality of much of the coal were other factors and as the best coal was removed and the pits worked out, it became less economic and the pits slowly closed. The building of the railways spelt the end for pits which could not compete in price or quality with coal by the train load from Lancashire and Yorkshire.

Coal mining at Ludworth came to an end in 1980 when Derbyshire County Council granted planning permission for the area to be mined by the open cast method. Strip mining was employed which allowed the restoration of the site and today sheep graze where once men toiled below the earth. Open cast mining could not have been employed earlier because neither the capital nor the equipment was available.

When these small local pits closed, we lost an industry, and the men who knew how to work the local seams, but we also said goodbye to a lot of hard, dirty and dangerous work. Imagine lying on your side in water working a narrow seam or pushing a loaded tub with 4 cwt of coal along a crude railway track whilst bent double because of the low roof. It seems that for all the hard work put into extracting coal in the area, none of the colliers or farmers made their fortunes. Lord Howard, on the other hand, who owned the mineral rights until Nationalisation in 1948 received a useful income during the life of the pits.

Firebricks

The Ganister coal seam in places was very thin but the ganister or fireclay was extracted and made into refractories and the like. Not all the old adits which are to be found around Chisworth and Ludworth are those of coal mines; some on the Chisworth-Charlesworth boundary near Rose Grove Cottage below Lee Valley Mill were to extract ganister. There was once a beerhouse at Fattinghey called the Ganister Arms. In 1877, the North Derbyshire Fire Brick and Tile Company found coal and fireclay at Mill Clough, near Mill Brow and commenced the manufacture of sanitary pipes, ridge tiles, fire-backs, chimney pots, and roof tiles. The fire brick works at Furness Vale was in production until much more recently and I am indebted to a gentleman who worked there both before and after WW II for a description of the work involved.

"We would set off from New Mills at half past five in the morning and walk along by the Goyt until we reached the Peak Forest Canal which we followed to Furness Vale. Close by was the mine where there were good seams of coal and ganister so that there was ample coal to fire the bricks. The mine was a drift mine and the coal of good quality; it only closed because the drift eventually reached a point under thick woodland where an air shaft could not be sunk to ventilate the mine. Besides being used for making firebricks, the ganister was supplied to a Sheffield steelworks.

After the ganister had been extracted it was left to settle and then put into a mill fitted with gratings and ground to dust. We had to keep a sharp lookout for nodules which could easily jam in the gratings and stop the steam engine. The steam engine naturally was run on coal from the mine. Measured quantities of ganister dust and water were then thoroughly mixed in a mortar mill until of the right consistency when the mix was hand moulded into bricks which were left to dry on a steam heated floor until they turned white and were strong enough to be handled. Then they were stacked in the kiln taking care not to damage the edges and fired. Each day 4,500 bricks were made in this way."

Other Industries

Stone to build the mills had to be quarried locally to keep down the transport costs especially before the railways were built. As a result there were many small quarries dotted about the Longdendale valley with perhaps a couple of men working in them cutting stone to order. It is no coincidence that many of these quarries are beside the old turnpike roads.

Today quarrying is highly mechanised with pneumatic tools and great earth moving machines. In the 19th century it was virtually all heavy hand work with hammers, punches, and crowbars, which no doubt is why the workmen in old photographs look so worn. Many of the old skills are lost to us but recently a farmer got a surprise when he wanted a drystone retaining wall on his land. After a search he found an old quarryman who was prepared to do the job and at the appointed time the quarryman duly turned up complete with wheelbarrow, crowbar and a selection of chisels, hammers and punches. The farmer was puzzled that the quarryman was prepared to build a wall without any stone. but this minor problem was solved when the quarryman took a good look round the field and after picking a suitable spot started to dig. The farmer left him to it and when he returned found that he was now the owner of a small quarry from which the quarryman was removing stone with apparent ease with the aid of his simple hand tools. This sort of scene must have once been commonplace when the drystone walls were being built to enclose common land.

The Top Chapel

There is a legend relating to Charlesworth Chapel that a Catholic priest on his way from Manchester to London, in crossing this part of the Peak was overtaken by one of those storms that sweep down with great suddenness, wrapping the hills in a dense and almost impenetrable mist. A comparative stranger to the neighbourhood, yet conscious of the wild and dangerous character of the district through which he was travelling, he feared to proceed lest the next step should launch him over some precipice. or entangle him in some equally dreaded bog. He could therefore do nothing but pray for guidance and wait for the storm to pass. Kneeling on the spot where he stood, he besought the help of heaven, and vowed a solemn vow that if preserved and taken to the end of his journey in safety, on that spot he would build a house of prayer and dedicate it to his patron saint. In a short time the storm ceased, the sky began to clear, the mist rolled away from the hills, and to his great joy he found himself on the hillside overlooking the place where Charlesworth now stands. Marking the spot where deliverance had been so wonderfully, and he believed miraculously, vouchsafed to him, he continued his journey, but did not forget his vow, and returned soon after to fulfil it. He built a small chapel or oratory near the spot where the Charlesworth Chapel now stands.

This story may be a flight of fancy, and the chapel was probably erected by one of the Abbots prior to 1291. At the dissolution of the monasteries by Henry VIII in 1536-39, the chapel escaped being seized, but Queen Elizabeth became possessed of it in 1559, and the lands belonging to it, but neglected the chapel, which then came into the hands of the Independents.

John Ward, F.S.A. writes relating to the chapel "In the early part of Henry VIII (from 1509) a chantry was founded in the chapel of Charlesworth by William Woodley, of Riber, in the Parish of Matlock, who left certain lands in Chesterfield, Newbould, Tapton, and Dronfield, which lands had been given to him by Ralph Heathcote, bell-founder of Chesterfield, to provide a priest to say Mass for his soul." This endowment escaped the attentions of the Commissioners, who drew up the Chantry Roll, but shortly afterwards, in the second year of Queen Elizabeth, the land was taken from the chapel and conferred on Sir George Howard.

The chapel also appears to have been transferred with the land to the Howards, and as they remained firm in their attachment to Roman Catholicism, it is probable that no effort was made either to preserve the fabric or to provide for the performance of the reformed service. The Parliamentary Commissioners of 1650 report of Charlesworth Chapel "that it is fit to be disused, and the place united to Glossop," from which it would seem that it was then occasionally used for service, which at that time was Presbyterian. After the Restoration of the Monarchy, the chapel was allowed to remain in the hands of the Presbyterians by the Howards. In 1797 the chapel was entirely rebuilt, and not a trace of the original edifice remains.

Being a stronghold of the Independents and situated at a distance from the parish church at what is now Old Glossop, the Charlesworth Top Chapel was held in high regard by those closer at hand. Few bothered to travel to the parish church except when forced to do so.

Sir Robert Peel's Act in 1844 created Charlesworth, Chisworth and Simmondley into the Ecclesiastical Parish of Charlesworth. There was no Established Church before that date in Charlesworth. As a result of this Act, the Rev Goodwin Purcell was instituted to the living at Charlesworth. *"The Bishop of Lichfield appointed me to labour in this new parish,"* was how he expressed it. The Rev Purcell immediately set about collecting a congregation and raising the money to build a church. He set out the story of his struggles in a book entitled *Stone upon Stone* and the following is one of many amusing extracts:

"I next took a journey to London, but I had little success in that field.... On one occasion, when urging the claims of Charlesworth, a Bishop, with whom I was acquainted in early life, greeted me warmly on entering the room. This succeeded me in procuring a subscription. I called upon a member of Parliament for a county in which I had a small freehold, and after laying my case before him, he laid a sovereign on the table. This I did not appear to notice, and spoke of an anticipated election, and mentioned casually that I had a vote and some interest there. He added four sovereigns to the one on the table, which I gladly received."

The Rev Purcell was not welcomed by Chapel people some of whom were so bitter as to spit at the new church when it was built in 1848. The stories of antagonism between Church and Chapel at Charlesworth would fill a volume. Anyone interested in learning more should read the Rev Purcell's book and another called *Memorials of Charlesworth* written by the Rev T J Hosken who was the minister at the top Chapel from 1884 to 1888. Ill feeling between Church and Chapel continued well into the 20th century. There was one Vicar whose conduct left something to be desired, but his congregation did their best to cover his tracks. Years after he had left, one villager said to me. "When the new Vicar came, two lorry loads of whisky bottles were carried away from a shed at the back of the vicarage." Naturally my informant was a Chapel man.

Some confusion exists concerning the relative sizes of Glossop and Charlesworth. Before Glossop gained its charter in 1866 all the townships on the Derbyshire side of the Etherow were part of Glossop-dale but thereafter Glossop was the area set out in the charter. In 1894 the Parish Council Act was passed and those portions of the Hamlets of Simmondley, Chunal, Whitfield, Glossop, Hadfield and Padfield that were outside the Glossop Borough area were formed into No 2 Ward of the Parish of Charlesworth. As a result Charlesworth Parish Council were responsible for a far larger area than Glossop and it meant that places like Moorfield Mansion, Hurst Reservoir, Swineshaw Reservoir, parts of Woodhead Reservoirs and the Great Central Railway, came within its jurisdiction and paid them rates. This was most important for the Charlesworth Parish Council by reason of the large assessments. An interesting situation arose where some of the houses immediately above the Royal Oak were in Glossop and those higher up were in Charlesworth. necessitating a long trip for the Charlesworth refuse cart. These divisions were of interest to children living on the boundaries of Glossop because they were able to see the Charlesworth Police approaching from a considerable distance. For example to get to the bottom of the Snake Road, a Charlesworth policeman had to cycle along Derbyshire Level where he was in full view from Sheffield Road.

Robin Hoods Picking Rods

One medieval relic in the district is the so called Robin Hood's picking Rods situated at the junction of the Township boundaries of Mellor, Chisworth, Ludworth, and Thornsett. The very idea of Robin Hood or anyone else for that matter using the upright stones to string his bow and then shooting an arrow from that point using the Mare's Back about a mile away is of course pure fantasy. Goodness knows who thought up the name, but then we have plenty of other places with Robin's name attached, such as Robin Hood's stride. Another suggestion is that it is

Robin Hood's Picking Rods.

linked with ancient druids, but this can be dismissed as well as a product of a time when anything which could not be explained was put down to the druids.

On a map of 1640 it is marked as the Maiden Stones which tells us no more about its purpose. While there is no doubt as to its position as a boundary marker we can only guess as to whether it was placed there for that purpose or whether it was there long before the Township boundaries were fixed and used as a convenient point for that purpose. The most likely explanation is that the Picking Rods are the rounded shafts of Mercian crosses similar to the Bow stones near Disley. The Bow Stones and the shaft of Whitfield Cross are also cylindrical and closely resemble each other. It could well be in the case of all these that the tops of the cross have been deliberately broken off.

The Picking Rods stand on the route of an old track leading from Plainsteads Farm on Monks road and heading towards Marple Bridge. The suggestion that it is in too swampy a spot for a preaching cross might carry some weight but there are wayside crosses beside far worse tracks; the Lady Cross for example. The Picking Rods have been vandalised and overthrown on more than one occasion. In 1900 twelve men of the Hayfield Antiquarian Society set it up once more.

Crosses were put up for various reasons including to mark the boundaries of monastic lands and as a preaching centre where folks could gather to hear some itinerant preacher in the days before a church could be built for example. When placed by by roadsides and on hill tops they were intended to call the thoughts of the passer by to a sense of religion, doing duty as boundary markers, or guide posts at the same time. Where the township boundaries make a sudden change of direction the point of deviation is often marked with a cross.

Stockport Chronicle 5.9.1840: Serious Affray with Poachers: On the night of Monday week, a most serious engagement took place between the watchers employed by the Duke of Norfolk and a gang of poachers. It appears that six of the tenters went out to watch a preserve called Ernocroft Wood, and about half past eleven, a gang of seven or eight poachers came into the field where they had lain down in a hollow place under a hedge. One of the poachers advanced to within two or three yards of them when they jumped up with the intention of seizing them and immediately the whole gang attacked the tenters with bludgeons and stones and a general fight ensued which lasted about twenty minutes and ended in the tenters capturing two of the poachers and taking two bags of nets, two bundles of pegs for setting them, a hat, a rabbit, and three bludgeons. The poachers were armed with bludgeons and the tenters are all more or less hurt, some of them very severely. Thomas Stansfield received a blow from one of the poachers when struck upon the breast with a large stone, it ruptured a blood vessel internally, and caused him to vomit a great quantity of blood, and his companions thought he would have died upon the field. A surgeon having been sent for, he was bled and put to bed; he is now going on pretty well and it is hoped that that with care and attention he will recover. James Wood is kicked and bruised all over from head to foot; and it is a mercy he was not killed on the spot, as he was attacked by three of the poachers, two of them holding him down, kicking him and striking him with their fists, while a third was was beating him about the head with a large bludgeon for upwards of five minutes, until one of his companions, seeing the situation he was in flew to his rescue and succeeded in beating off his assailants. His wounds are all external and it is hoped that in the course of a few weeks he will be not be much worse for them. The poachers had a large dog with them which at the onset flew at one of the tenters seized him by the breast and tore his waistcoat but did not injure him. One of the tenters shot the dog, and thought he had killed it but it could not be found next morning. The men who are taken are William Rowland, of Hyde, hatter; and Thomas Woods, of Haughton Green, collier, and they have been committed to take their trial at the next quarter sessions at Derby. The whole gang are supposed to come from Hyde; and it is hoped that a clue will be obtained by which the remainder of the gang will be apprehended and brought to justice.

Compstall Print Works.

The Athenaeum, Compstall.

CHAPTER FIFTEEN
COMPSTALL

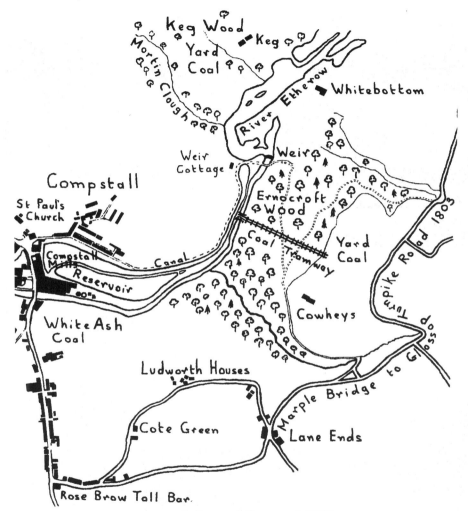

Map 10. Compstall around 1895.

The present village of Compstall was once part of the ancient township and Manor of Werneth, recorded in the Domesday Survey as being a manor held by Hugh Lupus, Earl of Chester. Werneth is next mentioned in an inquisition after the death of Hugh de Davenport in 1370. This family held Werneth for generations until the last male heir, William Davenport died in 1640. His only daughter, Isabel married Sir Fulke Lucy in 1664 and in 1678 Lucy sold part of Werneth to Reginald Bretland of Mottram. When Tobias Bretland died in 1710 the Werneth land was bought by William Egerton of Tatton one of whose descendants sold a piece of 600 acres to George Andrew of Compstall in 1817.

Just where is Compstall? Is it between the Windsor Castle Hotel and the bridge over the Etherow, or is it the village on the north side of the river? The answer depends on whom you ask and when. According to Bulmer's Derbyshire in 1895 Compstall Road was a considerable village on the Derbyshire side of the River Etherow, which was here crossed by a bridge, on the other side of which was Compstall in Cheshire. The Compstall Road area was formerly part of the Township of Ludworth which was in Derbyshire before the alteration to the county boundaries in 1936. Indeed Ludworth was once one of the outer Townships of Glossop, which seems somewhat distant from Compstall. The village on the north side was formerly known as Becum after a property now demolished called Beacom Fold beside the road up to Mortinfold, and we still have Beacom Houses on the side of Werneth Low. I say we still have, but I note that the someone involved in preparing the latest Ordnance Survey map has decided that the correct spelling is Beacon. Here we have a fine example of the danger of education. His job is to faithfully record matters to the best of his ability. But no, he spots the spelling Beacom and assumes that local folks know no better and promptly alters it to beacon. Why was it called Beacom? I do not know, perhaps a family of that name lived there years ago. Certainly we have places called after the former inhabitants in the locality, Warhurst Fold and Rhodes Fold spring immediately to mind.

The name Compstall Bridge is of some antiquity. On the 6th of December, 1639, the death of Margaret, wife of William Tomlinson was entered in the records of Mellor church. Her address is given as Comsty Bridge. A few years later, on the 13th of August 1666, a second Margaret Tomlinson de Comstybridge died; her will however states that she lived in Ludworth. At this date the bridge might well have been built from timber, or at best a simple packhorse bridge.

The present bridge was erected in 1819 and evidence of the causeway of a ford was discovered during sewering work in 1961. There were certainly bridges at an earlier date; Burdett's map showing a bridge circa 1760. Both Burdett's and Aikin's Maps show Compstall Bridge but the later map gives no indication of any houses which suggests that no factory existed at that time.

Before the Industrial Revolution, Compstall existed only as tiny hamlet; suddenly coming into prominence due to the efforts of the Andrew family, who in the early nineteenth century transformed it into an industrial village. Most of what is known about the Andrew family and the development of Compstall can be learned from a book written by R. E Thelwall entitled *The Andrews and Compstall Their Village.*

The Andrews family seem to have come from a different social and financial background to the cotton masters we met higher up the valley. They came originally from the Rochdale area but at the time they purchased land at Compstall they were living in Harpurhey which was still a country village. Thomas Andrew lived at Harpurhey Cottage and had two sons, Thomas born in 1778 and George in 1779. The older Thomas owned land in Blackley and Crumpsall and in 1788 had a printing and dyeworks containing four block printing tables besides the nearby river Irk. So the Andrews knew something of the textile trade before moving to Compstall. Blackley, Crumpsall and Harpurhey are all districts with the Irk flowing through them which have been swallowed up to form part of North Manchester

Manchester Mercury 7.1.1794.

COMPSTALL FOR SALE. "An estate called Compstall upon a good road about 4 miles from Stockport, upwards of 70 acres of land, the River Mersey extends about a mile through it which commands a great fall and is never in any respect injurious in the greatest flooding. There are several good springs which may be conveyed to any part of the land, all of which is dry soil and lies in a full south aspect. There is good marl in some of the higher land to the river banks, and in all of the low ground is plenty of rock stone.

There are collieries now working at a distance of half a mile, and the line of the intended canal from Derbyshire to Manchester is near the end of the estate. The neighbourhood is populous; adjacent are several established concerns, among others beyond are the very extensive works of Mr Samuel Oldknow, and a little below are the print grounds of Messrs Rose and Kershaw at Chadkirk.

The estate possesses every advantage desirable to a printer or bleacher, and for any extent of business that requires great power of water and number of hands. It will be let together or separately for any term that may be agreed of years or perpetual chief rent, and may be entered upon at pleasure or the expiration of a year from May next.

Apply Robert Grimshaw at Gorton House, Manchester."

In the same paper on 12.11.1805.

PEAK FOREST CANAL. "The public are hereby informed that the locks uniting the upper and lower levels of this canal being now completed for navigation, the canal is open for Through-Fare Trade which holds out a very advantageous prospect to persons desirous of establishing connections for the conveyance of goods and merchandise upon the canal, and enables the proprietors to offer the following reduced prices, viz: Limestone scrap to be delivered at Bugsworth. 2s 2d Limestone scrap to be delivered at Manchester. 6s 0d. And at intermediate places in like proportions. Apply to Mr William Wright at Marple."

The Manchester Mercury was forced into bankruptcy in 1822 by the Tory government of the day, because of its support for the Radical movement before and after the Peterloo Massacre, and for its of exposure of widespread government corruption. In its last edition it urged its readers to support the Manchester Guardian which started publication in the same year.

This advertisement certainly refers to some of the land which the Andrews later used for their factories, but as it coincides with the period of the Napoleonic Wars the actual sale of the land for commercial purposes could have been delayed for some time.

George Andrew came to Compstall in 1815 which, if the experience of others is any guide, appears to have been a good time to enter the textile industry. He lived for a time at Werneth Hall, high on Werneth Low, and it is possible that he started printing cloth on the site. The land on which the mill and village were built was purchased by a Thomas Andrew, but it is not certain whether this was George's father or brother.

The brothers George and Thomas Andrew together with two partners, set up business in Compstall at some date prior to 1820 and the first buildings for cloth printing were erected. They started by dying and printing cotton, but soon expanded their activities into spinning and weaving because George realised that if he wove his own cloth instead of buying and dying that of others the profits would be increased. By June 1824 the first cloth was being woven at the site probably on hand looms, but soon power looms were installed. Before the use of chemicals for bleaching it was the practice to bleach the cloth by spreading it on fields and over frames and reminders of this practice come down to us as place names including the word croft, such as tentercroft. Note that Ernocroft is just across the river, and could have been used as a bleaching field.

The Andrews also erected streets of cottages to accommodate the workers. The streets were given the names of members of the Andrews family. Later, more houses were built on the Ludworth side of the river on land leased from Lord Howard. In 1839 the building of St. Paul's Church was commenced, and it was completed in 1841. The cost was about £2,000 of which sum £1,500 was provided by George and Thomas Andrew. The remainder was made up of donations by village residents with probably some help from diocesan funds. The first school may also have been built by George Andrew. Clean water was important for dying and printing, and George Andrew diverted the small Gigg Stream which rises on Werneth Low through a tunnel under the road and stored the water in a new reservoir. Later this water was used to power a small turbine and the exhaust water used for washing the printed cloth.

Some textile employers made it their business to own farms so that food could be supplied to the workers who were working such long hours that they could no longer grow their own. Some took advantage of the fact that the workforce was often compelled to make their purchases from the company store and charged exorbitant prices. The position was made worse because wages were paid a fortnight in arrears so that the workers were usually, if not always in debt. Unlike other employers, George and Charles Andrew played a leading part in promoting and encouraging the Compstall Cooperative Society which was founded in 1851, with Charles as the first elected president. The first meeting was held in the mill office and capital was raised by members taking up £1 shares. This money was obtained by deductions from the wages of those members who worked at the mill or printworks and when the accumulated deductions reached £207, a manager was appointed. The society had a hard time to keep afloat during the cotton famine of the 1860's when the members could not afford to buy meat, and credit for this must be given to the ordinary villagers who showed that they had the ability and determination to keep the society going under such disadvantageous conditions. Short time working during the cotton famine lasted for almost four years.

The Andrew brothers had the foresight to see the potential of the site for industrial development. There were deposits of the White Ash and Yard coal seams close by, suitable stone for building and ample water power supplied by the river. The possibilities for extracting water power before the building of the Longdendale reservoirs were exceptional once substantial civil engineering work had been carried out. Before work started on the site there was already a waterfall flowing over a natural weir and the river below this point was fairly fast flowing in a narrow gorge. By building a weir using the local stone on top of the existing waterfall and diverting the water into an artificial canal it was possible to provide a far greater head of water for the two giant water wheels at the mill known as the North Wheel and the Lily Wheel respectively. This water source was further improved by building a reservoir alongside the lower part of the canal to provide a reliable source of power at times when rainfall was low. The canal and reservoir were at a higher level than the river and were supported by an embankment built once more from the local flag stone. The capacity for water storage was also increased by the weir itself which held back considerable quantities of water by flooding the fields upstream. On the embankment beside the weir stands a red brick building which houses the the gear for controlling the flow of water from the river above the weir into the canal.

The giant Lily wheel, built by Fairbairn and Lilley and erected in 1838-9, was reputed at the time to be the largest of its type in the country. It was seventeen feet wide and fifty feet in diameter and capable of producing eight hundred and fifty horse power. Presumably the manufacturers had their name cast into some prominent part which gave rise to the name Lily Wheel.

The Lily Wheel.

At one stage, the total water requirement for producing power at Compstall was forty million gallons for a ten hour working day. The impounding of water by Manchester Corporation led to a diminishing supply at Compstall and in 1881 two more efficient water turbines were installed to replace the Lily wheel which stood idle until it was demolished in 1906. Its site was filled by a new engine house with a steam engine capable of developing six hundred horse power. During 1915 the works were completely electrified.

These developments did not exhaust the possibilities of the

Gearing for a sluice on the canal.

natural advantages of the site. Coal extracted from mines in Ernocroft and Keg Woods was transported cheaply in quantity straight to the mill by loading into iron barges. The rusting remains of the last of these iron barges can still be seen in the pool at the weir end of the canal where it was widened to allow boats to manoeuvre. This relic is 22' long, 6'5" wide and 3' high and is constructed of cast iron plates joined with rivets. Fitted to its upper deck are towing rings and one of originally four rowlocks used for steering. When fully laden, this vessel held 8 tons of coal.

Fireclay also occurred under the coal seam and was used in the manufacture of bricks and tiles close to Weir Cottage. These finished goods were then transported by the canal for use at the mill, or for delivery elsewhere by the turnpike road. The new turnpike road conveniently passed through Compstall and gradually an extensive complex of mills and other buildings grew up on both sides of the road, until by 1840 George Andrew's property consisted of a printworks, cotton mills, a house built in 1824 known as Green Hill Hall, and later as Compstall Hall, and 200 mill workers houses.

The Andrews and their partners must have had considerable capital at their disposal to complete all the work involved in the mills and their power supply. The weir and canal had to be built to supply water with a suitable head and after the water had driven the wheel it had to be able to run back into the river lower down by means of tunnels. All this civil engineering work found employment for a small army of stonemasons, carpenters and millwrights and it also gives an indication of how advanced the technology of the men supervising the schemes had become.

Despite the advertisement in the Manchester Mercury extolling the advantages of the area, flooding could be a very real danger. To combat this, spillways were incorporated into the system so that water could be by-passed from the canal and the reservoir into the lower reaches of the river. Later, when Montagu Woodmass ran the works a direct telephone line was installed between the mill and a point several miles upstream so that advanced information could be obtained on flood conditions higher up the valley. A further telephone connection went to the weir cottage where the man who operated the main sluice gates between the pound and the canal lived. These precautions were necessary since it is quite possible for Compstall to be basking in sunlight at the same time as a cloudburst is occurring over Glossop or Woodhead.

The first George Andrew was the founder of the village and his second son, also named George carried on his father's work. This was a period of rapid expansion and technical development in the textile industry and the second George and his brother Charles were quick to recognise the possibilities of the new methods and machines. The works were progressively enlarged and small steam engines were used for the individual drives of the rotary printing machines. With the introduction of steam power more coal was required and this was obtained from local mines; the Rose Brow Pit, a drift mine in Ernocroft Wood and the Cowlishaw Pit. White's History and Gazeteer and Directory of Cheshire for 1860 states that the establishment of George Andrew at Compstall Bridge gave employment to upwards of 2,000 persons.

The railway reached Marple in 1865 and in the North Cheshire Herald of 24.2.1872 we read:

NEW GOODS STATION. "This building is now ready for goods traffic and is expected to be declared open for public use very shortly. It must certainly be a considerable convenience to the Mellor manufacturers who have hitherto had to cart their goods to the canal wharf at the top of Brabyns Brow, for they will thus be enabled partially to evade the heavy incline from Marple Bridge, as well as to dispatch and receive goods with greater promptitude. Other business people will doubtless soon discover the new goods shed an advantage."

The second George Andrew died in February 1873 and his funeral was attended by three thousand people as his loss was much mourned by the village.

From 1869 to 1873 Montagu Woodmass who was married to Edith Alice Andrew, the third daughter of George Andrew, held a half share in the Compstall business which he purchased from his wife's uncle Charles Andrew. The second George Andrew had no sons and because of his high opinion of Woodmass he left the remaining half of the manufacturing and printworks shares to him. Thus Woodmass became the sole owner with the exception of the village houses, coal mines and monies. During the period that the Woodmass family ran the factory, their behaviour was that of the squire and his lady rather than that of a cotton master. Montagu Woodmass was said to be happiest with his dog and gun rather than with a bobbin of weft. It was he who widened the river above the weir to form a fishpond. The technical control of the business was left in the hands of managers and foremen. Although he was not a descendent of Thomas Andrew of Harpurhey, there is something of the clogs to clogs tradition about this pattern of behaviour.

In 1887 a bay cob belonging to Mr Woodmass which had been stolen eighteen months earlier was found in Yorkshire. John Saul who prior to the horse being stolen had worked for Mr Woodmass for some time was charged with the theft but due to the long time since the theft the case was not proceeded with. Two years later the same John Saul was sentenced to nine months imprisonment for stealing a horse and trap.

Mr Woodmass liked to remind the villagers of their proper station in life. Girls had to curtsy and boys remove their hats when the carriage from the big house passed by. Failure to comply with this practice resulted in the parents being reprimanded in the mill office concerning their children's behaviour.

So many printing factories were built and machinery exported to competitors abroad that there was considerable over capacity in the industry. Various attempts were made to standardise practice within the British industry by the larger concerns and eventually in 1899 the Calico Printers Association was formed. George Andrew and Company joined the association when Montagu Woodmass sold both the business and the village to the C.P.A. Some of the problems were due to the older factories being more expensive to maintain, equipped with outdated machinery, and not being located in the best positions for transport of goods. The owners not being intimately involved in the day to day running was another factor. As we have seen, during the nineteenth century, the textile workers had been very militant but this could not be said of the twentieth and the blame for the decline of the textile industry cannot be laid on the unions. There is a lot of truth in the adage that the neck is at the top of the bottle. Straightaway the C.P.A. began to close uneconomic works and the printing section at George Andrew and Sons was closed by 1901.

The closure was a disaster for the people of Compstall and in 1926 worse followed with the closure of the spinning section. Many people were never employed in textiles again and had to take any work on offer.

The final break with the name Andrew was in 1936 when what remained of the business changed its name to Gartside and Company which was a branch of the C.P.A. During the Second World War the firm was occupied making shirtings for the forces and at a later stage of the conflict, parachute fabric. Like many other textile concerns the factory was kept busy for some years after the War and during this period the looms were converted to individual electric drive. The mill was closed in 1966. There was a tendency at this time for young people to avoid entering the textile industry and so the experienced workers were often in demand in other mills that were still busy. It was a common practice to provide buses to collect these workers from areas where mills had closed and take them to and from work each day.

Ernocroft Wood

Map 9 on page 194 shows many of the mine workings in the area. Some explanation of their names is necessary because this varied with the access to the seam. The Ludworth Colliery which was also known as Rose Brow Pit to differentiate from the Ludworth Moor Colliery had workings which extended from the Etherow above Compstall Bridge under what is now a new housing estate to the south and also under Brabyns Park. It was worked by the Jowetts but the Andrews also had an interest.

The manner of working at Ernocroft Pit shows how the site was used to the best advantage. The entrance to the drift mine was on the hillside above the river and from the entrance a tramway on an earth embankment led straight downhill to where a bridge spanned the river. The coal was carried by this tramway which had two lines of narrow gauge track. The system was self acting using the weight of a descending coal wagon to haul an empty one back up the track. The two wagons were connected by a chain which passed round a winding mechanism at the mine entrance. Once across the river the wagon could be unloaded on to waiting barges which were drawn by horses along the canal to the works at Compstall.

It is possible that coal was mined in Ernocroft Wood as early as the Middle Ages, when this land was held by the Abbots of Basingwerke Abbey, the records of such monasteries include many of the oldest references to coal. Documentary evidence from the North West indicates that mining grew in importance from the 16th century, coinciding with a decline in the availability of timber for fuel. Sledges discovered at the western end of Ernocroft Wood, near Compstall Bridge, provide evidence for the exploitation of the local coal measures in the 17th century. The fullest evidence dates from the 19th century. In 1811, in his Survey of Derbyshire, John Farey included "Ernocroft" in a list of collieries either then or previously in use.

In 1828 George Andrew leased the right to mine coal in Ernocroft Wood from the Duke of Norfolk, who owned the wood as part of the Manor of Glossop. This lease was for a period of 20 years and stipulated that Andrews was to pay the Duke an annual sum amounting to one eighth of the selling price of the coal he extracted or a minimum rent of £10, whichever was the greater. The accounts of the Duke's Glossop estate show that Andrew began mining in Ernocroft almost immediately and that between 1828 and 1838 he paid the Duke between £33 and £42 per annum. This is a relatively small amount compared with the rents for the other local mines recorded in the Norfolk accounts; in 1839 John Thornley paid over £2100 rent for Chisworth colliery. It is likely that most of the coal dug in Ernocroft Wood by George Andrew was for use in the Compstall works, although in both the mid 1820's and in the early 1830's Andrew also appears in trade directories as a coal merchant.

The lease for mining Ernocroft expired in 1848, and by the 1860's the Andrew family's mining activities shifted to the area known as 'The Keg,' further upstream above the weir.

In this century mining took place at Dog Clough in the north-eastern spur of Ernocroft Wood, during the miner's strike of the 1920's.

Today the main attraction for many people at Compstall is the Etherow Country Park which is well worth a visit as it has something of interest to offer for most tastes; the bird life on the reservoir and in the woodlands; the wide variety of the flora, and not least the industrial archaeology. The practice of feeding the ducks on the reservoir has led to an explosion in the numbers of water birds. Most of these are of common varieties but it is worth taking a closer look because rarer birds occasionally use the water as well but are not normally as tame. There is scope for the fisherman and the model boat enthusiast as well. There is ample car parking and at Compstall much of the industrial complex has survived and we can still gain some understanding of what the original must have been like in its heyday.

For anyone walking around Compstall, starting from the car park, there are several buildings worth noting - the gate house, boiler house, base of the turbine house, the steam engine house which is now used a an electricity sub-station, two extensive mills, and two former weaving sheds. To the rear of the car park is the remnant of what was known as North Mill which is now reduced to three storeys. In 1840, it had four floors; the top floor for carding, the two middle floors for spinning, and the ground floor for weaving so that the material flowed down through the mill as it passed through the various processes. The north section of this mill was demolished around 1970 and is now a car park. What remained of the North Wheel was taken away at the same time.

There is a substantial bridge over the Etherow built to carry the turnpike road in the early 1800's when the Andrew brothers were trustees. Like many bridges originally built to carry horse drawn traffic it has probably been rebuilt and strengthened since that date.

From the entrance to the former printworks, on the opposite side of the road the only remaining building of the printworks can be seen. This stone building with an arched entrance was known as the bleach croft. The building with stone exterior facing the road is a building erected in 1916 to house the warp sizing department on the site of the filled-in print works reservoir.

The public library is housed in a fine stone building called the Athenaeum, built by the second George Andrew in the mid-1860s for the recreation and education of adults; the building acted as a cultural centre for the community. From the 1870s until the 1960s it was used as the village school when it reverted to being a library.

Following the path from the car park between the river and the reservoir, on the right is a weaving shed just past the mill, at one time the site of the gasworks. The mills were lit by gas made by burning coal from 1834. Many of the larger mills had their own gasworks several years before gas lighting became available to householders. Marple gasworks for example was not built until 1845. At Compstall the gas was used for house lighting and the mains were even taken across the river to supply houses in Compstall Road as far as the Windsor Castle Hotel.

At points along the reservoir embankment are spillways to allow excess water to flow into the river. Before leaving the reservoir behind cast your eyes towards the island which is a haven for great crested grebes.

The yard coal seam outcrops in the stream bed and in Ernocroft Wood. At the site of the bridge, which was used to carry the coal over the river, is a sign illustrating what the installation was like. Below the stone abutment of the bridge remains.

When the path reaches the end of the canal, the river can be crossed by a wide bridge from which there is a good view of the weir. By crossing this bridge and following the paths it is possible to see the remains of the tramway embankment and places where the ground has been disturbed by early surface workings. The Ernocroft Drift Mine is outside the part of the wood with public access. Where a coal seam was exposed by a stream the early miners would notice it easily, but the flora growing on the coal measures is usually noticeably different to that on the millstone grit higher up the valley and I wonder if this guided them in their search for seams.

Quite apart from inspecting industrial archeological remains, the paths which go on past Weir Cottages are worth exploring together with the fish ponds and Keg Cottage. The park is quite extensive and too large to view in a single visit. I doubt if the local farmers would agree with me, but it is a great pity that the Etherow-Goyt Valley Walk cannot continue from the end of the park to Botham's Hall, although the existing route does take in Beacom Houses and some fine views of the valley from Werneth Low.

After returning to Compstall by the opposite side of the canal, after the canal starts to broaden out, there is a green in front of the terraces along Montagu Street. Between 1820 and the late 1830's a considerable number of houses were built for the mill workers and those engaged on the building works. Rows of houses, named streets, were given the Christian names of various members of the Andrew family. Note that the houses are typical for the time; more recent occupants have replaced the old sash windows with more modern designs, but there are no fanlights over the doors. One good feature is that many are raised above street level and entered by a short flight of steps. This would help combat the problems with rising damp in the days before the introduction of damp proof courses.

Not only the streets carry Andrews names; there is an Andrew Arms next to the Methodist Chapel built in 1887 replacing an earlier chapel of 1826. Adjacent is the original Sunday School. A letter to the local press in 1894:

"Sir, The playground near Pleasant View has become the meeting place for young men who play "peggy" for money. Those who frequent the place can ill afford to lose their money. The language they indulge in is dreadful etc."

For the benefit of those who have never experienced the delights of Peggy I should perhaps explain that this is a game played with a block of wood known as a peggy, shaped rather like a small anvil which has to be struck with a stout stick. The peggy is placed on a level surface such as a flat stone and made to rise into the air by a smart tap on the point; it is then struck to propel it as far as possible. The best stick for striking was held to be a hickory picking peg off a loom. Having struck the peggy to a distance the striker would estimate the number of strides necessary to cover this distance and announce a number slightly smaller. If no one could cover the distance in this number of strides then the striker scored the number he had given. On the other hand if another player could manage to do it within this number then he was credited with this score.

North Cheshire Herald 6.1.1872.

PENAL SERVITUDE. "John Thompson of Compstall was brought before Mr Thornley at Hyde Police Court charged with stealing a pair of trousers. He was sent to Knutsford for trial on Wednesday. He pleaded Not Guilty, but the jury sentenced him to seven years penal servitude."

Seems a bit steep after John Saul got away with a mere nine months for stealing a horse and trap; surely it is the judge who awards the sentence not the jury, but then reports in local papers - or any other paper - warrant careful study.

Few things attract the attention of newspaper reporters more than a spot of scandalous behaviour on the part of respectable citizens. Hence it hardly surprising to read in the Ashton-under-Lyne Reporter of 19th May 1906 the lurid details of a shocking case at the Stockport County Police Court involving a certain Miss Mary Ann Shaw of Compstall who was fined for being drunk and incapable in the village. Unfortunately for both the Reporter and Miss Shaw, the culprit was a tramp passing through the village who happened to have the same name. The resident Miss Shaw was naturally none too pleased with the report and the following week the paper had to make an abject apology to Miss Shaw who was described as a woman of exemplary character.

Some of the figures that have emerged during the journey indicate the original size of the Etherow. 20 million gallons daily allowed in compensation water for the mills below Bottoms Reservoir; between 24 and 48 million gallons daily taken by Manchester as drinking water; 40 million gallons per day to power the Andrew's mills at Compstall. It must have been an impressive stream as it passed under Compstall Bridge. We may never see the salmon making their way upstream again, but with improvements in water quality, trout have returned in places. Some idea of the former rural nature of Compstall can be gained by the fact that a cormorant was shot at Compstall Bridge in 1825.

And there we reach the end of our journey having descended 390 metres from our starting point at Redhole Spring. The river goes on to meet the Tame, and other lesser streams, until it joins the sea, but that would require another book.

The End